Leonard L. Berry

ON GREAT SERVICE

A Framework for Action

THE FREE PRESS

NEW YORK   LONDON   TORONTO   SYDNEY   TOKYO   SINGAPORE

The Free Press
A Division of Simon & Schuster Inc.
866 Third Avenue, New York, N.Y. 10022

Printed in the United States of America

printing number
1 2 3 4 5 6 7 8 9 10

Library of Congress Cataloging-in-Publication Data

Berry, Leonard L.
    On great service: a framework for action / Leonard L. Berry
        p.   cm.
    Includes bibliographical references and index.
    ISBN 0–02–918555–6
    1. Customer service—Quality control.   2. Customer service—United States—Management—Case studies.   I. Title.
    HF5415.5.B483   1995
    658.5'62—DC20   94–41391
                                                          CIP

To my wife and sons,
who practice the principles of great service in their endeavors:
Nancy as a leader of community and state organizations,
Matthew as a writer for television,
and Jonathan as a retailer.

CONTENTS

ACKNOWLEDGMENTS

I have written this book with a strong sense of urgency and personal commitment. Many companies are struggling to improve their service quality. Some companies are not even trying to improve. We can do better. We must do better. Much is at stake in the service quality journey, from company market share to country market share.

This volume concerns how to improve service quality. It is a book about implementation. I have devoted my academic career to studying and writing about services marketing and its foundation—service quality. I have tried to bring every relevant lesson, every insight, from this career experience into this volume.

Many people have contributed their time, energy, wisdom, skills, and encouragement to this book. Had the Marketing Science Institute (MSI) not believed in a team of three researchers who wanted to investigate the elusive subject of service quality, this book, and two earlier volumes, would never have been written. In the early 1980s, most of the published work on quality concerned manufactured goods quality. A. (Parsu) Parasuraman, Valarie Zeithaml, and I, colleagues on the marketing faculty at Texas A&M University, wanted to study service quality. The Marketing Science Institute provided the initial research funding and continues to sponsor our research. Our research program, with five distinct phases now complete, is the longest-running in MSI's history. My participation in the MSI studies has profoundly shaped my views on service quality. Every chapter in this book has benefited from my involvement in this work.

I am grateful for the opportunity to have worked so closely and for so many years with Parsu Parasuraman and Valarie Zeithaml. I have gained much knowledge and inspiration from this collaboration. Parsu and Valarie join me, I am sure, in expressing appreciation to the Marketing Science Institute. Paul Root, MSI's president, and Katherine Jocz, Director of Research Management, have been champions of our work for years and deserve a special thank you.

Part of the research for this book involved on-site observation and interviews at ten of America's finest service organizations. I am indebted to the dozens of individuals who participated in the interviews and candidly shared their ideas and experiences. The pages that follow are filled with quotes and examples that come from this process. At each company, one or several people went to great lengths to make sure my visit was successful. I am especially grateful to these individuals:

- Richard Hart and Garrett Jamison of Bank One Texas Trust Division
- Larry Harmon of De Mar Plumbing, Heating, and Air Conditioning
- Harold, Darryl, and Michael Wiesenthal of Harold's
- Michael Redwine, formerly of Hard Rock Cafe
- Dr. Phyllis Watson of Lakeland Regional Medical Center
- Greg Penske, Becky Cabot, and John Dinsmore of Longo Toyota and Lexus
- Richard Bartlett of Mary Kay Corporation
- Joyce Meskis of Tattered Cover Book Store
- Bruce Simpson of Roberts Express
- Russell Vernon and Kathryn Lowe of West Point Market

George Rieder, one of my closest friends and an expert on human resources management, provided valuable ideas and secondary research information for Chapters 11 and 12. Glenda Bessler, my long-time administrative assistant and great friend, supported this project in myriad ways, including typing every word in the manuscript and verifying information in telephone interviews. This is the fourth book Glenda has helped me prepare for publication. She epitomizes the meaning of great service. So does Shirley Bovey, an associate editor with the Real Estate Center at Texas A&M University, who moonlighted to provide editorial assistance. Shirley, a firm believer in the virtue of short sentences, has been a wonderful teacher to me in my quest to be an effective writer. This is the second book on which Shirley has assisted. Bob Wallace, senior editor at The Free Press, and Elena Vega, assistant editor, have been enthusiastic supporters of this book from the beginning of the process. Their advice and encouragement have been invaluable. To George, Glenda, Shirley, Bob, and Elena I offer my heartfelt thanks.

Finally, I thank my wife, Nancy, and sons, Matthew and Jonathan, for understanding how important writing this book was to me, and for saying they were proud of me as I sat at my desk in my home, day after day, and endeavored to make every word count.

Leonard L. Berry

AUTHOR'S NOTE

A number of individuals provided original material for this book by participating in interviews or preparing written responses to questions. Individuals who are quoted without an accompanying citation provided material expressly for use in this book.

CHAPTER 1

A FRAMEWORK
FOR GREAT SERVICE

Manager, West Point Market   July 14, 1994
1711 West Market Street
Akron, OH 44313

Dear Sir or Madam:

I feel compelled to write to tell you how much I enjoyed my trip to the West Point Market last weekend, and particularly how good the service was at the market.

From time to time, I drive all the way from Columbus to shop at your market because I have found no place like it in the State. What a delight it is to be able to find everything I could possibly need for even the most exotic recipes in one store!

Last weekend, in addition to the wonderful food, I found that the service was particularly good. In the produce department, a young woman got a special container to pack my fresh figs in, so that they would not get smashed on the trip back. Also while I was shopping for my produce, I asked one of the employees what lychee nuts were. She not only explained where they come from and how they are served, but she sliced one open and offered me a sample.

Then I ordered my lunch at the deli counter, and found when it arrived that I could not carry my tray very well because I was holding my baby son. An employee who was apparently on her lunch break gave up her place in line right behind me to carry my tray to the table. The young men at the checkout counter also noticed that I had my arms full of baby, and packed all of my groceries in bags with handles. One of them then helped me out to my car and loaded the groceries inside.

Each of the employees who helped me out did so without my asking, and seemed happy to be of assistance to me. It is so rare

1

to find such service at any store these days. Please know how much I enjoy and appreciate the top-notch service and the delightful shopping experience that West Point Market offers. I intend to shop there for many years to come.

Very truly yours,
Ronda Shamansky

West Point Market delivers great service. Doing business in Akron, Ohio, since 1936, it is a gem of a retail store that sells specialty foods of exceptionally high quality. What makes the store so special, however, is that the service is of exceptionally high quality, too. Ronda Shamansky's letter conveys the attachment many customers feel toward this store. Customers love West Point Market, principally because West Point Market loves its customers. West Point Market's prices are not low. It doesn't matter. Without low prices, it still competes on value. Many customers, including Mrs. Shamansky, come from out of town just to shop at the store.

Infused throughout this book are practical lessons from West Point Market and many other companies that deliver great service to their customers. Among the companies readers will meet in this book are:

- Longo Toyota and Lexus, one of the most successful automobile dealerships in the world
- Mary Kay Cosmetics, a magical company that has produced more female millionaires than any other company in the world
- Roberts Express, a trucking company, and De Mar, a plumbing, heating, air conditioning and refrigeration company, that operate 24 hours a day, 7 days a week, and thrive on helping customers with emergencies solve their problems
- Tattered Cover Book Store, one of America's largest independent bookstores that is remarkable in its passion for books and customers whom they help find that one elusive title
- Hard Rock Cafe, a restaurant and merchandiser that attracted hordes of customers on its first day and still does more than 20 years later
- Lakeland Regional Medical Center, a pioneer in introducing patient-focused health care in America

- Bank One Texas Trust Division, which made service quality the centerpiece of its strategy, and grew to more than $4 billion in trust assets in its first three years of operation
- Harold's, an upscale clothing store in business since 1950 that grows more than 10 percent each year despite infrequent sale events and a location long past its prime

Great service is rare, but it is not an impossible dream. American companies in every industry are delivering great service and profiting handsomely from their excellence. The companies just mentioned and numerous others discussed in this book are role model companies that have implemented great service and are highly successful because of it.

The purpose of this book is to teach the lessons of service quality *implementation*. The book focuses exclusively on *how* to improve service quality. The book's research and writing required one and one-half years. Site visits and interviews at each of the companies just mentioned composed part of the research. Considerable secondary research and follow-ups with many other firms also were undertaken. My service quality research collaboration since 1983 with colleagues A. Parasuraman and Valarie Zeithaml, a research stream sponsored by the Marketing Science Institute, provided the vital backdrop for this work.

The inspiration to write this book was borne of frustration over the many companies that are investing large sums of money to improve service but still are struggling mightily to succeed. Even more frustrating are the companies that are not even trying to improve service, companies whose managements deem service quality a low priority or a fruitless pursuit.

Everyone loses when service is poor. Customers lose. Employees lose. Senior managers lose. Suppliers lose. Shareholders lose. Communities lose. The country loses. Poor service has no redeeming virtue, nor does mediocre service for that matter. Service excellence is more profitable, more fun, and more conducive to a better future.

Delivering great service, one customer at a time, day after day, month after month, is difficult. Nothing in this book suggests that the excellent service journey is easy. It is not. But it is immensely rewarding, not just financially, but spiritually. Excellence nourishes the soul.

Why "great service?" What is wrong with "good service?" Good service isn't good enough to insure differentiation from competitors, to build solid customer relationships, to compete on value without competing on price, to inspire employees to want to become even better at their work and at their lives, to deliver an unmistakable financial dividend.

Most companies need to set their service aspirations higher. This does not mean throwing money breathlessly at service improvement. It does not mean dozens or hundreds of task forces and projects followed by an overnight conversion to the service quality religion. Rather, it means an integrated, holistic improvement journey that never ends, a journey anchored in a mission of high purpose, rock-solid values, and a fundamental belief in the capacity of human beings to rise to excellence. The seeds of great service are sown in the collective commitment to daily improvement.

In a 1993 presentation at a meeting of services marketing professors, AT&T executive Merrill Tutton stated that it was high time to "get excellent service off of the viewgraphs and into the market place." I agree. The "talking-about-quality" era is past. This is the "improving-quality" era. It is time to replace the struggling with genuine progress. It is time for action.

This is a book of ideas on how to pursue great service. The ideas are presented within a framework of essential steps, a road map for implementation. The framework, Exhibit 1–1, is a picture of the book. Each part of the framework is a chapter in the book. Chapter 2 emphasizes the leadership qualities that inspire service achievement in organizations. It discusses ways to nurture service leadership skills and values throughout the firm. Chapter 3 stresses the need for systematic listening to the voice of the customer. Conducting a study is insufficient. Companies need to build a service quality information system. Research approaches that can be used in such a system are discussed.

Listening to the customer provides the basis for establishing an overall service strategy, the subject of Chapter 4. The service strategy is a company's "reason for being"; it provides the focus and inspiration that is characteristic of all great service companies. Because quality service underpins value creation for customers, it always must be emphasized in the strategy. Chapter 5

Exhibit 1–1
FRAMEWORK FOR GREAT SERVICE

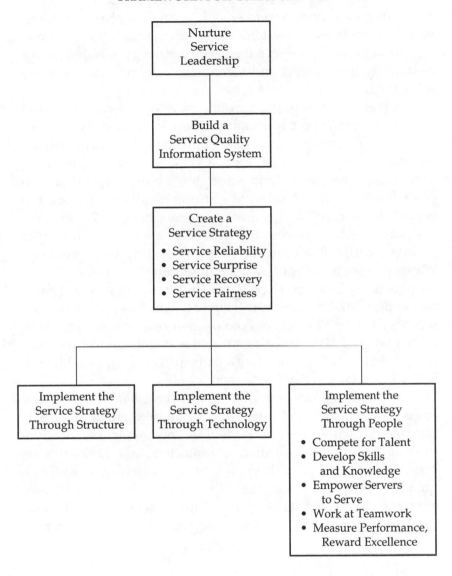

discusses four principles of service quality—reliability, pleasant surprise, recovery, and fairness—integral to the strategy. The nature and importance of these principles are described and suggestions for implementing them are presented.

Chapters 6 through 12 discuss implementing the service

strategy through structure, technology, and people. Chapter 6 presents structural forms that companies should consider in organizing for service improvement. Special emphasis is on service delivery teams. Chapter 7 examines the need for a technology strategy to implement the service strategy. Guidelines for technology investments and technology's service-improvement roles are discussed.

Chapter 8 discusses the pivotal issues of whom to hire and how to attract the best applicants. When the product is a performance as in service businesses, competing for talent helps a company compete for customers. Chapter 9 stresses preparing service providers to perform through ongoing skill and knowledge development. Job-relevant learning builds competence and confidence—essentials for great service. Chapter 10 addresses the issue of empowerment but probably in a manner dissimilar to many readers' accustomed understanding of the subject. Ways to create feelings of ownership within the organization are emphasized. Chapter 11 conveys the theme that quality is a team sport. Methods for nurturing collaborative power are presented. Chapter 12 discusses the roles of performance measurement and rewards in building an achievement culture. The integration of measures and rewards into a broader human resources approach that fits the service strategy is stressed.

Companies compete with value in the 1990s. Value is not price. Value equals benefits received for burdens endured. Price is but one burden to endure. Rudeness, incompetence, inconvenience, carelessness, inflexibility, unfairness, lack of concern or caring—these are a price that many customers refuse to pay. High quality directly affects the value of a service by increasing its benefits and decreasing its burdens. How to deliver great service need not be a mystery. We have a road map. It is time for action.

CHAPTER 2

NURTURE SERVICE LEADERSHIP

G reat service is not a pipe dream. Companies in every indus-try have surmounted the operational complexities, external market forces, and short-term earnings pressure that encourage service mediocrity. The key is genuine service leadership at all levels in an organization—leadership that inspires achievement.

"Managing workers" does not result in great service. The stresses of service performance are simply too great. The constant pressure of "being on stage"—serving many customers in a short time, enduring conflicting demands, suffering customers who are disagreeable, rude, or worse—frequently leads to fatigue and discouragement.

Service providers need a vision of work that is worth believing in, a vision that challenges them, provides emotional energy, and generates commitment. They need to feel a sense of teamwork and belonging within the organization that sustains them on the difficult days. They need contact with role models who set high standards and show the way. They need to taste the elixir that comes from having to think on the job, to be creative, and to venture outside of the routine. They need to experience the stimulation of forward motion, progress, achievement—both personal and organizational. These are the fruits of service leadership. Without inspired leadership, service mediocrity prevails. As Bell South executive Lee Harkins states: ". . . leadership is *the* make-or-break quality issue."[1]

Nurturing the development of service leadership values and skills is the most important step an organization can take in the service quality journey. And this nurturing must occur throughout the organization. Service leadership at the top of the company is critical, but so is it at all other levels. A prominent bank marketing executive makes the point well:

> The weakest link in banks, which is an undermining factor of service quality, is middle management. That's where it falls apart. This comes from high turnover at this level, lack of commitment, lack of understanding "the big picture," lack of motivation, and lack of senior management communications.[2]

Most service jobs have high discretionary content. The maximum amount of energy and care an individual can bring to the service role and the minimum amount required to avoid penalty are quite different. Thus, the energy and care levels of service are up to the service providers' discretion.[3] Companies delivering great service have providers who live near the maximums; most companies do not. Service leadership is the difference. Peter Drucker urges executives to consider employees "volunteers."[4] Most employees will show up for work without leadership; however, going beyond the ordinary for a customer, trying a second solution when the first one fails, contributing ingenuity to the task at hand—these are voluntary acts.

Joyce Meskis, owner of the Tattered Cover Book Store in Denver, states: "Diligence and doggedness are what we do best. We search for the elusive title wanted by the customer." This is not an owner's illusion. From Tattered Cover floor manager Sidney Jackson: "Just this morning, a couple came in looking for Christian videos that we didn't have. I said, 'Let me call a store or two and find them.' The customer said, 'You'll do that?'" Floor manager, Neil Strandberg, adds: "We try to say 'yes' to everything." And from general manager Linda Millemann comes this thought: "We have always been willing to special order. Managers from other stores say 'Well, you are big enough to do that,' but that is how we got big."

QUALITIES OF SERVICE LEADERS

In their book, *Leaders: The Strategies for Taking Charge*, Bennis and Nanus distinguish between *leaders* who emphasize the emotional and spiritual resources of an organization, and *managers* who stress the organization's physical resources, such as raw materials, technology, and capital.[5] Although managing is critical to organizational efficiency, too few firms are tapping the emotional and spiritual energy of leadership that characterizes all great service companies.

Much has been written about leadership. Far less is written about *service* leadership—the specific qualities that foster service achievement in organizations. Service leaders exhibit most if not all of the qualities often ascribed to leaders in general—vision, persistence, high expectations, expertise, empathy, persuasiveness, integrity. Yet, the focus on *service achievement* makes four qualities essential.

Service Vision

Service leaders view excellent service as the driving force of the business. Excellent service separates a company from its competition; it makes the essential difference. Regardless of the target markets, the specific services, or the pricing strategy, service leaders visualize quality of service as the foundation for competing. Larry Harmon, owner of De Mar, the highly successful plumbing, heating, and air conditioning company in Clovis, California, says: "Getting totally focused on customer satisfaction was the turning point for me." Tattered Cover's Joyce Meskis echoes Harmon: "Service has been the foundation to our business. We'll do everything it takes to put people and books together." These leaders know a customer is buying more than plumbing and books.

Service leaders continually sound the trumpet of excellence. Good service isn't good enough for a true service leader. Service leaders focus on the details and nuances of service. They see opportunities in small actions that competitors might consider trivial. They believe that how the organization handles the little things sets the tone for how it handles everything else. They also believe the details of the business add up for customers and make a difference.

Longo Toyota and Lexus in Los Angeles is the world's largest retail volume Toyota dealership. Longo adheres to a "one bumper rule" that requires the cars for sale to be perfectly aligned—a customer looking down a row of cars sees only one bumper. Says Longo president Greg Penske: "I am a fanatic on keeping the place neat and clean."

Longo sweats the details. Customers queuing up at the service entrance in the morning are greeted with coffee and the *Los Angeles Times*. Courtesy transportation is available to customers who leave their cars for servicing. A car rental outlet with discounted rates is on the premises. A porter covers the car's steering wheel, seats, and floors before service work commences. All serviced cars are washed and vacuumed before being returned to their owners. The showrooms are colorful, carpeted, comfortable, and clean. There are no "closing" rooms for negotiations. Instead, salespeople and customers sit at small tables in an open area within the showroom. Longo's sales force speaks 38 different languages. A special department serves Asian customers. At Longo Toyota and Lexus, service standards are high.

Service leaders define the service vision for their organization. They not only articulate it in words, they model it daily in their behavior. The West Point Market in Akron, Ohio, is a specialty food store with the feel of a fine department store. It is a sea of colors, an adventure in discovery, a store of temptation with its killer brownies, walnut nasties, and peanut-butter krazies. Many grocery retailers view food as commodities and compete primarily with price. West Point owner, Russ Vernon, views food as fashion products and competes primarily with merchandising, atmospherics, and service-driven value. He charges more than competitors but earns his margins with product selection and quality, innovative display, and do-whatever-it-takes customer care.

Russ Vernon's vision is in three parts:

- "Our market is the business/professional clientele looking for product convenience and service not met in conventional stores. We go where others do not in search of wonderful products. We get ideas from everybody and everywhere. We are a cook's resource."
- "People spend money where they feel good. We set the stage for the product. We want to slow the customer down, relax the customer. We are theatrical with our lighting, with

our special events, with classical music. Our store is an entertainment center. We do not want to look like a supermarket."
- "Bonding with customers is a key in this business."

Russ brings his vision to life by the example he sets. Kim Kowalski, West Point's head cashier states: "The customers love the fact that Russ is here. He carries out the groceries. He is always greeting people, helping them." Specialty foods buyer Cindy Yost explains: "Things never get stagnant here. Russ keeps moving ahead. We are all running hard to keep up with him and that keeps us motivated. He always has a new idea, yet he takes our ideas and builds on them too. We all have a voice in West Point Market." And from Carol Moore, director of food service: "Russ is a leader. He sets the example. We know what he wants and he excels in it. Russ is our giant-killer and we all learn from him. He attends to the details and we learn to do so, too."

Vision empowers. The power of the service vision is the guidance it offers service providers. The stronger the vision—the greater its clarity and emotional buy-in—the thinner the company service policies and procedures manual. Cindy Yost remarks: "Russ lets us buy into our own jobs. When I took over the cheese department, he allowed me to purchase the cheeses I wanted. It was always up to me. It would be difficult if I was told to buy twenty cases of this or that, and I didn't believe in the product." Carol Moore states: "Russ truly empowers us to serve our customer."

Belief in Others

Service leaders believe in the fundamental capacity of people to achieve and view their own role as setting a standard of excellence, providing the tools needed for success, and encouraging leadership behavior throughout the organization. Because service leaders believe in the people who work with them, they make communication with them a priority. Service leaders listen to the sounds of the business; they remove obstacles to improvement, communicate the business's vision, and teach its craft.

Their most fundamental service is to serve the server. Service leaders are not bosses; service leaders are *coaches*.

De Mar's Larry Harmon has only one word on his office door: coach. Harmon is not joking. He even signs his correspondence "president/coach." Harmon runs his business like a football team: continuous training, constant repetition of the central strategy ("people will pay if you solve the problem and leave them with good feelings"), individual responsibility to the team, high expectations, high rewards. Harmon says: "I try to keep making the team better. I try to give people the tools and direction they need and not pound on them when things go wrong."

De Mar offers guaranteed same-day service to customers requiring it, and 24-hour-a-day, 7-day-a-week service at no extra charge. It is a challenging place to work, as Harmon readily admits: "It is incredibly demanding to work at our company. If someone calls us at 3:00 A.M., we will have someone there at 3:30 A.M. . . . We have some of the highest paid service advisors in the entire industry—but they are also the hardest workers." De Mar clearly is not for everyone. But the right kind of person thrives in this culture of high expectations/high payoff. Norik Cohn, lead dispatcher, is one of those people:

> I've been here two years now. I've seen a lot of people come and go. You have to want to work hard here or you won't be able to cut it. You must do whatever it takes. On a really hot day, the phones just ring constantly. On a busy day, our guys may work from 6:00 A.M. to midnight. I have a set schedule but I never stick to it. . . . I just care about this job. Personally, I have learned so many things that I can't put a price on. Larry gives you so many chances to do things and learn. I've grown so much in this job.

Larry Harmon makes a strong point when he says: "All the rules in the world won't bring out the best in people. It's more important that they buy into the values." Joyce Meskis, Greg Penske, and Russ Vernon would agree.

Love of the Business

The best service leaders love the business they lead; they love their immersion in the intricacies of the business, the problems that test them, the sense of accomplishment after a good day; they love the action. Service leaders would rather be running the business than doing anything else. They have deep feelings about operating the business well, about making it grow, about creating something special.

Love of the business brings to full flower the enthusiasm and ebullience that characterize so many great service leaders. The combination of natural enthusiasm *and* the right setting in which to express it contributes to the emotional energy of true leadership. It is difficult to imagine Tattered Cover's Joyce Meskis in any business other than books. She is passionate about books and fervent about serving her employees and customers. Nor is it possible to imagine Longo's Greg Penske in a business that doesn't involve cars. He grew up in the car business; it is in his blood. "I love the business," he says.

Love of the business motivates service leaders to teach the business, to pass on to others the nuances, secrets, and craft of operating it. Harold Wiesenthal and his sons, Darryl and Michael, run Harold's, a multimillion dollar clothing store in Houston. In business for 45 years at this writing, Harold's sells top-of-the-line men's and women's apparel at full price in a location long past its prime. Without the benefit of a mall location or frequent sales, Harold's grows more than 10 percent a year. Success keys include highly personalized service ("We know most of our customers by name"); highly knowledgeable service ("Our salespeople are all career people"); quick, accurate alterations with 15 tailors on the premises ("We just don't say no when it comes to alterations"); integrity ("Sell customers what they need and something that fits"); and community involvement ("Harold is everywhere. He gives away money. He visits old folks in nursing homes. You can hardly go to a charity function and not see Harold"). Charles Milstead, a longtime Harold's customer, states: "I get kidded by friends who say I can get the same thing for half the price. But I tell them I can't get the same thing. I can't get the service, the confidence that it's the right color, the relationship."

With six salespeople, plus Darryl and Michael, Harold teaches one-on-one most of the time. He is the ultimate coach, the ultimate role model. Salesman Ken Patterson says: "I learned Harold's way by just being here." Salesman Charles Bourg, whom Harold recruited from a country club pro shop, remarks: "Harold can give me a look that sets me right if I'm going in the wrong direction." And from Robert Duncan, who annually sells more than a million dollars of clothing, comes this reflection: "I thought I knew how to sell but I really didn't know selling and service until coming here."

Harold Wiesenthal loves the business of helping customers look good. His zest for the business and his deep, personal commitment to it are contagious. He has inspired his sons to love the business, too. Harold says: "I've never seen two young fellows work as hard in retailing as Michael and Darryl." Michael and Darryl relate some of the retailing lessons Harold Wiesenthal has taught them:

1. Customers are the reason we are here. Take care of them. Follow-up. Deliver. Make sure they are happy.
2. Sell customers what they need and what fits. If they need a 44, don't sell them a 46 or a 42.
3. Emphasize quality of merchandise. Do not put anything in the store that you wouldn't be willing to wear yourself.
4. Be on the floor. The floor is everything. If you don't take care of the floor, little else matters. The customer wants to see the owner.
5. Make customers part of the store. Put their pictures on the walls, include them in the TV ads and radio spots, send them thank you letters.
6. Know your stock; know where things are.
7. Show the merchandise. Spend time on the little items, such as the ties to complement the suit and make the customer look good.
8. Always smile. The customer wants to see you smile.
9. You sell more than clothes. You sell yourself. People buy from us because they are our friends.
10. Promote the store 24 hours. If you go to the gym, wear a Harold's tee-shirt.

Love of the business fosters service leaders' high standards. The leader not only teaches the business operations but also exemplifies its style, its values, its excellence. Study Harold Wiesenthal's principles. Think about his lessons. Harold isn't just teaching the business; Harold is teaching service leadership.

Integrity

Service leaders do the right thing—even when inconvenient or expensive. They place a premium on being fair, consistent, and truthful with customers, employees, suppliers, and other stakeholders, thereby earning the opportunity to lead. As Peter Drucker wrote in a 1988 *Wall Street Journal* essay: "The final requirement of effective leadership is to earn trust. Otherwise there won't be any followers—and the only definition of a leader is someone who has followers."

Personal integrity is an essential service leadership characteristic. It is more than a philosophy; it is the ethical gyroscope of the organization. Through their integrity, leaders maintain a true orientation and direction regardless of pressure from other forces.

If we think of integrity as "psychological and ethical wholeness, sustained in time" that is "not a painfully upheld standard so much as a prolonged and focused delight,"[6] then its central role in service leadership becomes more apparent. Integrity is the source of a leader's commitment to fair play and truthfulness. Integrity propels the leader's vision of what the organization must be. Integrity assures consistency, which evokes trust.

Observe the finest service leaders carefully and listen closely to their words. Integrity dominates. Harley-Davidson CEO Richard Teerlink refuses to use alternative channels to market much-in-demand Harley-Davidson insignia products. He says matter-of-factly: "We will not compete with our dealers." Southwest Airlines CEO Herb Kelleher ignores enticement packages offered by city governments seeking to attract the airline. His reasoning: "We will only go into a market where we can make it work on our own. That way we won't have to pull up and leave."

Longo's Greg Penske states: "We teach our people: 'Don't sell customers a car, help them buy a car. Then you make a friend.'" All Longo salespeople are required to sign a code of ethics. De Mar's Larry Harmon says: "I feel all good relationships have to be built on trust." Harmon adds: "Would the people who work here want their kids to work here? I ask myself this all the time." Harold Wiesenthal says, "Once you tell a customer not to buy something because it doesn't fit or doesn't look right, then you have a customer for life."

These leaders bring vision to their organizations. They believe that "jobs can be elegantly conceived and gracefully done."[7] Their integrity enlivens fidelity to this vision.

Great service requires extraordinary effort; integrity generates such effort. Integrity inspires.

CULTIVATING SERVICE LEADERSHIP

Service leadership is the engine of service improvement. Without the energizing vision of leadership, without the direction, the coaching, and the inspiration, the idea of quality improvement is not transformed to action.

Great service is a matter of mentality. The quest to improve is unrelenting; ideas are part of the job; the spirit of entrepreneurship is strong. Values guide, not policy and procedure manuals. Mentality is a matter of leadership.

Are leaders born, or can they be made? The answer to this ageless question is "yes" and "yes." Some people are naturally gifted in ways that support leadership behaviors. Equally true, however, is the statement of Lieutenant General William Pagonis who led 40,000 military personnel in the Persian Gulf War: "I'm convinced that anyone who wants to work hard enough and develop these [leadership] traits can lead."[8] How can an organization cultivate the service leadership potential of its employees? Exhibit 2–1 portrays four ways.

Promote the Right People

The surest way to nurture service leadership in an organization is to use service leadership criteria in promoting people to positions of greater responsibility. Four good things happen when individuals who possess service leadership qualities are promoted. First, these individuals can develop their leadership capabilities further by virtue of their increased responsibilities.

Exhibit 2–1
FOUR WAYS TO NURTURE
SERVICE LEADERSHIP

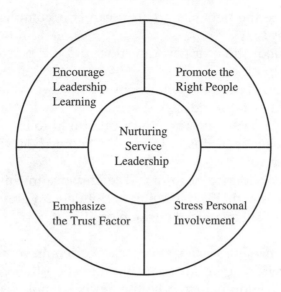

Second, through their new responsibilities, they have a greater opportunity to help the firm improve its service. Third, as people with a service philosophy move upward, other employees perceive service leadership as winning behavior. Fourth, and most importantly, placing service leaders in charge of other employees provides a service-minded role model from whom aspiring leaders learn. Modeling leadership behaviors is a particularly powerful way to cultivate leadership values and skills. Placing a true leader in charge helps transform followers into leaders themselves.

Few, if any, organizational decisions have a more profound impact on actual service improvement than who gets promoted and who does not. Excellent promotion decisions require approaches different from those used in many companies. Here are three recommended tests:

1. *The footprints-in-the-sand test.* The best predictor of a person's future performance is past performance. It is important to study a person's past qualitatively, not just quantitatively, and to

examine methods, not just outcomes. Questions to ask and answer include:

- What are the person's greatest career accomplishments—and why?
- What innovations or new directions did this person sponsor in prior positions?
- What is this person's philosophy of service? What evidence suggests that this individual will be a *service* leader?
- Does this person inspire others and build followership? Do others believe in this individual? Do they believe in his or her integrity?
- Is there evidence of informal leadership in this person's background, that is, the ability to influence a group without the benefit of an official position or title?

2. *The stand-for-something test.* True leaders have a vision for the future. They are clear about the direction they wish to go and why. They do not straddle the fence, are not wishy-washy, do not play it safe. As Peter Drucker has written, the leader's first task is to be the trumpet with a clear sound.[9] Thus, a crucial leadership test is the extent to which an individual's beliefs and priorities are on the table, visible for all to see.

3. *The outside leadership test.* In large organizations especially, the budding leadership potential of individuals not in management positions may be hidden. How can these individuals be identified and considered for faster-track assignments? One way is to encourage employees to become involved in volunteer activities outside of work. Not only can volunteerism be good for the community, it can be good for the volunteer. Involvements in professional societies, cultural and service organizations, non-profit social agencies, and the like can furnish creative outlets for developing and demonstrating leadership capabilities.

A leadership assignment in a volunteer organization can be a rigorous test of leadership potential, given the financial constraints under which most volunteer organizations operate, the emotion-laden issues that many such groups confront, and the reality that volunteers "don't have to do anything." Success in leading a volunteer organization requires vision, organizational and political skills, communications and consensus-building skills, patience, persistence, and resilience. Companies intent on cultivating service leaders would do well not only to encourage volunteerism among employees, but to stay abreast of employees' involvements and achievements in an organized way.

The footprints-in-the-sand, stand-for-something, and outside leadership tests offer additional criteria for making promotion decisions. With only 16 percent of employees of American companies believing they are well-managed according to a 1991 Hay Group study, much room for improved leadership exists.[10]

Stress Personal Involvement

Personal involvement in service improvement builds insight, fosters commitment—and stimulates leadership. When people in organizations are invited to participate in service improvement, to become genuine partners in an endeavor as challenging, sensible, and potentially gratifying as service excellence, many will give their ideas, energy, and spirit to the cause. Only in the most unhealthy organization, in which management has lost all credibility with the employees, will personal involvement efforts fail to bear fruit. Stated differently, unless people in organizations have given up completely, efforts to tap into the diversity of their gifts will be rewarded.

Every employee in the organization should be asked to assume personal responsibility for service improvement. Customer-contact employees must be involved because they deliver the end service to customers. Internal service providers must be involved because their performance affects the quality of service delivered to end customers. Middle managers must be involved because everyone in the organization (except top managers) works for them. And top executives must be involved because they set the tone for the entire organization; only they can commit a company to a new direction or a higher level of achievement.

Firms should use multiple personal involvement methods. Milliken & Company, a winner of the Malcolm Baldrige National Quality Award, sponsors *sharing rallies* in which employees from various parts of the company formally present the content and results of specific quality improvement efforts. Peers and management compose the audience at these two-day meetings in the company auditorium. No limits are imposed on the format or style of these presentations, which may involve skits or videos. Peer voting determines the winning presentations. Management views the sharing rallies as celebrations that recognize excellent work, cross-fertilize good ideas, and reaffirm every employee's role in quality improvement.

Many service-minded companies systematically solicit employees' ideas for service improvement with *employee suggestion systems*. Well-operated employee suggestion systems give servers closest to the work and to customers the chance to be heard by management and to help themselves, customers, and the company. Prompt responses to the suggestions and rewards for those who make them stimulate creative energy in the organization. People are encouraged to think about novel ways to solve problems; they are encouraged to get involved.

Preston Trucking, featured in the book, *The 100 Best Companies to Work For in America*, generated 7,882 employee suggestions in 1991, and 74 percent of them were implemented. This figure was up from 4,412 ideas in 1988. Each suggestion is published in the company's newsletter. Rewards for ideas are simple but plentiful, e.g., reserved parking spaces and Preston jackets.[11]

When First Drewitt Bank launched its 30-day GOOD Idea program in 1989, all 125 employees contributed 550 ideas on how to improve service, increase customer satisfaction, and lower costs.[12] Delta Dental Plan of Massachusetts's Keep It Simple Suggestion (KISS) system encourages employees to contribute solutions inside and outside of their department. The KISS system resulted in the implementation of 128 quality improvement ideas from the 338 suggested between February 1991 (the inception of the program) and June 1993. Biweekly, the president awards winning employees a sweatshirt, and their suggestions are printed in the organization's newsletter. Employees' performance reviews consider the degree of involvement in activities such as KISS. Managers are evaluated on whether they create a work environment that encourages employee involvement and risk taking.[13]

Book reports are another personal involvement device. No company uses book reports more diligently than Bank One Texas Trust Division. Management selects a set of service quality books that makes sense to them and then asks various units in the company to work with the books. Typically, an individual in a work group is named discussion leader for a chapter of the selected book. The work unit meets one hour a week to discuss the chapter. They may spend several weeks on one chapter. Everyone is expected to have read the chapter before the discussion day. The leader's task is to focus the discussion on the chapter's content and how to apply it to Bank One Texas Trust Division.

Richard Hart, chairman of the trust committee, is zealous about every level of the organization participating in service improvement. Books are an important tool. Hart states: "What I see missing in the service quality efforts of many companies is the use of books. It is imperative to understand the academics. Research is available, and it is silly not to use it."

At least one competitor agrees with Hart. The *Productivity Views* newsletter published the following passage about First Chicago Trust's Senior Vice President Joe Spadaford:

> After Spadaford had read a number of books and articles on empowered teams, he encouraged his senior managers to explore how employee teams could work in their units. His managers' reactions were less than enthusiastic.
>
> Undaunted, Spadaford tried another tactic. He bought copies of books about employee work teams and empowerment. Then he invited all his managers to a day-long off-site meeting, scheduled two weeks in the future. The purpose of the meeting was to involve the entire management team in exploring how employee empowerment and self-directed work teams could fit their business. Spadaford passed out the books he'd collected— one to each manager. He asked each to read the assigned book and prepare a one-page report of the book's key messages. How managers could apply the messages to success in their own operation were to be included in the report.
>
> The results surprised Spadaford. As managers presented their book's main points, they got excited. They saw the possibilities for applying the main lessons in their own shops and each manager became an advocate for some of the points of the book he or she had read.

By having to present to other members of management, each built understanding. The desire to sell others on the book's best points developed commitment to apply those methods at First Chicago.[14]

Still another means for galvanizing participation in service improvement is an *internal quality competition*. Many companies that apply for but do not win the Baldrige National Quality Award report significant benefits nonetheless. Not only does the application process offer a framework for thinking about quality and a mechanism for identifying weaknesses, but also the process itself requires broad participation and leadership.

Medium-sized and larger companies should consider in-house quality award competitions that may involve more employees than external competitions. First Union National Bank, headquartered in Charlotte, North Carolina, established such an internal competition in 1991. Eleven units of the bank participated. They were selected based on interest in participating and unit autonomy. The 11 units underwent a four-phase, 18-month process that started with a quality assessment based on Baldrige criteria and culminated with each unit completing an actual Baldrige award application. Baldrige examiners judged the applications, and three of the units were selected for site visits. First Union's Home Equity Corporation won the competition, receiving a prize of $100,000. Approximately 5,000 First Union employees from the 11 competing units participated in the training and served on the teams that prepared analyses and documentation. The company's management and leadership development department performed a facilitating role in the competition, including training, help in questionnaire design, and planning assistance.[15]

With the competition, First Union's management unleashed a powerful cultural force inside the company. With 5,000 people involved in learning and thinking about service improvement and having to apply the teachings to their work units, management couldn't turn the clock back even if it wanted to.

Participation on *quality improvement task forces* is yet another way to cultivate service leadership values and skills. A common tendency in organizations facing a service problem is for upper management to attempt to fix it. Potentially more beneficial is to assign the job of fixing it to a task group of employees who are close to the problem. The mental energy from a challenging, personally important issue and from working within a group, the motivation from being asked by management to solve such a problem, and the insight from being close to the problem in the work role frequently will result in a successful solution. And in addition to a solved problem are the benefits of participation: service quality awareness and interest, and leadership practice. As consultant Beth Summers writes: "Since learning is engaging and efficient only when applied to solving work problems, the best way to help people learn quality is to engage them in solutions to real company problems."[16]

RE/MAX International, a large real estate company with more than 30,000 salespeople, faced the problem of slow delivery of sales and training materials from its distribution center to the field force. It was taking three to six weeks for salespeople to receive materials. Management asked the 12 distribution center employees to develop a plan of improvement within one week. The group was empowered to revamp and reassign tasks and responsibilities as they saw fit. The result: a new distribution process in which orders were shipped within 48 hours and received within ten days. Says president Robert Fisher: "I'm not sure what they did." Fisher adds: "Let the people who do the job have more say about what they do."[17]

Assuming the customer's role also can foster service quality insight and commitment. Some companies incorporate "mystery shopping" exercises into their training programs. Employees assume the role of a customer and sample their own company's service and possibly the competition's. Then they come back into the training class to share what they experienced and learned about good and bad service. Going undercover as a customer can offer a fresh and invigorating perspective of what the organization must do to improve service—and why.

Masquerading with a fake identity, wigs, and scarves, New York City's welfare commissioner Barbara Sabol posed as a welfare customer on and off for nine months. Sabol says she wanted to experience the service system as her clients did. Sabol saw broken furniture and cockroaches in some of the offices. Privacy was sometimes violated as names were called over a loud-speaker. At one office, she was identified only by her zip code even though she protested that she had a name. At another office, she was scolded by a welfare worker who denied the office had made a mistake. Still, Sabol praised the majority of welfare personnel and said she did not intend to punish those who gave her poor service.[18]

Of course, employees need not be mystery shoppers to experience their companies' service. They can become actual customers. Bank employees, for example, need to do their banking somewhere. Why not the bank where they work? Management should encourage this so that employees have continuing exposure to the customers' reality. Training sessions and staff meetings could include discussions of service improvement from employees' perspectives as customers.

Hands-on involvement in service improvement can be enlightening, exciting, and motivating. No longer a theoretical matter, no longer empty rhetoric, no longer "management's problem," service improvement is a personal issue as well as an organizational one. People who participate in service improvement often become converts to the cause, supplying creativity, coaching, role modeling, and other service leadership contributions to the organization. Personal involvement nurtures the development of service leadership values and skills.

Emphasize the Trust Factor

Trusting the judgment, ability, and goodwill of employees cultivates leadership. Trust inspires a sense of ownership in the enterprise, which in turn inspires leadership behaviors. People who feel like owners think more about how to improve the business, work harder to make it grow, and assume risks to achieve success. An organization characterized by trust will be characterized by leadership as well. One of the ways true service leaders lead is by trusting.

How can companies emphasize the trust factor? Springfield Remanufacturing Corporation (SRC) does it with *open-book management*. The company teaches each employee to read an income statement and balance sheet and shares all financial performance data with employees. Employees own 100 percent of SRC's stock. Financials and other corporate matters are discussed at a weekly company meeting called The Great Huddle. Jack Stack, president and CEO of SRC, states:

> There's arrogance among those who manage financials and ignorance from those with no exposure to them. You can't make good business decisions with arrogance at the top and ignorance at the bottom. . . . The biggest myth is that people on the floor can't understand useful information. . . . Job security is about the balance sheet. If you show this to people and let them make their own decisions, they go from an employee mentality to an employer mentality. They see how their own performance affects the bottom line.[19]

Tattered Cover Book Store and Mary Kay Cosmetics operate their businesses on the *basic assumption that their employees are honest and worthy of complete trust*. As Tattered Cover general manager Linda Millemann puts it: "We run the business for the 98 percent of our people who are honest, not the 2 percent who are not." Tattered Cover gives all employees a key to the store on their first day of employment. Owner Joyce Meskis started this practice in 1974 when she bought the store and continues it to this day, even though the company now has more than 320 employees. The key symbolizes to employees that Tattered Cover is their store. Kathy Langer comments: "I remember when I started to work in 1977. The key made me feel that I was part of the store. I was more than an employee; I was part of the Tattered Cover." Tattered Cover employees can borrow any of the books in inventory to read—a policy that creates more informed floor personnel and symbolizes complete trust.

At Mary Kay Cosmetics, the word of its 300,000 beauty consultants (salespeople) is gospel. Sherrill Steinman, a top-producing sales director who has been with the company for more than 15 years, says:

> The company believes me. My word is golden to the company. They believe me if my shipment is missing something. I have never been questioned about anything I have said was wrong with the order. It's a good feeling.

Sales director, Mary Diem-Scott, a 17-year veteran, adds: "I feel like a big girl in this organization. I feel like an adult."

Harold's leverages the trust factor by *allowing employees to show what they can do*. Harold's youngest salesperson is Charles Bourg, who was hired in 1990 at the age of 18 to be a stockboy. One of the salesmen was ill on Bourg's first day, so Bourg worked the sales floor instead of the stockroom. He had sales of $3,800, and on day two he was a salesman. Bourg rose to the level of opportunity afforded him—perhaps even beyond it. He is, to put it mildly, a "go-getter." He is constantly trying to expand his product knowledge and likes to accompany Michael Wiesenthal on buying trips when possible. He stays in touch with customers and prospects, routinely making 20–30 phone calls on a Tuesday morning "to set the tone for the rest of the week." Bourg always puts the customer first. "If someone needs his suit by 6:00 P.M. and I have a date, I put off the date." Bourg thrives on the work, on the pace. He says: "When I have a customer, things are moving. I am racing around making things happen." He adds: "I take a lot of pride working for Harold, Michael, and Darryl. They place trust in me."

Baptist Hospital of Miami, with more than 2,000 employees, treats more patients than any other private hospital in the area. The hospital's management conveys trust by *seeking staff input and granting autonomy*. Medical technologist Kay Ferris states: "Our ideas and suggestions are taken seriously." Materials management director Frank Fernandez explains:

> We are allowed a lot of freedom. There is not some power that is watching over our shoulder to see what we do. We are allowed to make mistakes, and we do make mistakes and we learn from those mistakes. The level of autonomy that we have is quite remarkable. That makes us grow and be more confident in what we do.[20]

In a Baptist Hospital staff survey, 91 percent of employees agreed with the statement, "I am trusted to do my job without someone unnecessarily checking on me."[21]

Trusting employees helps them to flourish, like Mary Kay's Sherrill Steinman and Harold's Charles Bourg. Trust nurtures leadership behaviors. The open sharing of important company information, the assumption that employees are honest rather than dishonest, the opportunity for people to demonstrate their abilities, the chance to shape the job, to give input, to be heard— these *qualities* lead to *quality*. People at work feel like owners— and owners have reasons to lead.

In twenty years, have any Tattered Cover Book Store employees abused the key-to-the-store policy? A few have. But the powerful message the practice conveys about the company's values and vision outweighs these disappointments. Tattered Cover Book Store did not become one of the largest one-store booksellers in the world, with double-digit volume increases every year, by following a risk-minimization strategy with employees.

Encourage Leadership Learning

Service leadership values and skills can be learned. Companies aspiring to excellent service should be prepared to invest in leadership learning on a continuous basis and on multiple fronts. One alternative is *challenge learning*, which involves placing individuals or groups in work situations that require leadership behaviors to succeed. New learning, new thinking, new approaches are required. The old ways of doing things are insufficient to surmount the challenge. Timidity doesn't suffice. Safe solutions are no longer safe. In effect, the new situation calls for a higher level of leadership.

Challenge learning is why Milliken & Company sets such aggressive goals for its strategic business units. As Milliken president Tom Malone says: "We've learned that stretch objectives are absolutely crucial to force new thinking."[22] Challenge learning is why Joe Scarlett and Gerry Newkirk suddenly switched jobs at Tractor Supply Company, a successful chain of more than 150 farm stores. Scarlett, currently chief executive officer, worked his way up through store operations. Newkirk, the president, was the company's senior merchandising executive. Then, in 1990 they suddenly switched functions. Newkirk took over operations and Scarlett merchandising. The switch forced them to use greater leadership skills to overcome their lack of technical experience. Conceptual and interpersonal skills (including visioning, communicating, and team building) would have to become paramount as Newkirk and Scarlett learned new disciplines.

Judy Frow is a personal trust administrative assistant in the Houston office of Bank One Texas Trust Company. She was selected by her manager, Mark Day, to create detailed service maps of key trust services. The maps were to be used throughout the trust company for such purposes as improving service design, training, and employee orientation. Frow had never faced such a daunting, unfamiliar task before. In fact, this was the company's first experience in service mapping, a difficult, arduous process when done properly. Frow worked day and night on the project for six weeks to prepare the maps for presentation at a management meeting. Gathering input from employees involved in the actual services, she prepared maps of the testamentary trust, 401K, custody, cash-management, and escrow account services. Frow, not her manager Mark Day, made the presentation at the management meeting. Says Frow: "I have personally blossomed at Bank One. I have discovered qualities that I didn't know I had. I didn't know that I had the analytical mind to lead the mapping process."

Imitative learning is another form of leadership learning. Imitation can be a particularly effective means of learning. Visible, accessible leaders inside and outside the organization who model service leadership behaviors can have a strong, positive impact.

Mary Kay Cosmetics asks successful people in its field sales force to teach the courses in its annual Dallas "Seminar," which in 1993 attracted 36,000 saleswomen. Mary Kay is tapping the power of imitative learning. The company is attracting thousands of women to Dallas every summer to expose them to role models—role models who teach and, during "Awards Night," are lavished with praise, awards, and gifts in a huge arena in front of thousands of peers.

It is doubtful that any company in America does a better job of nurturing the development of service leadership values and skills through a combination of challenge and imitative learning than Mary Kay Cosmetics. Meet Mary Beth Slattum, formerly a hospital operating room nurse, now a successful Mary Kay sales director with more than 100 saleswomen in her unit:

I am my own boss. I am in complete control of my own schedule. Many women in management positions in medicine were
not trained in management methods. But with Mary Kay you
have to be a leader. Because you are independent, you are making decisions all the time. You begin to become successful in
small steps, and you develop confidence. You are able to assess
yourself more objectively, not only your weaknesses on which
to improve, but your strengths. Mary Kay instilled in me to find
role models and to learn by their example. One lady, for example, helped me so much. I listened to her tapes, took classes
with her, and observed her in action.

Companies can facilitate imitative learning by asking strong
role models to teach the orientation and training classes, by
encouraging and rewarding one-on-one leadership mentoring, by
establishing leadership forums in which outstanding leaders from
within and outside the organization are invited to speak on leadership topics, and by redoubling efforts to promote high-potential
leaders to positions that offer upward reporting relationships with
people who are themselves leaders.

Challenge and imitative learning can apply to individuals;
collective learning applies to groups. Companies should encourage leadership learning at the group level, not just the individual level. Several years ago, Milliken sent its top 24 executives to
Japan for 18 days to learn from Japanese companies. The actual
trip followed several weeks of group training to prepare for the
trip. And while the top 24 executives were in Japan, the next 100
executives were undergoing the two-week preparation course
taken earlier by the senior executives. The middle managers
would then be "ready" for the senior managers when they
returned from Japan with new ideas. This is collective learning
in action.

Milliken's management is so committed to collective learning that it no longer receives companies wishing to learn from it
unless the top 10 to 12 executives are part of the group. Tom
Malone explains: "It seems inefficient to send 10–12 people from
the same firm for learning. However, the reverse is true. When
you only send a few, change is difficult."[23]

Service leadership learning should not be left to chance.
Challenge, imitative, and collective learning approaches culti-

vate the development of leadership values and skills. Companies such as Mary Kay Cosmetics and Milliken are benefiting enormously from the fundamental belief that leadership can be learned.

SUMMARY

Leadership is the make-or-break service quality issue. With it, great service is possible; without it, great service is a pipe dream. Companies need excellent service leadership at all levels of the organization. The reason middle managers are called middle managers is because they are in the middle of everything. What companies aspiring to great service really need in the middle are "middle leaders."

Much has been written about the broad subject of leadership. In this chapter, the focus is on qualities most important to driving service achievement, that is service leadership. Service leaders inspire followers with a vision of service excellence, with a belief in the capacity of the followers to excel, with their love of the business and desire to teach the business's values and craft, and with their integrity. True service leaders engage followers in realizing their full potential at work, including their leadership potential.

Nurturing the development of service leadership values and skills is the single most important step an organization can take in the service quality journey. It paves the way for everything else a company might do to improve service. Companies can nurture service leadership by promoting the right people into management, stressing personal involvement, emphasizing the trust factor, and encouraging leadership learning.

Here is an action checklist of questions that executives can use in discussing company strengths, weaknesses, and priorities in service leadership development:

1. *Do we distinguish between leading and managing in this company?* Do we use the terms interchangeably or do we see a difference?
2. *Do we connect quality of leadership and quality of service?* Do we view leadership development as an important issue in service improvement?

3. *Do we have a service "mentality" in this organization?* Do we aspire to great service or is good service good enough? Do we seek continually to improve our service? Are we aggressive in service improvement, ambitious, bold?
4. *Do we use service leadership criteria in promotion decisions?* Do we take sufficient care to put service coaches and role models in charge?
5. *Do we actively solicit each employee's personal involvement in service improvement?* Do people in our organization feel involved in the company's quality improvement efforts? Do they feel that quality improvement is part of their responsibility?
6. *Do we trust our employees?* Do we believe in our employees judgment and goodwill? Do we give them the freedom to create for their customers, to make decisions on their own, to make and learn from mistakes? Are we cultivating an "ownership" feeling among our employees?
7. *Do we invest in service leadership learning?* Do we believe that leadership values and skills can be learned? If the answer is "yes," are we strategic and systematic in encouraging leadership learning?

CHAPTER 3

BUILD A SERVICE QUALITY INFORMATION SYSTEM

Service leadership alone cannot achieve great service. Leaders must establish the course of the service-improvement journey. But what is the proper course? What are the improvement priorities? How should resources be allocated? What are the essential elements of an effective service quality strategy? Answering these questions requires continuous listening to the voices of customers.

A common mistake that companies make in service improvement is focusing on internal processes with no clear link to customers' service priorities. Without the voices of customers guiding the service quality strategy, the best that can be hoped for is marginal improvement.

Quality is defined by the customer. Conformance to company specifications is not quality; conformance to the customers' specifications is quality. Spending wisely to improve service comes from continuous learning about the expectations and perceptions of customers and noncustomers.* Customer research reveals the strengths and weaknesses of a company's service from the perspective of those who have experienced it. Noncustomer research reveals how competitors perform on service and provides a basis for comparison. Important expectations for the service that competitors fulfill better offer an agenda for action.

---

*Generic phrases such as "listening to the voices of customers" refer to all customers of a service category, i.e., a company's customers and its competitors' customers.

This chapter champions listening to customers before allocating service improvement resources, before acting. Spending to improve service and failing to do so is not only wasteful but also hurts the credibility of the service quality cause. When invested monies do not produce results, management has little incentive to spend more.

Companies need to establish a service quality research process that provides timely, relevant trend data that managers become accustomed to using in decision making: *companies need to build a service quality information system, not just do a study*. Conducting a service quality study is analogous to taking a snapshot. Deeper insight and an understanding of the pattern of change come from an ongoing series of snapshots taken of various subject matter from different angles.

SYSTEMATIC LISTENING

Building a service quality information system is not just for big companies. Systematic listening to the customers' voice is just as necessary—and practical—for small companies. A small company's service quality information system may differ from a big company's, but it still can have all the necessary features. Simply stated, a service quality information system *uses multiple research approaches to systematically capture and disseminate service quality information to support decision making*.

The use of multiple research approaches is important because each approach has limitations as well as strengths. A combination of approaches enables a firm to tap the strengths of each and compensate for weaknesses. Continuous data collection and dissemination informs and educates decision makers about the *patterns* of change, for example, shifting service priorities for customers (or a segment of customers), declining or improving service performance in some facet of the company's service, declining or improving service performance of competitors. An effective service quality information system can offer a company's executives a big-picture view of service quality with its composite of many smaller pictures. It can teach decision makers which service attributes are important to customers and

Exhibit 3–1
**PRINCIPAL BENEFITS OF AN EFFECTIVE
SERVICE QUALITY INFORMATION SYSTEM**

Service Quality Information System

Encourages and enables management to incorporate the voice of the customer into decision making

Reveals customers' service priorities

Identifies service-improvement priorities and guides resource-allocation decisions

Allows the tracking of company and competitor service performance over time

Discloses the impact of service quality initiatives and investments

Offers performance-based data to reward excellent service and correct poor service

prospects and which are not, what aspects of the firm's service system are working well and what aspects are breaking down, and which service investments are paying off and which are not. A service quality information system can focus service improvement planning and resource allocation. It can help sustain managers' interest in service improvement by comparing the service quality of various units in the organization and linking compensation to these results. And it can be the basis for an effective first-line employee reward system by identifying who is delivering excellent service and who is not. Exhibit 3–1 summarizes the principal benefits of a service quality information system.

CAPTURING SERVICE QUALITY INFORMATION

What research approaches are useful in developing a service quality information system? This section overviews nine types of service quality research to consider:

- transactional surveys
- total market surveys

- mystery shopping
- service reviews
- customer advisory panels
- new, declining, and former customer surveys
- focus group interviews
- employee field reporting
- employee research

A firm normally would not use all of these approaches in the same information system; too many different studies can cloud rather than illuminate significant findings. Conversely, just one or two of the approaches will be insufficient; certain information that would influence decisions remains undisclosed.

Readers should consider the research approaches discussed here carefully, evaluating their "fit" with each other, the company's existing research program, the needs and habits of decision makers, and the nature and characteristics of the service and industry. Three of the methods are essential for any service quality information system: transactional surveys, total market surveys, and employee surveys. Other methods that should be used depend on "fit."

Transactional Surveys

Transactional surveys are done with customers in the aftermath of a service transaction with the firm. The purpose is to measure customers' satisfaction with the service experience and reasons for these perceptions while the experience is still fresh. Thus, most transaction surveys are administered immediately after the service experience, or within a few days. For infrequent, high-risk, high-involvement service experiences (such as taking a cruise), leeway exists on the amount of time that can pass prior to administering the survey. Customers are likely to remember these experiences for some time. For most services, however, survey timeliness is critical.

Transaction surveys can be conducted with a sample of customers or all customers. Longo Toyota and Lexus surveys by telephone each car buyer and service customer, making 40,000 telephone calls a year for this purpose. If the surveys are not administered daily, they should be conducted frequently enough to provide *ongoing* feedback on the quality of customers' service experiences. The continuous nature of the surveys facilitates early detection of developing trends so that the firm can take corrective actions. Points of weakness (in specific facilities, or with specific services, for example) should be easily spotted. The surveys also can facilitate corrective actions *with dissatisfied customers*—that is, service recovery—if the customer is identified.

Transactional surveys enable firms to *track* service quality on a timely basis; this is their principal benefit. Their focus on customers' most recent service experience rather than on overall perceptions of service performance, and their exclusion of noncustomers, are inherent limitations.

Taco Bell conducts transactional surveys at its company-owned restaurants. The questionnaire is distributed periodically and collected over the course of a day by a professional interviewer. An outside research firm administers the surveys, lending credibility to a research process used in the performance evaluation of managers. The questionnaire includes service elements that are important to customers and controllable at the restaurant level, such as cleanliness, speed of service, staff friendliness.[1]

Marriott's Fairfield Inn asks guests during check-out to rate check-in and check-out efficiency, exterior and room cleanliness, staff hospitality, continental breakfast, and overall value. The guest answers questions directly on a front-desk computer terminal, a simple process that takes little time. Thirty-three percent of the guests respond. Fairfield's system identifies which employees were on duty when a guest reported good or bad experiences, allowing the company to reward excellent service. The company pays annual bonuses on the average of more than $900 per employee based on guest satisfaction scores.[2]

Norrell Services, a temporary-employee provider, surveys clients every week through its Integrated Research Information System (IRIS). Norrell offices track each job in a computer database. Three times a week, headquarters personnel scan the database to see which jobs have been completed and send a survey directly to the supervisor to whom the temporary worker reported. The supervisor rates the employee(s) and returns the survey to headquarters where the data are summarized and disseminated to the branch offices. The survey form uses a four-point rating scale—exceeded my expectations, met my expectations, below my expectations, and poor, not acceptable—for such items as productivity, job skills, attitude, and communication skills. Branches follow up within five days with any client giving a below-expectations or poor rating. Client ratings are linked to service associates' and managers' compensation. The payout is determined by whether branches match or exceed their division's average score and whether they show improvement.[3]

Total Market Surveys

Total market surveys are less frequent but more comprehensive than transactional surveys. Whereas transactional surveys measure customers' satisfaction with a recent service experience, total market surveys measure customers' overall assessment of a company's service. Customers' evaluation of a recent, specific service experience may differ from their overall perceptions of the company's service, which come from accumulated experiences over time. Services are performances, and one service experience is no guarantee of the next experience.

When well designed and executed, total market surveys provide a range of information unmatched by any other method. Among the information that should be gathered (for reasons developed later in the chapter) are customers' service expectations and perceptions, the relative importance of service dimensions, and customers' behavioral intentions—for example, intention to repurchase from the firm and willingness to recommend the firm.

A critical facet of total market surveys (and the reason for using the word "total") is the measurement of competitors' service quality. This requires including noncustomers in the sample to rate the service of their suppliers. One common approach is to use probability sampling for the total market to survey an appropriate mix of customers and noncustomers. Respondents identify their primary supplier on the questionnaire and then rate that company.

Companies that survey only customers miss a rich source of information. *Noncustomer research reveals how competitors perform on service and provides a basis for comparison. Important service expectations that competitors fulfill best must not be ignored in service-improvement planning.*

Like transactional surveys, total market surveys facilitate performance tracking over time. Exhibit 3–2 illustrates competitive tracking for one service attribute for companies A, B, and C, using SERVQUAL, a methodology that A. Parasuraman, Valarie Zeithaml, and I developed for measuring customers' expectations for the service category and their perceptions of the company supplying the service.[4] A negative score results when perceptions fall short of expectations. In the exhibit, company A's performance is solid on this particular service attribute, company B was improving until period 4 and may have a problem developing, and company C is clearly losing ground and, depending on the attribute's importance, may want to take corrective action.

Exhibit 3–2
COMPETITIVE TRACKING OF SERVICE QUALITY SCORES

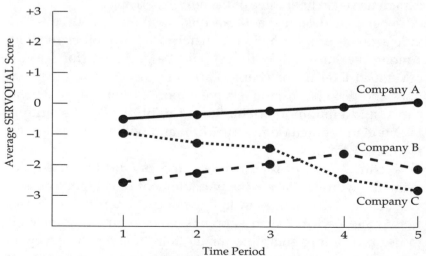

Source: A. Parasuraman, Leonard L. Berry, and Valarie A. Zeithaml, "Guidelines for Conducting Service Quality Research," *Marketing Research*, December 1990, p. 38.

By virtue of their scope, total market surveys are not inexpensive. Frequency of surveying is a function of budget realities and the service category's sensitivity to market changes. Quality of services that are used often or subject to competitive innovation should be measured more, rather than less, frequently. At the very least, total market surveys should be conducted annually. Two to four surveys per year should be considered, as should subdividing the sample for a monthly "running" survey.

Roberts Express, a freight company specializing in emergency, time-sensitive shipments, tracks customer service perceptions monthly. Roberts telephones 150 customers per month, asking questions such as:

- How satisfied are you with the service from Roberts Express?
- Why are you satisfied or dissatisfied?
- How likely are you to use Roberts Express?
- How likely are you to recommend Roberts to others?
- What is your satisfaction with the value of Roberts Express?
- How did Roberts do based on your expectations?
- Why choose Roberts instead of another carrier?

Roberts Express issues a monthly research report to every employee. The report includes summary results, month-to-month trend charts for each question, and verbatim responses to the "why" questions. What the reports do not include is meaningful competitive intelligence—a weakness of this survey. The monthly reports do not gather dust on employees' desks given that bonuses for *every* Roberts employee depend, in part, on the company's customer satisfaction scores.

Mystery Shopping

A variation of transactional surveys is "mystery shopping." Mystery shoppers are researchers who pose as customers to evaluate directly the quality of service delivered. Following the service encounter, the researchers use a rating form to systematically and comprehensively record their evaluations.

Mystery shopping enables a company to measure the performance of individual service providers. Transactional surveys completed by actual customers normally do not identify the individual service provider. Accordingly, companies often use conventional transactional surveys and mystery shopping in combination. Transactional surveys typically provide less in-depth appraisals of service units from large samples of actual customers. Mystery shopping typically provides more penetrating appraisals of individual service providers, but they are based on far fewer encounters.

The assessment of individuals' service behaviors via mystery shopping makes the data particularly useful in identifying employee-specific coaching and training needs. Mystery shopping data also can be used to recognize and reward excellent service performance. Aggregated mystery shopping data reveal systemic deficiencies that require corrective action.

The phrase "mystery shopping" sounds sinister and makes some executives uncomfortable. However, when executed properly, mystery shopping is a positive for most employees, especially those who are able and motivated. As noted in the last chapter, most service work is high in discretionary content. Servers who work hard for their customers will not be displeased if others in the organization (including management) learn about the good work they do. Mystery shopping is a way to reveal individual excellence.

Keys to proper usage include educating employees on why and how mystery shopping will be used and using the research in positive, constructive ways, such as rewarding servers who receive outstanding scores and helping those with poor scores to improve. It is necessary to shop service providers multiple times during a performance appraisal period to minimize the potential bias of just one measurement encounter.

One company sold on the benefits of mystery shopping is Hard Rock Cafe. The company uses professional researchers to shop both its restaurants and on-site merchandise stores every two months. A report is issued to every location following each two-month period. Individual servers shopped receive a numerical rating and a narrative description. Each location's shopping score trends are charted and compared to other units.

Juli Powers, a regional director of merchandise operations for Hard Rock Cafe, comments: "Shoppers' reports are beneficial because the staff can see the customers' perception of their service. This is one way we motivate staff to want to succeed. And it is important for us in management to see how trends are developing." Rob Perez, general manager of Hard Rock Cafe Orlando, has even used his own employees as shoppers. Perez explains:

> We had a problem. Our shopping ratings were slipping. So I had every member of the staff assume the role of a shopper. They had to stand in line, go through the whole experience of a customer, and then write a shopper's report. That process helped motivate us to change some things.

Service Reviews

Service reviews are periodic visits with customers (or a class of customers) to discuss the service relationship from A to Z. In effect, service reviews are in-depth personal interviews with customers to assess their satisfaction with various aspects of the service and to identify improvement priorities.

Service reviews should be a formal process involving a standard set of questions that are always asked, the written capture of responses, and follow-up correspondence to the customer summarizing salient conclusions and improvement priorities agreed upon. A common format should be developed for incorporating service review data and materials into the service quality information system.

Questions that might be asked in a service review are the following:

- What is the most beneficial part of our service to you?
- What is the least beneficial part of our service to you?
- Do you receive the information from our company that you need?
- Do our personnel deliver the type and quality of services that you need?
- What are the most important ways we could improve our service to you?

- Are there services we do not provide that you wish we did?
- Do you believe you are receiving good value from our company?
- Is our service good enough that you would feel comfortable recommending our company to a friend?

These questions suggest the rich, detailed dialogue between company and customer that is possible from service reviews. Customers stand to gain by cooperating, which they are most likely to do if a credible executive in the company other than the account representative conducts the service review. It would be awkward, for example, for a customer to comment about the poor responsiveness of the account representative *to* the account representative.

Because service reviews by their nature are time consuming and expensive, they are most appropriate for businesses marketing complex services on an ongoing basis. They are best suited to companies seeking to develop genuine customer relationships.

The Houston office of Bank One Texas Trust Company holds a year-end service review with each corporate client. At this writing, the manager of employee benefits, Marshall Shanklin, conducts the reviews, doing several a week. Although account administrators meet periodically with clients during the year, they are not present at the service review. Following the review session, Shanklin prepares his notes and meets privately with the account administrator to discuss points of concern and an improvement plan. Shanklin then sends a letter to the client summarizing the main points from the review session, and the changes, if any, that will be made. Clients are also asked to complete and return a questionnaire at this time.

Is such an intensive listening process worth the investment required? Houston manager Mark Day says yes: "We find out a lot of things. The administrator may think everything is great because there are no complaints. But in these sessions, when you specifically ask clients if they are satisfied, you learn more." Not all Bank One Texas trust offices conduct service reviews at this writing, so Day's assessment of costs and benefits are not shared uniformly throughout the organization. To be sure, service reviews, if conducted properly, represent a major resource commitment. In addition to the resources required to conduct the reviews are the resources required to act on what is learned. Companies making such a commitment do strengthen the foundation for relationship marketing.

Customer Advisory Panels

Customer advisory panels are another way to listen. The firm recruits a sample of customers to provide periodic feedback and advice. Panels can be formed strictly for service quality research or to provide information on various subjects, including service quality. Data typically would be obtained verbally in panel meetings or telephone interviews, or in writing via mail questionnaires.

This approach requires only that a company be able to identify and contact its customers. Many services of course involve a customer application or sign-up process (telephone or insurance services, for example) in which the requisite information is captured. However, even self-service retail businesses can obtain customer names, addresses, and phone numbers with some ingenuity, e.g., customer sign-up sheets in the store to qualify for gift sweepstakes.

Customer panels can produce unusually high levels of respondent cooperation because of the "membership" nature of the group. Customers agreeing to serve on the panel will feel more obligated to cooperate in a study than if they simply received a questionnaire in the mail. This sense of commitment also allows more in-depth questioning. Another advantage of customer panels is fast access to the customers' point of view when decisions affecting customers must be made quickly.

Panels can be created for specific groups, such as high-volume customers, or new customers, facilitating the monitoring of particular groups' service quality assessments. A panel of high-volume customers is certainly one way to keep management interested in service improvement. Management is likely to listen if this panel complains about service.

Managing customer panels is no small task. A system must be developed for rotating old members off the panel and recruiting new members. Members must be compensated. Overuse or underuse of the panel must be avoided. Overuse wears out the panel. Underuse undermines credibility, suggesting that the company isn't serious about wanting input.

Customer panels have the inherent limitation of being confined to customers. Moreover, a panel is not normally projectable to a company's entire customer base because of panel size or selection considerations. A customer panel can be a valuable part of a service quality information system; it should never be the sole source of service quality information.

Pier 1 Imports, a home furnishings, housewares, and apparel chain, formed a Customer Advisory Board (CAB) in 1985. The CAB is composed of approximately 1,200 preferred customers representing a range of age and income levels. Eighty-five percent of the members are women. CAB members receive detailed mail questionnaires three or four times per year. Five dollar gift certificates for Pier 1 purchases accompany each questionnaire. Through the years, the CAB has been surveyed on topics such as advertising, holiday shopping, in-store signage, and service quality.

A recent service quality questionnaire sent to the CAB achieved a response rate of 46 percent despite being 11 pages long. The questionnaire included rating scales for respondents to indicate the importance of various aspects of customer service (for example, salespersons' attitudes, helpfulness with merchandise, and knowledge), and how well Pier 1 performs on these service attributes. Open-ended questions were included, for example, "What could Pier 1 do to better serve you? Please be as specific as possible." The results from this particular survey were a deciding factor in Pier 1's rollout of a new selling skills training program to all of its 6,000 store associates during 1993.

New, Declining, and Former Customer Surveys

One way to rivet management's attention on service improvement is through surveys that suggest the *profit impact* of service quality. Surveys of new, declining, and former customers can identify the consequences of a firm's service quality performance.

New customers are attracted to a company and existing customers buy less or leave altogether for various reasons, including service quality. Identifying these reasons, determining their relative impact, and monitoring trends in the data will illuminate the value brought by excellent service and the damage by poor service.

The first time former customer research is done, executives frequently are surprised by the sizeable percentage of customers who defect for service-related reasons. If a commercial bank, for example, does closed account surveys and adds up the percentages of customers leaving for service-related reasons (e.g., long lines, inconvenient operating hours, statement errors, staff attitude), it may discover that poor service is the primary cause of customer defections, greater even than change of residence. If the bank further analyzes the cost of acquiring new customers to replace lost ones and the cumulative profitability of retaining certain types of customers for one, three, five, and ten years, executives would become instant converts to the service-improvement cause. Moreover, if the bank takes several other steps, such as reporting closed-account data by office, territory, or strategic business unit, and setting compensation-based goals for improvement, middle managers will become more interested in service improvement, too.

Monitoring declining customer patronage also can be valuable as a barometer of customer loyalty and predictor of future customer defections. Why are some customers buying less service or fewer services than formerly? Can the former level of business be recaptured? Which of the reasons for declining patronage are correctable and which are not? Declining customer measurement is especially important for businesses that sell multiple services and have a high cost of acquiring and installing new customers. In these firms, the profit impact of selling five services to a customer for a long time, instead of one or two services for a short time, is significant.

New customer surveying helps a firm track the primary influences in customer attraction. Asking new customers why they have become customers is a powerful question. Executives can monitor the relative impact of influences such as specific marketing campaigns (e.g., new advertising, sales promotion activity) and service indicators, such as the company's service reputation or positive word of mouth.

New, declining, and former customer surveys are easiest to conduct in businesses in which customers continuously or periodically use the service(s), and sales or transactional activity on a per-customer basis is captured. However, with some imagination, virtually any business can conduct this type of research. Staples, the Boston-based office products retailer, offers its customers membership cards to use when they pay for their purchases. To obtain the card, customers must provide background information, including mailing address, on an application. While the membership card gives customers access to special discounts and promotions, it allows Staples to track an individual customer's frequency of visits, plus the size and type of purchases made.[5] Staples can readily conduct the type of research discussed in this section if it chooses to do so.

Focus Group Interviews

Focus group interviews involve directed questioning of a small group, usually eight to twelve people. The questions concern a specific topic or issue, hence the use of the word "focus." Interviews normally last from one to two hours, allowing the focal issue to be thoroughly discussed.

Focus group interviews are popular in service quality research because they are relatively simple to implement and can be administered quickly. Unfortunately, focus groups are often used incorrectly. It is tempting for a company's management to sponsor customer focus groups to be able to claim that the firm does service quality research. However, focus groups are not a substitute for quantitative research; they can play a complementary role, but they should not stand alone.

A focused interview with a small group enables a researcher to probe for insight, to delve beneath the surface of an issue. In service quality research, focus groups are an ideal forum for customers to discuss service problems they are experiencing and suggest ideas for improvement. Customers can discuss the criteria they use to judge service quality or provide quick feedback on a service initiative the company is planning. Employee focus groups can be convened to discuss ways to overcome certain service problems or to offer prompt feedback on proposed operational changes.

Focus groups, in effect, are brainstorming sessions. They can provide managers with new ideas and different perspectives. The information, however, is not projectable to the population of interest. If several people in each of three customer focus groups complain about an insurance company's slow claims processing, the company still does not know the extent of the problem, the relative importance to customers of claim processing speed versus other service attributes, or how the firm compares on this attribute with competitors.

Focus group research is most valuable in service improvement when it is coupled with projectable research. Projectable research gives decision makers data from which they can make inferences about the population under study; qualitative research, such as focus groups, gives decision-makers context and sensitivity for interpreting the data. *Focus group research brings to life the computer printout numbers.* The combination of "Mary" in a videotaped customer focus group passionately denouncing the runaround she experienced with her insurance claim, and a computer printout statistic of 37 percent of recent claimants rating their claim processing experience negatively, may move management to act.

Qualitative and quantitative research used in tandem can improve the design of both. Themes from qualitative research can be explored further in empirical surveys. Empirical data can highlight specific service issues for deeper probing in focus groups.

Employee Field Reporting

Another form of qualitative research that can be incorporated in a service quality information system is employee field reporting. Many companies fail to capture what customer-contact personnel are learning about customers because no systematic means for gathering and sharing such information exists. Providing a formal mechanism for capturing and sharing this market intelligence is the basic idea of employee field reporting.

Why ask employees what customers are saying and doing when the company is already using surveys to ask customers directly? There are three reasons. First, employee reports can reinforce certain themes from the customer research, underlining their urgency. Second, employees can report on what they are observing, not just hearing, and thus provide a different slant on the information. Whereas a survey of supermarket customers may reveal their disdain for long checkout lines, a survey of supermarket cashiers about customers may reveal the problem of some customers in long lines abandoning their full carts and leaving the store. Third, employee field reports can cover a wider range of issues than those normally covered in customer research, for example, competitive strategies.

Respondents in employee field reporting can be salespeople, service technicians, telephone receptionists, service recovery personnel, store managers, bank tellers—anyone having extensive contact with customers. Companies can gather the information through questionnaires, call reports, employee focus groups, or other means.

One company using employee field reporting effectively is Omega, a San Francisco-based bank training and consulting company. With offices in several U.S. cities, and in Toronto, London, and Sydney, Omega has representatives from each office contribute written monthly statements that are consolidated into a single report. The consolidated report is then distributed throughout the company. Respondents report on a variety of topics:

- what clients are saying
- what I learned last month about banking
- competitive information
- major accomplishments and successful tactics
- business development
- quality ideas, accolades, or problems
- how I'm feeling about the business

Aside from these regular issues, respondents gather intelligence on an assigned special topic for the monthly report. The special topic recently was how banks are handling the training needs of part-time employees.

Although the Omega system covers more than service quality intelligence, its application to service improvement is clear. The following few excerpts from a lengthy "what clients are saying" section of a monthly report (with proprietary information deleted) illustrate the potential richness of field report data:

Respondent #1

Although the recently completed Credit Skills Assessment went well at the point of administration, the client is frustrated at the delays encountered by the test scoring company. Earlier promises may now not be met. Naturally, we are working hard to ensure that the test scoring vendor makes up for lost time. The point here is that the client will always hold us responsible even when certain project activities are outside our direct control. The importance of obtaining service quality guarantees from our suppliers has certainly been reinforced in this current project.

Respondent #2

I have been interviewing retail bank managers about their perceived need for satellite delivery of training and information to branch staff. The clearest message I'm hearing is that staffing is very tight and so is time available for training. At _____, there is the assumption by the training department that "there is zero time available for training." The implications for Omega are startling—we don't serve our clients well if training takes people out of the branches, and takes days to complete.

Respondent #3

_____ was pleased with the content and workshop delivery of the customized version of Analyzing Personal Cash Flow. They particularly like the emphasis in the workshop on making analytical judgments based on the cash flow computations. However, they wish for a "simpler worksheet" and to have the worksheet available for use on a computer diskette.

Respondent #4

This month's special topic is timely. I have never heard such a unanimous outcry for any single training need as I have heard from clients about managing part-time tellers. I've summarized their comments in the special topic section.

Respondent #5

During this visit, _____, head of the Retail Bank at _____, commented a number of times on the quality of teamwork which the Omega people displayed. He was very impressed with the lengths which our people went to help each other and to help the UK business. He is presently grappling with team-work issues at the highest level with his own organization and saw before him a model of how things could be.

Omega's field reporting system is a simple way to capture and share market intelligence that, for the most part, probably would be lost otherwise. Moreover, the discipline of preparing monthly answers to established questions reinforces the staff's need to listen to customers and to reflect on what they say.

Employee Research

Researching employees' experiences as internal customers also is critical in service improvement. Employees after all perform the services customers evaluate; to a degree, employees *are* the service to customers. Yet many companies do little or no employee research to buttress their service-improvement efforts. They may spend considerable sums researching the customers' perspective but nothing to learn the service providers' perspective.

Employee research makes internal service quality measurement possible. Because employees are the customers for internal services, they are the only people who can evaluate internal service quality. Because internal service quality affects external service quality, it is essential to measure the former, not just the latter.

People working in organizations know that management measures important employee performances. Management rhetoric about internal service quality carries little weight in the organization without measurement. Nor will management know what the internal service priorities should be without research. Baldrige winner Solectron Corporation uses a simple internal customer report card to measure the quality of support services such as telephone, information systems, and E-mail. One Tuesday each month, internal service providers distribute report cards to their customers. The card lists performance attributes vertically (for example, communication) and letter grades (from A to D) across the columns. Respondents check the appropriate grade for each performance dimension and write comments at the bottom. The comments can be ideas for improvement or explanations for the grade given.[6]

San Diego Gas and Electric sends an internal service survey to everyone in the company annually. The questions are broad enough to apply to diverse services; they are rated on a five-point scale. The 1993 version of the questionnaire contained 11 questions, including: "They have the knowledge and skills to give me what I need," "Overall, the people are easy to work with," and "They respond promptly to my phone calls and messages." Employee respondents evaluate the departments that have served them over the past year. Survey results are linked to managers' compensation and internal service improvement has become one of the company's key strategic goals.[7]

Employee research can help expose the root causes of poor service. Employees experience the organization's service delivery system daily. They see more than customers see and from a different vantage point. Employee research helps reveal *why* service problems occur and *what* companies must do to solve the problems. Consider, for example, what can be learned about service quality problems and priorities by asking employees twice a year to complete an anonymous survey that contains questions such as:

- If you could make one change in the company to improve employee motivation, what change would you make?
- What is the biggest problem you face day in and day out trying to deliver a high quality of service to your customers?

- If you were president of the company and could make only one change to improve service quality, what change would you make?

Answers to these questions can be especially valuable in starting or revitalizing a service-improvement effort because the questions will cut through surface issues to identify service obstacles in the organization.

Employee research also can serve as an early warning system. Employees' intensive exposure to the service delivery system often enables them to see the system breaking down before customers do. In a study of a large industrial services company, my colleagues and I asked both customers and employees to evaluate the company's service quality. As illustrated by Table 3–1, employees' ratings were significantly less favorable—perhaps because employees simply knew more about weaknesses in the firm's service system.

Companies that forego employee research are missing out on a vital source of service-improvement information. Customer and employee research play complementary roles; one is not a

Table 3–1
EMPLOYEE AND CUSTOMER RATINGS
OF AN INDUSTRIAL SERVICES COMPANY

Illustrative Service Attributes Included in the Study*	Average Rating on a 7-point Scale	
	Employees	Customers
Coordination of company's activities to ensure customer satisfaction	3.26	5.00
Preparation of employees to sell company's service	4.29	5.65
Ease with which customers having problems or special needs can reach appropriate company personnel	3.26	5.33

*Additional information about this study is available in Leonard L. Berry, Jeffrey S. Conant, and A. Parasuraman, "A Framework for Conducting a Services Marketing Audit," *Journal of the Academy of Marketing Science*, 19, 3 (1991), pp. 255–268.

substitute for the other. One caveat with employee research is that management must be prepared to act. To be ignorant of legitimate employee concerns and problems is bad. To know of them and do nothing is worse; it conveys the message that management cares little about employees.

A company conveying the message that management *does* care is Rosenbluth International, one of America's largest travel agencies with hundreds of offices. Management uses multiple methods to listen to employees. The Associate Hotline enables any associate to contact CEO Hal Rosenbluth directly through his 800-number voice mail. Quality assurance teams composed of nonmanagers visit branch offices, asking associates to review the performance of their managers, then asking those managers to review their managers, and so on. Twice a year, Rosenbluth also spends a day with 18 randomly chosen associates who complete surveys and discuss staff morale.[8] Hal Rosenbluth sends crayons to associates and asks them to draw pictures that express how they feel about the company. He likes the crayon exercise because "it elicits feelings that aren't going to come out in a survey."[9]

Occasional Snapshots Not Enough

The nine service quality research approaches discussed in this chapter underscore the philosophy of using multiple listening methods to guide the service-improvement process. Although a company normally would not use all nine approaches, it does want to use the combination that will provide decision makers with a current, comprehensive picture of what is happening in service quality, why, and what needs to be done.

An effective service quality information system is one that *informs and supports service improvement throughout the organization. It reveals service quality patterns and trends, identifies service-improvement priorities, and motivates service performance.* The research approaches that best deliver these benefits should be included in the service quality information system.

It is beneficial to incorporate relevant internal operating performance data into a service quality information system to supplement research-based information. Among the internal measures that might be included are service failure rates, service response times, customer and employee turnover statistics, training participation rates, and service costs.

A service quality information system does not replace the need for decision makers to interact directly with customers, prospects, and employees. Knowing what is going on and what needs to be done involves more than reading computer printouts. It also means spending considerable time listening and observing in the field. Airline executives should ride their planes, inconspicuously, to listen to passengers and to experience firsthand realities such as sitting in the middle seat in the coach cabin. Retailers periodically should accompany customers through their stores—asking them about what they see, what they like, and what they would change.

A service quality information system should give decision makers an overall—yet detailed—view, a current—yet historical—perspective. Required is a rich mix of data: present and past, quantitative and qualitative, internal and external, company and competitor, research and operating. Occasional snapshots are not enough.

CHARACTERISTICS OF AN EFFECTIVE
SERVICE QUALITY SYSTEM

This chapter focuses on the concept, purposes, scope, and methods of a service quality information system. Creating such a system is an important step in building the foundation for great service. Systematic listening improves service-quality decision making, the ultimate test of a service quality information system. A service quality information system requires certain features regardless of its specific design. Ongoing data collection through multiple research approaches is a necessity. Transactional surveys, total market surveys, and employee research should always be included. We turn now to other essential characteristics of a service quality information system.

Customers' service expectations should be measured. Measuring service performance *per se* is not as meaningful as measuring performance relative to customers' expectations. Customers' service expectations provide a context for their assessment of the service. Assume, for example, that a company only measures customers' perceptions of service performance using a 9-point scale. It receives an average perception score of 7.3 on the service attribute "performs the service right the first time." How should managers interpret this score? Is it a good score or not? Without knowing what customers expect, this is a difficult question. No context exists for gauging the rating; there is no frame of reference. Managers' interpretation of the 7.3 perception score likely would be far different if customers' average expectation rating for this attribute was 8.2 rather than 7.0. As researchers John Goodman, Scott Broetzmann, and Colin Adamson write:

> How satisfied is a satisfied customer? When is good, good enough? Unfortunately, companies that ask their customers how satisfied they are but fail to research customers' expectations cannot answer these questions.[10]

Exhibit 3–3, presented strictly as an illustration, shows that customers' service perceptions of attribute A have remained fairly stable over five time periods. However, their assessment of the company's quality of service on this attribute has declined sharply in periods 4 and 5 because of rising expectations. Managers in this company would have been oblivious to this deterioration in quality had they measured customers' perceptions in absolute terms rather than in relation to expectations.

Measuring the relative importance of service quality attributes is critical. Companies commonly invest in the wrong service priorities. Determining which service attributes are most important to targeted customer segments and which attributes the company underperforms on relative to key competitors and to customers' expectations establishes a sound basis for service-improvement priorities.

Measuring the importance of service attributes is not the same thing as measuring customers' service expectations, although they are closely related. Customers' expectations are the comparison standards they use to judge the performance of various service attributes. Customers assess service performance on two standards: what they want (desired service) and

Exhibit 3–3
WHY MEASURING CUSTOMERS'
SERVICE EXPECTATIONS IS IMP0RTANT

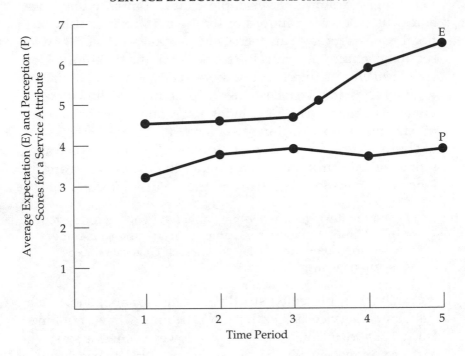

Source: A. Parasuraman, Leonard L. Berry, and Valarie A. Zeithaml, "Guidelines for Conducting Service Quality Research," *Marketing Research*, December 1990, p. 36.

what they will accept (adequate service).[11] The service attributes are not uniformly important to customers, however, and it is beneficial to specifically measure their relative importance.

One simple approach for measuring importance is asking respondents to rank order the service attributes. This does not establish the degree of difference in importance among attributes, however. Managers learn that the second-ranked attribute is more important than the third-ranked attribute but not how much more important. Asking respondents to allocate a total of 100 points across the various service dimensions based on their importance overcomes the problem. This method works well for a small number of service attributes but becomes too complex for more than ten attributes.

Having respondents rate service attributes on an importance scale, for example, "not at all important" to "extremely important" is another alternative. Unfortunately, respondents may award high scores to all the attributes, rendering the data ineffectual. Bernard Chudy and Roger Sant suggest presenting respondents with a pack of cards, with each card describing a different service attribute. Respondents are asked to place each card into one of four importance groups: of overriding importance, of key importance, of some importance, of limited importance.[12] This method overcomes to a degree the limitations of other approaches but does require a personal interview format.

Only a few of the direct ways to measure service attribute importance are discussed here. Each approach has pros and cons. A popular *indirect* method is to use regression analysis to analyze the proportion of variance in an overall service quality measure caused by specific service attributes. The more variance attributable to a service attribute, the more important it is. The purpose here is not to present an exposition on how to measure service attribute importance but, rather, to stress the necessity of doing so.

Measuring customers' service expectations and service attribute importance contributes to *actionability*, another essential characteristic of a service quality information system. The information generated must be sufficiently aligned with the organizational structure so that it is clear *who* needs to take action. The information must be specific enough so the managers will know *what to do*.

Discovering that a company's service is "unreliable" is not actionable. Actionability comes from determining which aspects of the service are unreliable, why, and who is responsible for fixing the problem. Without a link to a managerial process, it is not possible for anyone to take ownership of the information.[13] Researcher Brian Lunde makes the point when he writes:

> One of the worst criticisms that could be made by a line manager about a company's . . . information is that it is "interesting." "Interesting" is code for "useless." The information simply must be specific enough that executives . . . can take action—make decisions, set priorities, launch programs, cancel projects. . . . [14]

Measuring the market impact of service quality is also essential. Why should anyone care about delivering quality service? How significant is service quality compared to other investments a company can make? If the answers to such questions do not come from the service quality information system, from where will they come?

A service quality information system should disclose the market gains and damage attributable to service quality performance. New, declining, and former customer surveys can help in this regard, as discussed earlier. Additionally, customers' behavioral intentions can be measured in both transactional and overall service quality surveys. Customers can be asked, for example, to rate their likelihood of recommending the company to a friend, purchasing from the company again, buying additional services from the company, and paying 5 to 10 percent more for the company's service than competitors charge. Measures such as these then can be correlated with customers' service quality ratings of the company to reveal the extent to which the dependent variable (the customers' behavioral intentions) moves with the independent variable (the customers' service quality rating).

A service quality information system should not only guide managers on what to do to improve service; it should also motivate them to act. Measuring the market impact of service quality leads managers to implement needed changes.

A service quality information system must be more than a data-collection system; it must also be a communications system. The system can be beneficial only if decision makers use it. Eli Seggev and Denise Lapnow describe some of the guiding principles for the development of AT&T International's service quality information system:

- *Timeliness*—Management receives monthly reports no later than ten days after the month. Managers know when to expect the information.
- *Uniformity*—The monthly reports are as uniform as possible, familiarizing managers with the information and helping them locate key data quickly.
- *Presentation*—The operative guideline is that pictures are better than numbers, numbers are better than words, and, if words are necessary, fewer are better than more.[15]

The service quality information system should disseminate relevant service information to *everyone* in the organization. Why, for example, should customer-contact personnel not receive information about the expectations and perceptions of the customers they serve? Contact personnel might be given the information in different forms than senior managers—for example, in training classes, newsletters, and videos—but they should receive it. Executives miss a golden opportunity when they assume that employees lower in the organizational hierarchy have no need for or interest in details about the company's service performance. Southwest Airlines shows front-line employees videotapes of passengers who have complained about the service. Colleen Barrett, executive vice president for customers, states:

> When we show the tape, you can hear a pin drop. It's fascinating to see the faces of employees while they're watching. When they realize the customer is talking about them, it's pretty chilling. That has far more impact than anything I say.[16]

Service quality information is meant to be shared. One of the principal design challenges is determining who receives what information in what form when. The information needs of people at different levels in the organization vary; packaging the right information for each audience is a success key. As Peter Drucker states: "Knowledge is power. In post-capitalism, power comes from transmitting information to make it productive, not hiding it."[17]

SUMMARY

The voice of the customer must guide service improvement. Investing service-improvement resources in ways that do not improve service occurs frequently. It is common even in companies that conduct service quality research. Companies need a systematic, multiple-approach process for continually capturing and disseminating useable information for decision makers. What is needed is a service quality information system. An individual service quality study is but a snapshot. A system that provides an ongoing series of snapshots of various relevant subject matter taken from different angles is part of the foundation for great service.

The chapter presents nine service quality research approaches:

- transactional surveys
- total market surveys
- mystery shopping
- service reviews
- customer advisory panels
- new, declining, and former customer surveys
- focus group interviews
- employee field reporting
- employee research

Transactional surveys, total market surveys, and employee research are essential in any service quality information system. Additional approaches depend on company-specific issues. Internal operating data such as service response times and service costs also should be incorporated into the system.

Managers can assess where their company is in the development of a service quality information system by discussing the following questions:

1. *Do we listen to the voice of the customer systematically?* Is there a continuous flow of relevant data on which to base service decisions? Does the service information we collect reveal the patterns of change?
2. *Is the service quality information collected useful in guiding decisions?* Is the information considered interesting or essential? Are the data *actionable?*
3. *Are we using a portfolio of research approaches to learn about service quality?* Are we taking different types of service snapshots? Are we getting a comprehensive view?
4. *Do we know which service attributes are most important to our target markets?* Do we know how we perform on these attributes relative to key competitors and to customers' expectations?
5. *Are we aggressive in sharing service quality information within the organization?* Are we reaching everyone in the organization with infor-

mation that can help them improve service? Are we getting the right information to the right people?

6. *Does the service quality information we collect motivate service improvement?* Do we capture and convey the market payoff from great service and the market damage from poor service? Is service quality information a catalyst for change in our firm?

CHAPTER 4

CREATE A
SERVICE STRATEGY

S ervice leadership produces a service mentality in the organization. Service listening reveals what is important to customers, what is occurring in service performance and why, and what should be done to improve it; it also provides the basis for establishing an overall strategic direction—a service strategy.

All great service companies have a clear, compelling service strategy. They have a "reason for being" that energizes the organization and defines the word "service."

With a clear, compelling service strategy, decision makers know better which initiatives to approve and which to reject; the strategy is the guide. With a clear, compelling service strategy, service providers know better how to serve customers; the strategy is the guide. Thick policy and procedures manuals are unneeded.

A service strategy is a mission, *not* a mission statement. Mission statements are often nothing more than fancy words in internal and public documents that mean absolutely nothing to people in organizations who do the work. A mission, on the other hand, is galvanizing; it is a goal, a direction, a calling. It binds people in an organization together in a common purpose. It brings meaning to work. As James Collins writes: "A true mission . . . focuses people's efforts. It is tangible, specific, crisp, clear and engaging. It reaches out and grabs people in the gut."[1]

A service strategy captures what gives the service value to customers. To forge a path to great service, a company's leaders must define correctly that which makes the service compelling. They must set in motion and sustain a vision of service excellence, a set of guideposts that point to the future and show the way. It is not easy—which is why this book opened with the subject of leadership.

The service strategy usually can be expressed in a few sentences or words. Its value is in guiding and energizing; thus, the words serve their purpose only if they embrace a company's core beliefs, touch the human spirit of achievement, and are internalized. If employees have to look up the company's service strategy in a manual or planning document, the company doesn't have a service strategy.

TACOS, PLUMBING, AND SHIPPING— AT THE CUSTOMER'S BECK AND CALL

Researching this book led to many companies with strong service strategies. We review briefly the service strategies of three companies to illustrate the concept and its importance.

Taco Bell's service strategy is to offer the best value fast meal whenever and wherever customers are hungry. To implement this strategy, Taco Bell discarded traditional approaches to the business that gave the consumer only 27 cents worth of food for each dollar expended. Today's customers receive more than 45 cents worth of food per dollar. Through technology, training, job redefinition, and empowerment, Taco Bell increased span of control from one supervisor for five restaurants in 1990 to one for 30 (or more) in 1993. By developing technology that reduced the labor intensity of taco preparation, moving food preparation off-site, and turning restaurant kitchens into strictly assembly areas, Taco Bell was able to reallocate restaurant space from 70 percent kitchen/30 percent seating to 70 percent seating/30 percent kitchen. Store construction and operating costs plummeted, and customer waiting time decreased by more than 70 percent.

Taco Bell is now embarking on an ambitious journey of taking the "restaurant" to where customers already are via carts, kiosks, and vending machines. Management envisions growing from 4,500 fixed restaurant locations in 1993 to 200,000 distribution points at stadiums, schools, offices, airports, and other locations within ten years. In 1993, Taco Bell served 50 million customers per week. This number may soon seem small. Chairman and Chief Executive Officer John E. Martin states: "If there is a hungry stomach, we want to fill it."[2]

De Mar, the Clovis-Fresno, California, plumbing, heating, air conditioning, refrigeration company, has a simple but powerful service strategy: *solve the customer's problem no matter what, solve the problem when the customer needs it solved, and make sure the customer feels good when you leave.* De Mar offers guaranteed, same-day service for customers requiring it. The company provides 24-hour-a-day, 7-day-a-week service at no extra charge for customers whose air conditioning dies on a hot summer Sunday or whose toilet overflows at 2:30 in the morning. As Janie Walter, assistant service coordinator, puts it: "We will be there to fix your A/C on the fourth of July, and it's not a penny extra. When our competitors won't get out of bed, we'll be there!"

De Mar guarantees the price of a job to the penny before the work commences. Whereas most competitors guarantee their work for 30 days, De Mar guarantees all parts and labor for one year. The company assesses no travel charge because "it's not fair to charge customers for driving out." Owner Larry Harmon says: "We are in an industry that doesn't have the best reputation. If we start making money our main goal, we are in trouble. So I stress customer satisfaction; money is the by-product."

As discussed later in the book, De Mar uses selective hiring, ongoing training and education, performance measures and compensation that incorporate customer satisfaction, strong teamwork, peer pressure, empowerment, and aggressive promotion to implement its service strategy. Anne Semrick, credit and receivables manager, says: "The person who wants a nine-to-five job needs to go somewhere else." Janie Walter adds: "This job is wild."

Unlike Taco Bell with its low-price menu, De Mar is a premium pricer. Yet customers respond to both companies because both deliver value, that is, benefits for costs. In 1985, De Mar's annual sales were approximately $200,000. By 1993, they were more than $3.3 million.

Roberts Express's service strategy is transporting time-sensitive critical shipments door-to-door with uncompromised reliability and customized, personal service. Through a fleet of more than 1,500 multisized trucks owned and operated by independent contractors and an air charter service, Roberts Express transports shipments such as hazardous materials, emergency medical equipment and supplies, and parts for manufacturers using just-in-time inventory methods. Operating 24 hours a day, 7 days a week, Roberts Express picks up most shipments within 90 minutes of the order and delivers 95 percent of the shipments within 15 minutes of the promised time. The company backs up its time-sensitive shipping strategy with an explicit guarantee: 25 percent refund for shipments that arrive more than two hours late and 50 percent for shipments more than four hours late.

Roberts Express uses advanced computer and telecommunications technology to communicate immediately with every driver, predict where more drivers will be needed the next day, and, within seconds of a customer's call, calculate the precise pick-up and delivery times, and the customer's cost. As discussed in Chapter 6, Roberts Express uses teams to receive and dispatch job orders. Each team specializes in a geographic territory, which allows team members to develop working relationships with frequent customers. "We want to appear small in everything we do," states President Bruce Simpson.

Roberts Express is an ardent user of measures and incentives tied to customer satisfaction. The company has been measuring customer satisfaction on a monthly basis for years, as described in Chapter 3. Bruce Simpson says: "We are in the strategic management of perception." The strategy is working, with annual sales climbing from $3 million in 1982 to $125 million in 1993. Today, Roberts Express is the largest surface-expedited carrier in North America.

CHARACTERISTICS OF A SERVICE STRATEGY

The Taco Bell, De Mar, and Roberts Express examples illustrate the *central role of quality service in a service strategy*. A service strategy may encompass more than the delivery of quality service—for example, value pricing is a key element of Taco Bell's strategy—but quality service must be a point of emphasis for the strategy to be effective. Taco Bell's value pricing would not work if the restaurants were unclean, the lines long and slow-moving, and the hot food was served cold. The value prices would not offer much value.

The pivotal role of quality service in a service strategy means commitment to four quality service principles: reliability, surprise, recovery, and fairness. Reliability refers to accurate and dependable service; it refers to keeping the service promise. Surprise means finding ways to make the customer say "wow, these folks are good"; it comes from the unexpected extra. Recovery involves regaining the customers' confidence if the service is deficient; it means standing behind the service. Fairness requires a level playing field for company and customer; business is conducted in an ethical arena. These service quality principles—discussed in the next chapter—form the basis of a service strategy, as they do for Taco Bell, De Mar, and Roberts Express.

Roberts Express picks up and delivers shipments within 15 minutes of when promised 95 percent of the time—and is working hard to improve. The 95 percent standard holds regardless of traffic, weather, or mechanical delays. The company picks up *and* delivers 50 percent of its shipments by midnight of the same day. Another 30 percent is delivered by 9:00 A.M. the next morning. Roberts quotes the price of the service to the penny before the service commences and guarantees on-time service backed up by an explicit refund policy. Service reliability, surprise, recovery, and fairness are much in evidence in Roberts Express's strategy—and are contributing to the company's rapid growth.

An excellent service strategy *offers customers genuine value; it gives customers more for the costs they incur.* The strategy focuses on the few dimensions of performance that make the service valuable, even essential, to customers. Whether the price is low or high, customers believe they are getting their money's worth.

When a Fresno restaurant's air conditioning breaks down an hour before the lunch rush on a hot summer day, speed and service reliability—not price—are the critical determinants of value. Some air conditioning firms answer the phone with a recording. But to De Mar's Larry Harmon, ". . . when the customer's A/C breaks down, it's almost like a 911 call here." Service consultant Chip Bell advises, "Decide what you want to be famous for in the eyes of customers."[3] De Mar wants to be famous for treating an emergency like an emergency.

A company must live its service strategy. Wordsmithing does not give life to a service strategy; aligning the strategy with employee selection criteria, training and education, technology, performance measures, and reward systems *does* give life to a service strategy. The service strategy must embody the company's belief system. If the belief system contradicts the desired strategy, then the belief system must be changed or the strategy will fail.

Alignment vitalizes a service strategy. The correct question is not "what is the best technology?" The correct question is "what is the best technology to support our strategy?" The right question is not "which organizational structure is best?" It is "which organizational structure is right for our strategy?"

An excellent service strategy fosters genuine achievement in the organization. It challenges every employee to develop new skills and knowledge; it challenges them to raise their aspirations. An excellent strategy requires creativity and risk taking at all organizational levels, not just the management levels. It demands high discretionary efforts; minimum efforts do not suffice.

A service strategy should push the organization to perform beyond industry norms. The strategy should "stretch" the organization. Such a strategy is possible only in organizations whose managers fundamentally believe in the capacity of people to achieve—to grow in their work, to rise to the occasion.

Taco Bell operates 90 percent of its company-owned restaurants without a full-time manager. These locations are team-managed by their mostly-young-person crews who order inventory, schedule work hours, and recruit and train peers, among other functions. A manager-less restaurant defies convention; it also challenges the unmanaged service providers to assume greater responsibility, learn more, and work together as a team. Taco Bell's John Martin explains:

> Ask most young people who work at the crew level in the restaurant industry whether they'd rather chop lettuce or take the responsibility for transmitting a P&L statement via computer to their main office. The fact is, many of them would rather chop lettuce. Why? Because most of them don't believe that they can do the other. They don't believe it because they haven't had the experience. But give them the experience. Change their beliefs. Prove to them that they can do the job. And much more often than not, they'll do it.[4]

Taco Bell's service strategy is the product of "out-of-the box" thinking as revealed through their taking most of the kitchen out of the restaurant, making tacos with machines, operating manager-less restaurants, using mobile food distribution units. Out-of-the-box thinking fashions extraordinary achievement. The conventional wisdom breeds complacency.

In a speech to auto dealers, I commented on the need to offer evening hours for maintenance and repair service. Afterward, a dealer remarked that his mechanics would quit if they had to work at night. Perhaps they would quit, but this is a classic case of running the business by the conventional wisdom that auto mechanics work during the day, not in the evening, and nothing can be done about it. The problem with this conventional wisdom, of course, is that many car owners also work during the day, and evening service hours might be more convenient.

De Mar is a multimillion dollar business today because it defies the conventional wisdom of its industry. De Mar's Larry Harmon not only gets his employees to work at night; if necessary, he gets them out of bed. De Mar's service strategy requires unconventional thinking. So does the auto dealer's strategy if great service is the goal.

Taco Bell, De Mar, and Roberts Express all have a strategic "reason for being." Customers would miss these companies if they were suddenly to disappear—just as they would miss the other companies featured in this book. A clear, compelling service strategy generates great service. All the other components of service excellence emerge from the service strategy—manifesting it, refining it, implementing it.

IDENTIFYING A SERVICE STRATEGY

Knowing that a service strategy must emphasize quality, offer value to customers, be aligned with organizational practices and beliefs, and stimulate achievement is insufficient in and of itself. A firm still must identify a service strategy that will meet these tests.

Identifying a service strategy involves answering three pivotal questions:

- What attributes of service are—and will continue to be— most important to our target markets?

- On which important service attributes is the competition weakest?
- What are the existing and potential service capabilities of our company?

Answering these questions constitutes an opportunity analysis. Important service needs of customers that are undermet by competitors and can be met by the strategy-defining company represent an "open" service position in the market. Revealing these possible openings through research approaches discussed in the previous chapter is a prerequisite to creating a service strategy.

In analyzing what is important to target markets, decision makers should ask two subquestions: what is *essential* to the customer and what will make the customer say "wow"? The service strategy should incorporate both the essential attributes that will meet customers' expectations and the "wow" attributes that will exceed their expectations. This is why the service reliability, surprise, recovery, and fairness themes need to be considered in the service strategy's development. Reliability, recovery, and fairness are service essentials; surprise adds unexpected value. But these are broad themes. What type of reliability? What are the principal fairness issues? What does excellent recovery require? What kind of service surprises? And what else should be part of the service strategy?

De Mar is a good example of a company that provides essential and wow service with the same strategy. The company's technical excellence, same-day service, and guaranteed price quotes meet the essential-service test. Its 24-hour, 7-day service at no extra charge and the staff's service-minded attitudes provide the extra-differentiating "wow" effect. Make no mistake about it: Larry Harmon understands what is important to the customers.

Analysis of competitor service strengths and weaknesses is critical to assessing which strategies will be differentiating. Important service attributes on which competitors are mediocre or poor offer a better opening than attributes on which they are strong. Of course, key competitors may already be strong on the most important service attributes. If so, the challenge is to find or create an alternative opening, for example adding strength for one or more of the critical service attributes—and possibly several secondary ones—and creatively packaging and communicating these virtues. In general, strength versus vulnerability works better than strength versus strength.

Denver's Tattered Cover Book Store illustrates the power of service strength versus service vulnerability. Many bookstores, especially the chains, have used price promotion as a primary marketing strategy, attempting to compete by discounting titles on the best-seller lists. Some of these chains also are building spacious, attractive superstores that stock a large number of titles. The superstore trend is a development of the 1990s.

The Tattered Cover was a book superstore long before the industry trend developed, moving into a four-story, 40,000-square-foot building in 1986. But Tattered Cover's store size and huge selection of 150,000 book titles are not its only success factors. To customers, the store feels like home with wooden bookshelves, antique furniture and desks, and "151 comfy chairs and couches" as employee Tracy Holloway puts it. Sidney Jackson adds: "We've created an atmosphere that it is all right for the customers to touch the books. They can sit down and read the books and it's fine."

The key to the entire strategy, however, is Tattered Cover's service quality. The mentality of serving that is so alive in this store—the passion to help customers find the right book—is what transforms the huge store, huge collection, comfortable furnishings combination into a unique, impossible-to-imitate retail company. The Tattered Cover's competitive advantage is its people, its service providers. Customers feel good in this store, which is why they flock to it. Bookstore *service* was and is the Tattered Cover's opportunity in the market.

Finally, the strategy-defining company must carefully appraise its own service competencies, weaknesses, performance, and belief system. A market opening may exist but the company may not be prepared to seize it. It may lack the needed skills, knowledge, systems, financial resources, belief system, or reputation. Determining the gap between market opportunity and a company's capability and then deciding whether the firm is prepared to make the needed changes are requisite steps in the service strategy creation process.

A company's service strategists should be prepared to ask and answer questions such as these:

- What are the company's integral service competencies—the critical knowledge and skills that define and drive the firm, both philosophically and practically?
- What are the company's service incompetencies—knowledge and skill weaknesses that are hurting the company?
- What are the company's resource strengths and weaknesses? How does the firm compare to competitors in terms of financial, facility, technology, human, and other resources?
- What is the company's service reputation? How do customers, noncustomers, and employees view service performance?
- What is the company's belief system? What is valued within the organization? What is the company's core culture?
- What is the company's present service strategy? What is the firm's "reason for being" today?

Identifying a service strategy boils down to searching for a match between what needs doing and what the firm can do exceedingly well. It pays to do one's homework, for the service strategy provides the framework for all service-improvement investments. Excellent service strategies are remarkably enduring. Tactical enhancements and refinements are common, but the fundamental strategy changes rarely. The reason is that the best strategies tap basic human needs that change little over time.

Harold's, the Houston clothier, fills the basic need some customers have for an ongoing relationship with an honest, knowledgeable "clothing advisor." Hard Rock Cafe taps the need of its target market for sensory stimulation, for food *and* fun, not just food. Roberts Express fills shippers' needs for competence and speed when time is of the essence. When Joyce Meskis bought The Tattered Cover Book Store in 1974, she started with two people. Today, the company employs more than 320 people. Yet, the basic service strategy remains unchanged. As general manager Linda Millemann, who has worked at Tattered Cover since 1979, comments: "What I've noticed is how the store has stayed the same as we've grown. Our approach to each other and to the customer has stayed the same."

Exhibit 4–1 summarizes the principal analytical steps for identifying a strong service strategy. Handling these steps well produces an enduring pathway to the decisions and practices needed for great service.

Exhibit 4–1
IDENTIFYING A SERVICE STRATEGY

Determine the most important service attributes for meeting and exceeding customers' expectations.

↓

Determine the important service attributes on which competitors are most vulnerable.

↓

Determine existing and potential service capabilities of our company. Assess service competencies and incompetencies, resource strengths and weaknesses, service reputation, belief system, and "reason for being."

↓

Develop a service strategy that addresses important, enduring customer needs, exploits competitor vulnerabilities, and fits our company's capabilities and potential.

DEFINING THE SERVICE ROLE

The service strategy defines the broad parameters of the service providers' role. Explicit service standards clarify the service task and provide benchmarks against which employees can judge their own performance and managers can judge the employees' and organization's performance.

Properly developed service standards bring a customer focus into the service provider's day-to-day role and reinforce the implementation of the service strategy. Service standards reflect customer expectations in a way that is meaningful to employees; the standards are the specifics of the service strategy.

Many service organizations do not adequately define the meaning of excellent service to service providers. Executives may exhort employees to deliver excellent service but leave vague the meaning of excellent service. The result is service role ambiguity: the priorities for excellent service are unclear. The potential causes of service role ambiguity include the following:

- *No service standards*, which make the service role a guessing game.
- *Too many service standards*, which diminish employees' awareness of the most urgent service priorities.
- *General service standards*, which offer insufficient direction and a limited basis for performance measurement.
- *Poorly communicated service standards*, which is almost the same as having no service standards.
- *"Toothless" service standards*, which are standards unconnected to performance measurement and reward systems, thereby conveying their lack of importance.[5]

No company in America does a better job of defining the service role and linking it to the overall service strategy than the Ritz-Carlton Hotel Company, a 1992 winner of the Baldrige National Quality Award. Ritz-Carlton employees are focused on delivering the company's "Gold Standards," which are printed on a wallet-sized, plastic "credo" card that all employees carry; the card is considered part of the uniform. The card contains the company's credo (its service strategy), its motto ("We Are Ladies and Gentlemen Serving Ladies and Gentlemen"), its three steps of service, and a list of 20 Ritz-Carlton basics (the service standards).

A Ritz-Carlton employee who does not know and embrace the company's credo, motto, three service steps, and 20 service basics is rare. Ritz-Carlton selects employment candidates with its service strategy and standards in mind. All new employees undergo a two-day orientation in the company's service mission and receive intensive on-the-job training. The gold standards are reinforced by daily service personnel lineups, regular performance reviews, a job-certification process, and frequent recognition for extraordinary service.

The content of Ritz-Carlton's Credo card, presented in Exhibit 4-2, exemplifies the message of this chapter: *great service requires definition. Understanding the company's "reason for being" internally is a prerequisite to implementing it for customers. An excellent service strategy, effectively reinforced by service standards, brings focus and energy to service delivery.*

Exhibit 4–2
RITZ-CARLTON'S GOLD STANDARDS

THREE STEPS OF SERVICE

1
A warm and sincere greeting. Use the guest name, if and when possible.

2
Anticipation and compliance with guest needs.

3
Fond farewell. Give them a warm good-bye and use their names, if and when possible.

"We Are Ladies and Gentlemen Serving Ladies and Gentlemen"

THE RITZ-CARLTON

CREDO

The Ritz-Carlton Hotel is a place where the genuine care and comfort of our guests is our highest mission.

We pledge to provide the finest personal service and facilities for our guests who will always enjoy a warm, relaxed yet refined ambience.

The Ritz-Carlton experience enlivens the senses, instills well-being, and fulfills even the unexpressed wishes and needs of our guests.

THE RITZ-CARLTON BASICS

1 The Credo will be known, owned and energized by all employees.

2 Our motto is: "We are Ladies and Gentlemen serving Ladies and Gentlemen". Practice teamwork and "lateral service" to create a positive work environment.

3 The three steps of service shall be practiced by all employees.

4 All employees will successfully complete Training Certification to ensure they understand how to perform to The Ritz-Carlton standards in their position.

5 Each employee will understand their work area and Hotel goals as established in each strategic plan.

6 All employees will know the needs of their internal and external customers (guests and employees) so that we may deliver the products and services they expect. Use guest preference pads to record specific needs.

7 Each employee will continuously identify defects (Mr. BIV) throughout the Hotel.

8 Any employee who receives a customer complaint "owns" the complaint.

9 Instant guest pacification will be ensured by all. React quickly to correct the problem immediately. Follow-up with a telephone call within twenty minutes to verify the problem has been resolved to the customer's satisfaction. Do everything you possibly can to never lose a guest.

10 Guest incident action forms are used to record and communicate every incident of guest dissatisfaction. Every employee is empowered to resolve the problem and to prevent a repeat occurrence.

11 Uncompromising levels of cleanliness are the responsibility of every employee.

12 "Smile – We are on stage." Always maintain positive eye contact. Use the proper vocabulary with our guests. (Use words like – "Good Morning," "Certainly," "I'll be happy to" and "My pleasure").

13 Be an ambassador of your Hotel in and outside of the work place. Always talk positively. No negative comments.

14 Escort guests rather than pointing out directions to another area of the Hotel.

15 Be knowledgeable of Hotel information (hours of operation, etc.) to answer guest inquiries. Always recommend the Hotel's retail and food and beverage outlets prior to outside facilities.

16 Use proper telephone etiquette. Answer within three rings and with a "smile." When necessary, ask the caller, "May I place you on hold." Do not screen calls. Eliminate call transfers when possible.

17 Uniforms are to be immaculate; Wear proper and safe footwear (clean and polished), and your correct name tag. Take pride and care in your personal appearance (adhering to all grooming standards).

18 Ensure all employees know their roles during emergency situations and are aware of fire and life safety response processes.

19 Notify your supervisor immediately of hazards, injuries, equipment or assistance that you need. Practice energy conservation and proper maintenance and repair of Hotel property and equipment.

20 Protecting the assets of a Ritz-Carlton Hotel is the responsibility of every employee.

1092

SYMBOLIZING THE SERVICE STRATEGY

The examples in this chapter, from De Mar to Ritz-Carlton, illustrate the centrality of the service strategy in the firm's belief system. The more difficult it is to distinguish between a company's belief system and its service strategy, the better. In effect, in companies like De Mar and Ritz-Carlton, the strategy and the belief system are one and the same.

Like service standards, service symbols can convey beliefs, reinforce the service strategy, and meld the beliefs and strategy. Although symbols alone cannot change a company's belief system or give wings to its service strategy, symbols can underscore structural changes, technology investments, operating shifts, and other developments, signaling the realness of the firm's path. If aligned with what is otherwise occurring in the organization, symbols can help communicate what the firm stands for and where it is going.

Tangibles, language, and management behaviors are primary symbolization tools that companies can use to carry the intended message. Ritz-Carlton uses tangibles to enliven the guests' senses—and remind employees of the hotel's special mission. Fresh flowers are everywhere (because they smell good), luxurious terry cloth robes are in each guest room (because they feel good), and chandeliers hang in the public areas (because they look good). The company's language is purposeful and powerful. "We are ladies and gentlemen serving ladies and gentlemen" conveys the dignity of service so infrequently felt in many other companies. Employees respond to guest requests with "certainly" or "my pleasure," not with "OK." Ritz-Carlton "selects" new employees rather than "hiring" them. Horst Schulze, Ritz-Carlton's president, helps conduct employee orientation sessions at new hotels. Schulze and 13 other senior executives compose the company's quality management team, which meets weekly to review service quality performance, progress, and plans. The top managers devote about one-fourth of their total work time to quality-related matters. Management behaviors symbolize the service mission at Ritz-Carlton.

De Mar's Larry Harmon personally leads weekly customer service training and education sessions, which begin at 6:00 A.M. The training room is filled with employee photos, motivational signs ("Enthusiasm," "De Mar Co.—The Best," "Satisfied Customers"), and Dale Carnegie plaques, employee awards, and company trophies (the De Mar Wall of Fame). Following the Monday class on customer relations, De Mar has truck inspection. Service advisors cannot make their first call until their trucks pass inspection. De Mar trucks are painted bright yellow with red lettering. The lettering is reflectorized so it can be seen after dark—prime time for De Mar. The trucks are viewed as mobile billboards and are a key part of De Mar's marketing strategy. De Mar's Anne Semrick comments: "De Mar is very visible in the town. The lady at the bank said there are more De Mar trucks in Fresno than police cars. Everyone knows who we are. This puts on added pressure to live up to our reputation."

De Mar uses the term "service advisor" rather than "technician." Larry Harmon explains: "I don't want our people to think like a technician. I want them to think like businesspeople." De Mar service advisors conclude service visits with "Have a Dee Marvelous Day." De Mar sends a thank you card to customers after every job. All employees have business cards, which feature De Mar's Commitment to Service Excellence on the back: "Every De Mar customer should always feel they received the best service available . . . anytime, anywhere, at any price."

Bidding the customer a "Dee Marvelous Day" would seem silly or artificial in most companies. At De Mar, the language fits the company's belief system and service strategy; the language is appropriate because it is an honest reflection of what the company stands for, of its reason for being. Symbols must be authentic to be powerful.

SUMMARY

All great service companies have a clear, compelling service strategy. They have a "reason for being" that galvanizes the organization, gives it direction, gives it purpose. An excellent service strategy offers customers genuine value, is aligned with a company's operating practices and beliefs, and fosters true achievement within the organization. It emphasizes quality service, incorporating the service quality pillars of reliability, surprise, recovery, and fairness.

Identifying a specific service strategy that meets the above tests requires analysis of service attributes important to target markets, competitor strengths and weaknesses, and one's own company's strengths and weaknesses. The objective is to find some degree of market opening: a match between what is needed and what the company can do well.

Identifying a strong service strategy is a crucial step in service improvement for everything else revolves around it. Service standards and symbols should reinforce the service strategy. So should organizational structures, technology investments, and human resource practices—discussed in subsequent chapters. The importance of developing an excellent service strategy cannot be overstated. The wrong strategy puts into motion the wrong reinforcing and implementing initiatives.

Executives can use the following action checklist to discuss the service strategy issue:

1. *Is our service strategy clear and compelling to all of our employees?* Does it focus our efforts? Does it bring energy and meaning to our work?
2. *Does our service strategy deliver genuine value to customers?* Does it capture what is most valuable to customers? Does it guide us towards value-adding improvements?
3. *Does our service strategy emphasize excellent service quality?* Is it sufficiently focused on the service quality essentials of reliability, surprise, recovery, and fairness?
4. *Do we live our service strategy in this company?* Is it central to our belief system? Is it aligned with our structure, technology and operating practices?
5. *Does our service strategy demand superior achievement?* Does it require our people to grow in their work, to be creative, and to take risks? Does the strategy stretch us? Does it force unconventional thinking?
6. *Does our service strategy differentiate our company from competitors?* Does it capitalize on our strengths and competitor vulnerabilities?
7. *Do we reinforce our service strategy with explicit service standards that guide and energize employees?* Do our employees understand the meaning of excellent service? Do they know what the priorities are?
8. *Do we reinforce our service strategy with appropriate symbols?* Are we using tangibles, language, and management behaviors to convey to employees what the firm stands for and where it is going?

CHAPTER 5

COMMIT TO THE PRINCIPLES OF GREAT SERVICE

The most successful companies all have a "reason for being"; customers would miss these companies if they were suddenly to disappear. Service companies define their reason for being through their service strategy. The strategy guides and energizes the firm in creating value for customers.

Because quality service is integral to value creation for customers, it must always be a point of emphasis in the service strategy. Quality service underpins value creation; it is the necessary foundation for all else that the service strategy might entail. In turn, reliability, surprise, recovery, and fairness underpin quality service; these are the principles of creating great service. Reliability, recovery, and fairness are the basics of service. It is impossible to maintain the customers' confidence without these principles. Surprising service makes customers say "wow." It is difficult to exceed customers' service expectations without the element of surprise. Great service companies, regardless of the nature of their business, couple the basics of service with the art of surprise.

SERVICE RELIABILITY

Qualitative and empirical research that my colleagues and I have performed over many years suggests five broad dimensions that customers use as criteria to judge service quality.[1] The dimensions are not mutually exclusive, yet they provide a helpful framework in understanding customers' expectations:

RELIABILITY	The ability to perform the promised service dependably and accurately
TANGIBLES	The appearance of physical facilities, equipment, personnel, and communication materials
RESPONSIVENESS	The willingness to help customers and provide prompt service
ASSURANCE	The knowledge and courtesy of employees and their ability to convey trust and confidence
EMPATHY	The caring, individualized attention provided customers

Of these five service dimensions, reliability is the most important. Regardless of the service industry we studied, customers rated reliability as the single most important feature in judging service quality. Retail banking customers rated service reliability first in importance. So did product repair, securities brokerage, auto insurance, department store, credit card, life insurance, long-distance telephone, and computer manufacturing support service customers.

Evidence from elsewhere supports our research findings. From Union Pacific president and chief executive officer Richard Davidson comes this statement:

> . . . our senior management had been out talking to our major customers and asking them why the railroad share was not growing and about what the customers' perceptions of us were. The answer was that we really weren't offering the reliability that had to be there. It turned out that of all the factors that were prioritized by the customers being reliable was number one, and we just weren't measuring up.[2]

Findings such as this one buttressed Union Pacific's service improvement effort started in 1987 that *Railway Age* characterizes as "perhaps the most aggressive and advanced of any in the industry."[3]

Illinois Power, an electrical utility, surveyed its 400 largest customers and identified seven attributes that customers use to define service. The attributes fell into three tiers, ranked by importance. Gordon Spainhower, director of marketing, commented: "Reliability of service stands above the others as the single most important factor. It is about twice as important as any factor in the second tier of factors."[4]

Because services are performances rather than objects, they are difficult for customers to evaluate prior to purchase. A customer can test drive an automobile or try on clothing before deciding whether to buy. With services, however, purchase precedes experience. Customers open a bank account, check into a hotel, or buy an airline ticket before they experience the service. *Customers buy a promise and they must trust the company to deliver on its promises.*

Dependable, accurate service increases the customers' confidence in the company; frequent service mistakes destroy the customers' confidence. Most customers appreciate a sincere apology when a service problem occurs, but the apology does not erase the memory of a failed service. If a pattern of service mistakes develops, customers conclude that the company cannot be depended on to provide the promised service.

Challenges of Service Reliability

Service reliability poses some challenges different from manufactured goods reliability. Goods are first manufactured, then shipped, sold, and consumed. Services are first sold and then frequently produced and consumed simultaneously. The buyer of tangible products never sees what goes on in the factory. Manufacturing mistakes can be corrected before the customer experiences the product. With services, the customer enters the "factory"—the bank, dentist office, or restaurant—and is more likely to experience firsthand any production mistakes. If the restaurant waiter brings the wrong order to the table, or fails to return to the table with the promised margarine, the customer experiences the unreliable service directly. Customers' presence in the service factory and participation in the service process expose errors and give them a sense of immediacy.

The inseparability of production and consumption for many services necessitates decentralized production. A restaurant must locate in the city, perhaps even in the section of the city, in which it wants to do business. Thus, service businesses often operate a chain of service facilities. They bring customers not to one factory but to many factories.

Moreover, many services are labor intensive, introducing a greater degree of variability in the production process than if machines dominated the process. Human beings deliver a more variable service than machines. This is the reality of the human condition. Servers not only differ from one another in their technical skills, service attitudes, and personalities, but the same server can provide quite a different service from one customer to the next depending on the circumstances of each situation— customer attitude, server fatigue, complexity of the service requested. Labor-intensive services are more error-prone.

The conditions described above are common. Many organizations produce labor-intensive services in multiple service factories that customers visit. Delivering a consistently dependable service under these conditions is no walk on the beach.

Denny's, a family restaurant chain with approximately 1,500 U.S. outlets, illustrates the challenge. Most Denny's restaurants are open 24 hours a day. A new menu implemented in 1994 offers more than 150 entree choices in the breakfast, lunch, dinner, and late night categories. In a typical 24-hour period, Denny's serves more than 1,000,000 customers systemwide. Denny's has over 47,000 restaurant-based employees who greet customers, cook, wait and clean tables, accept payment, make change, wash dishes, and solve problems, among other functions. Each employee has numerous opportunities during a work shift to deliver promised services accurately and dependably or to fall short. Clearly, the potential for service mistakes is high. However, Ron Petty, who became Denny's chief operating officer in mid-1993, is determined that Denny's will become one of America's most service-minded restaurant chains. Service reliability is a cornerstone of his vision.

Petty has focused on improving service in the individual restaurant unit. He believes that the strength of the Denny's brand is a function of the value customers receive at the restaurant and that service quality determines value. "Everything we do is about service," states Petty. "Service is a total, integrated strategy that includes how you organize, how you hire, how you train, what you measure and reward, how you use technology, how you create an image."

Denny's reorganized field management so that regional managers now are accountable for all the restaurants in the region regardless of whether they are company-owned or franchised. Previously, responsibility was divided even though both company-owned and franchised units operated under the same brand name. The old bonus system excluded restaurant managers. The new system keys off the individual restaurant's performance; not only does it include the restaurant managers, but field managers earn a bonus only if the restaurant earns a bonus. A new field position of Operations Specialist was created to evaluate the operational performance of the restaurants.

The restaurants are now using automated systems to streamline inventory ordering and labor scheduling among other administrative functions, freeing restaurant managers to devote far more time to customer service. The standard restaurant manager training course has been extended from seven weeks to thirteen weeks.

Denny's is testing new kitchen technology to improve speed of service and meal preparation consistency. The clamshell grill involves cooking by computer instead of by sight. The cook presses a timer button to prepare a well-done steak. Cooking time is cut in half.

Marketing and image also are integral to Denny's service-improvement journey. By early 1994, Denny's had completely renovated all 21 of its Houston restaurants. New decor, colors, fixtures, signage—even a Baskin-Robbins dessert center near the entrance. The environment is not only new for customers but also for employees, symbolizing a new standard for service. Denny's units in six additional markets were remodeled by the end of 1994. Denny's has learned in recent tests that it can use advertised price specials to improve service quality. The lower price points drive customer counts up enough to justify higher staffing levels; for example, one waitperson serves four tables instead of six tables.

By eliminating a drab, out-of-date server uniform, Denny's aided hiring. Servers now wear their own clothing under a smock. In visiting one of the restaurants, Ron Petty complimented the manager on the service he received from a waitress. The manager replied: "We tried to hire her before, but she wouldn't work for us because of the uniforms."

Service Reliability Is Attitude

Errors occur in every service organization. The profile of Denny's reveals the inherent potential for errors in a complex service organization. However, some service organizations make many more mistakes than other, similarly complex organizations do. One difference is attitude. Companies that continuously nurture the values of accuracy and dependability prevent many errors caused by carelessness.

Some managers believe it is not practical to eliminate service mistakes. Others relentlessly work to minimize errors. Some managers stress speed of service delivery. Others stress accuracy over speed. Some managers are satisfied with a 98 percent reliability rate. Others view 98 percent reliability as a two percent error rate—and remind their direct reports of the actual number of customers affected by such an error rate (2,000 customers for a company serving 100,000 customers per week).

Wanting to be reliable is a key to actually being reliable. Karen Johnson is the president of Accu-Pay, a company that checks hospital bills for accuracy. She estimates that if the average percentage of hospital overcharges found by her company in one year (11 percent) were applied to the entire country, the total overcharge would be approximately $40 billion a year. Among the errors Accu-Pay found in its first year of operation: a male charged for a pregnancy test, a female charged for a sperm count, and another female charged for 32 hours of oxygen during a 24-hour period.[5] Attitude cannot prevent every billing error, but it certainly could prevent blatant errors such as these.

In 1991, the credit bureau TRW classified every taxpayer in Norwich, Vermont (1,400 people) as a bad credit risk when a worker mistakenly recorded the names of taxpayers instead of *delinquent* taxpayers. The repercussions were powerful—for Norwich citizens who suddenly were being denied credit, for TRW which received considerable negative publicity, and for the credit-reporting industry, the most complained-about industry in America even before this incident occurred. Surely, attitude could have helped prevent this service failure, perhaps by creating an exception-reporting system that would have flagged such an unusual occurrence.

Double Checking at Hard Rock Cafe. Performing the service right the first time is a bedrock value at Hard Rock Cafe, the immensely successful restaurant chain and merchandise retailer. Hard Rock Cafe emphasizes "double checking" to minimize errors. The message of double checking is: *Perform the service carefully to avoid mistakes. If a mistake does occur, correct it before it reaches the customer.*

Hard Rock Cafe Orlando implements double checking through two "extra" people in the kitchen. One is stationed inside the kitchen and the other at the kitchen counter. The inside person reviews everything that is going on, looking for signs of undercooked or overcooked meals, wilting lettuce, or any below-standard product or performance. The counter person, or "expediter," checks each prepared plate against the order ticket before the food is delivered to the table.

Is such a system needlessly expensive? Some readers may think so. However, the system seems to work well at the Orlando restaurant that on a busy day serves 6,000 meals to customers who may have waited in line for an hour or more.

Attention to Detail at Longo Toyota and Lexus. Longo Toyota and Lexus, America's largest retail volume automobile dealership, services 250 to 300 Toyota and 65 to 70 Lexus automobiles per day. Longo pays attention to the details in striving for reliable service, as demonstrated by the step-by-step service process Longo uses in its Toyota dealership. Managing the details of the service chain is emphasized to keep the service promise.

1. The customer drives the car to the service entrance. If a queue has formed, a numbered "hat" is placed on the roof of the car, indicat-

ing the customer's position in line and need to be greeted. The customer is offered coffee and a newspaper.

2. The service advisor greets the customer, asks what work is needed, and writes the repair order. The repair order indicates the work to be done, when the car will be ready ("the promise time"), and the cost estimate if the work is not under warranty. The customer signs the repair order and receives a copy.

3. The customer who waits on-site for the car to be serviced checks in with a customer assistance representative in the waiting room and is assigned a number. Shuttle vans transport customers who choose to leave and return later.

4. A porter drives the car to the parking area and places protective covering over the steering wheel, seats, and floor. Another porter takes the repair order to the designated work area and gives it to the group leader. The group leader, working with a team of four to five technicians, determines the start and finish times for the job and dispatches it to a technician. If the customer's promise time is 4:00 P.M. and the job is expected to take three hours to complete, the start time would be 12:00 noon, and the finish time 3:00 P.M. The extra hour is to accommodate unexpected delays and to complete the paperwork by the promise time.

5. The assigned technician requests the needed parts from the parts representative assigned to the team. A runner delivers the parts at about the same time as the car arrives at the technician's work station.

6. The technician commences work on the car. If he notices something extra that needs to be done, he notifies the service advisor who contacts the customer for permission to proceed and, if necessary, to revise the promise time.

7. The technician road tests the car after the job is completed.

8. The service advisor reviews the list of services and charges on the repair order for accuracy.

9. The car is washed, vacuumed, and put in the finish area while the repair order is being printed and taken to the cashier.

10. Through the paging system, the cashier alerts the waiting customer that the car is ready. The number given the customer is also flashed on a bingo-like board in the customer waiting lounge. A customer who is not present when the car is finished is telephoned.

11. The customer pays the bill and steps to the customer assistance desk to wait for the car. The porter delivers the car to the waiting customer, removes the protective covering, and thanks the customer.

John Dinsmore, director of service, states: "I have been in the automobile business a long time. I have seen a lot of dealerships. Nobody emphasizes customer satisfaction like we do. It comes from the top. Customer satisfaction is our absolute number one goal."

Service Reliability Is Design

Service reliability is a matter of design as well as attitude. Dependability and accuracy can be designed into the service system—or designed out of it. Not all service mistakes stem from carelessness. Frequently, the real culprit is a needlessly complicated and failure-prone service system. The flaw is in the design.

Exhibit 5–1 presents a five-step process for improving service reliability. Ideally, all five steps should be applied, which involves the use of service mapping to design new services (step 1) and to improve mature services (step 4). The process can be started at any of the stages; however, the earlier service reliability is emphasized in the service's design, the better.

A service map visually defines a service system, displaying each subprocess within the sequence. The map should revolve around the explicit actions the customer takes to receive the service. The specific contacts the customer has with contact personnel are mapped, as are internal services (invisible to the customer) that support contact services. The service map also depicts the physical evidence in the service environment that forms part of the customer's experience.

When drawn explicitly, the service map answers the questions: "What is the service?" and "How does it work?"[6] In effect, the map depicts the performance chronology that creates the service, and it shows the service from the customer's perspec-

Exhibit 5–1
IMPROVING SERVICE DESIGN

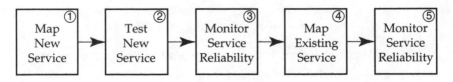

tive. The service map transforms a series of intangible processes into a tangible picture. This picture, in turn, enables designers of a new service system to better answer questions such as:

- Can the service system be simplified without compromising its value to customers?
- What can be done to help customers use the service correctly?
- What are the processes in the service system most vulnerable to failure (the "fail points"), and what can be done to prevent these failures?
- What knowledge and skills must service providers possess to deliver the service accurately and dependably?

Simplicity is a key to reliability, and the service map is a powerful tool for exposing needless complexity. Improving service quality not only involves understanding the customer; it also involves understanding the service. A service map helps decision makers to better understand the service, providing both a holistic view of the service and a sense of its details.

A new service needs to be thoroughly tested once it is designed. No legitimate reason exists for new services not being rigorously tested prior to full-scale distribution. The map of a new service may look quite promising. Transforming this picture into an actual service, however, will produce unanticipated problems and failures. A new service is a blending of server and customer performances, equipment, materials, and facilities. Many opportunities for glitches exist.

A bank wanting to market a new computer-based financial planning service for households should rigorously test the service first with a group of customers fitting the target market profile. The bank might even consider a two-phase test, first with a bank employee sample to remedy any major flaws, then with a customer sample. In exchange for receiving the test service free, sample members would provide specific feedback on their experiences and satisfaction with the service. Such feedback can lead to design changes before the service is marketed. As author G. Lynn Shostack puts it: "There is simply no substitute for a proper rehearsal."[7]

Pre-marketing testing and refining of new services are important because customers' early impressions are influential. Word-of-mouth communications are common in services because of the risks inherent in buying an intangible product. Customers who have tried a new service carry information that is potentially valuable to those who are interested in the service but have yet to try it. A new hotel in town, a new cellular telephone service, a restaurant chain with a revamped menu, the bank marketing the new financial planning service—these companies need to offer a strong, reliable service from the beginning because early triers are making up their minds about the service, deciding whether to use it again and what to tell others about it. Their first impressions are crucial.

Once a new service is launched, its performance should be monitored. Managers need to know the kind of reliability problems that are occurring, their frequency, and their root causes. Without monitoring, emerging reliability problems can go undetected—and uncorrected—for some time, weakening customer confidence in the service. How customers define reliability forms the basis for the reliability indicators that managers track. For a restaurant, these indicators might include customers' perceptions that their meals were prepared properly and that they received everything they ordered. Transactional surveys, as discussed in Chapter 3, can be used to monitor reliability indicators. Analysis of customer complaints also can be useful but is insufficient because many dissatisfied customers do not complain directly to the company.

Even if a service was mapped during its initial development, remapping it in a mature state can be useful. Technologies or knowledge not available when the service was first designed, or simply the accumulated weight of experience delivering the service, can contribute to improved service design. Thus, service mapping is recommended as step 4 in the reliability improvement process just as it is recommended in step 1. And because service monitoring is essential regardless of the stage in its life cycle, monitoring appears as step 5 as well as step 3.

Reliability is a core principle of quality service. An unreliable service is a poor service regardless of other attributes. Friendliness of the customer contact staff cannot rescue an unreliable service. Customers simply will conclude that the company is friendly but incompetent. Reliability must be a cornerstone for any effective service strategy. Attitude and service design are the keys.

SERVICE SURPRISE

Customers judge service reliability following the service experience. The promised service either was or was not delivered. Thus, reliability can be considered an "outcome" dimension of service. In contrast, customers judge the dimensions of tangibles, responsiveness, assurance, and empathy during the service process; these are "process" dimensions of service.

Although reliability is the most important dimension in meeting customers' service expectations, the process dimensions are most important in exceeding them. It is difficult for companies to exceed customers' expectations by reliably delivering the promised service. Banks are supposed to maintain accurate records of customers' accounts. Repair firms are supposed to keep their service appointments. Retailers are supposed to have the advertised goods in stock and on the shelves. Customers generally do not give firms extra credit for doing what they are supposed to do. Companies that surprise customers with unusual caring, commitment, or resourcefulness during the service process receive the extra credit. Exceeding customers' expectations requires the element of surprise, and the best opportunity to offer surprise is during the service process when customers interact with servers and experience the service environment.

A great serving company is outstanding on both the outcome and process dimensions of service. Service reliability allows the company to compete but generally is not sufficient to create a reputation for great service. Great serving companies go beyond competent, dependable service delivery and create emotional bonds with their customers. They do more than satisfy their customers; they "wow" their customers and build deeply felt loyalties. They do so by capitalizing on opportunities to impress during the service process.

Unfortunately, most service companies do not fully benefit from the potential of interactive service. In fact, many companies operate at the other end of the spectrum. They operate defensively to protect assets and maximize short-term earnings. Senior managers tightly control the business. Servers who interact with customers are disenfranchised to act like "owners"; they are discouraged from using their judgment, from being creative, from taking chances. The net effect is that employees spending the most time with customers have the least authority, incentive, or confidence to act on the customers' behalf. They work for the company, but it is not their company.

Firms that fit the description in the previous paragraph face a long journey of nurturing service leadership and changing attitudes. No magic formulas exist; no service quality pills are available. Surprising customers with service comes not from gimmicks but from inspiration and perspiration in the service factory where servers and customers meet. Genuine caring about customers and excellence—and the authority and confidence to exercise it—create emotional bonds with customers. A service company that sponsors "smile training" has no chance to be great. Only companies in which employees want to smile have a chance to be great.

Surprising Customers with Details

Great service companies "major in minors." They use details to be different and to signal customers that the company is special. Often, the "wow factor" in service is not one factor at all. Instead, flourishes of customer-pleasing creativity spring up in every facet of the service system. The "wow" is the total service experience; it is 101 little things done with the customers' interests uppermost in mind.

No company does a better job of surprising customers with details than Akron's West Point Market featured in Chapter 2. Started in 1936, West Point Market had undergone six expansions and 21 remodels by the fall of 1993, 57 years later. It is expanding its parking lot as this chapter is being written. Owner Russ Vernon comments:

This is a wonderful time for us. With all the alternative food formats entering our market, we are approaching double digit growth. There are so many customers "falling through the cracks," unsatisfied by discount formats, that we are expanding again. We need to have more room to park these disappointed shoppers seeking someone who cares. It's exciting!

At West Point Market, flowers are everywhere: in front of the store, complementing the parking lot, at the store entrance, in the aisles, in the merchandise displays. More than 80 trees are on the property. The delivery truck is painted with dancing vegetables. "Our truck isn't just a truck," says Russ Vernon. Merchandise signs are hand-drawn in soft colors by the same artist to insure a coordinated look. The exit signs are hand-carved wooden signs. Colorful balloons decorate the store. Information and recipe tags on the shelves educate shoppers on how to use the products: "This creamy mild cheese with caraway seeds slices well for ham sandwiches on hearty rye." Underneath custom-made wooden meat counters are wine racks, even though elsewhere in the store is the largest wine department of any food store in Ohio. This "second chance for customers to buy wine" adds sales of 350 to 380 cases of wine per year. West Point Market's "Customers of Tomorrow" program includes kiddie shopping carts and cookie credit cards (for children to receive a free cookie on each store visit). The restrooms have classical music, almond soap, indirect lighting—and, of course, fresh flowers.

Product tasting and demonstration events in the store are common. As many as four events may occur simultaneously on a Saturday, for example, one chef cooking pasta, another preparing salsa recipes, and another preparing a cold pasta with a new avocado dressing. And there might be a bread sampling table. Kaye Lowe, director of public relations, states: "One of the services we offer is customer education. We don't hesitate to let customers taste a product. Some people come in on a Saturday and eat their way around the store. Russ's favorite saying is: 'Come see the sights, smell the delights, and taste the wonders of WPM.'"

Customers visiting the store for the first time receive a personal thank you letter from Russ Vernon and a $2 certificate to use on their next visit. Each cashier in monthly meetings is responsible for reviewing ten customers by name with the cashier group: "Miss O'Neil comes in every night and always orders croissants. Sometimes she is not feeling well, so we go to the bakery and get them for her." Russ Vernon himself loves to stand near the store entrance to greet customers or carry out their groceries so he can strengthen the bond. Cindy Yost, the specialty foods buyer, enjoys teaching customers about unfamiliar foods and then following up: "If a customer buys a sauce I recommended, then the next time I see the customer I will ask how the sauce worked out. I don't always remember the customer's name, but I remember the products I sold to that customer."

The West Point Market is not for customers who wish to do their shopping anonymously in utilitarian surroundings. However, for customers who like to cook, who are looking for high quality and unusual foods, and who enjoy genuinely personalized service, West Point Market is a special place. Russ Vernon comments:

> From the very first day my father and his partners focused on the customers. They devoted their business life to probing and searching for new and exciting ways to please their customers. This is the kind of retailing that I learned. My competition is not willing to invest in the enhancements; I am.

Surprising Customers with Extra Effort

Companies earn extra credit with customers through extra effort. Customers remember when service providers go out of their way to help them, when they refuse to give up until a persistent problem is solved, when they throw out the "rulebook" if that is what's necessary.

Customers are so used to routine, "by-the-book" service that they are surprised by providers who go to extraordinary lengths to please. Although extra-effort service is by definition hard work, it also is more fun to provide. And why shouldn't it be? Being a star with the customer is fun.

Interviews conducted as part of the research for this book are replete with stories of extra-effort service. Darryl Wiesenthal of Harold's, the Houston apparel retailer, tells about a customer who needed a karate outfit for her grandson. Harold's doesn't sell karate outfits, but Darryl went to another store, purchased the outfit, and delivered it to the grandson. Darryl comments: "We do this everyday. It is a wow for the customer, but to us it is an expected level of service. It's a fun way to do business." Father Harold Wiesenthal adds: "You go into most stores and if they don't have it you are out of luck. We find the merchandise and if necessary we will pay retail for it."

De Mar once hired a helicopter to install an air conditioning unit on the roof of a house. President Larry Harmon explains:

> Last November, we won a bid on a residential air conditioner and budgeted $100 for installation with a crane. But then we got some real heavy rains, the kind Southern California's famous for. On the day we were supposed to do the work, the ground was too wet to get the crane in, and there was no asphalt to drive it onto near the house. But since we had promised the customer we'd complete the job that same day, we hired a helicopter for $500.
>
> Let me tell you, it was freezing and foggy, and then it started raining. But we got the air conditioner installed, videotaped the work, and gave a copy of the tape to the customer. The customer offered to split the extra $400 expense with us, but I wanted to stick to our bid. So we covered it.
>
> Well, that customer showed the videotape at his New Year's Eve party, and we got three new leads and one sale from that. The sale was a five-ton unit, and our profit was $2,400. So for an initial $400 investment in customer service, we figure our return was 600%.[8]

Terri Freiman, who works in the Wine Shop at West Point Market, recalls a customer who wanted a particular wine she had discovered at a Cleveland restaurant. Terri first called the restaurant and then the distributor, trying to get the wine. Neither firm would sell it to her. Finally, she telephoned the winery and got the customer her wine. Carol Moore, West Point Market's director of food service, says: "We get a lot of special requests. One customer wanted to serve duck for a big party. We don't normally sell duck but we did for this customer. We gave her recipes and sent our chef to her home to show her how to prepare the meal. We try to exceed the customers' expectations."

Service surprise plays a different role than service reliability. Reliability allows a company to compete; its absence shatters the customers' confidence. Service that surprises customers enables a company to develop a reputation for superlative service. Exceeding customers' expectations requires the element of surprise. And the best opportunity for surprising customers is during the service process when customers interact with servers and experience the service environment. Companies can surprise their customers by managing the details of the service experience and providing extra-effort service.

SERVICE RECOVERY

Another principle of great service is recovery, the company's response to a service problem. Some managers view recovery service as an expensive nuisance. This is a costly attitude because the customers' confidence in the firm is at risk when a service problem occurs. A company can act decisively and competently to restore the customers' confidence—at least to some degree—or it can make matters worse with a weak recovery.

A single service problem is unlikely to completely destroy a customer's confidence in the firm except under the following conditions:

- The service failure is so egregious that recovery of any type is ineffective. A service failure stemming from blatant dishonesty is an example.
- The service problem fits a pattern of failure rather than being an isolated incident.
- The recovery service is weak, compounding rather than correcting the original problem.

Even the most brilliant recovery strategy will not rescue a company from a serious error or a series of errors, as the first two points above suggest. How does a surgeon who operates on the wrong knee recover? How does a photographer who arrives at the wedding an hour late recover? How does a grocery store chain accused on national television of selling adulterated perishable foods recover? Recovery is not usually possible under such conditions, although the company should attempt to recover. Nor can the dry cleaners that loses a customer's shirt and three months later ruins the coloration of another of the customer's garments recover. The customer may give the dry cleaners another chance after the first failure—especially with a strong recovery effort—but the second failure clearly signals incompetence. The customer's confidence in the firm has been destroyed.

Although excellent recovery service cannot always keep customers from switching to competitors, often it can, and this is the message from the third point above. The reality of a deficient service and a weak recovery is a double failure. The customer may remain with the firm after a double failure but not with the prior level of confidence or commitment.

Research by my colleagues and me confirms the critical importance of effective recovery service. Satisfactory recovery service sharply increases customers' willingness to recommend the firm and significantly improves their perceptions of overall service quality as shown in Table 5–1. These data suggest that customers in general are far more forgiving of a service failure when the company makes a sincere, concerted effort to remedy the problem.

Customers usually have higher expectations for recovery service than for the original service. They have been disappointed or frustrated by the original service, and they expect the company to make amends. In a study of "critical service incidents" in which the researchers asked customers to recall especially positive and negative service experiences, almost 43 percent of the negative experiences mentioned were poorly handled recovery situations.[9]

Ron Zemke and Chip Bell wrote some of the first articles on service recovery. Based on their research, they propose these customer expectations for recovery service:

1. To receive a sincere apology
2. To be offered a "fair fix" for the problem
3. To be treated in a way that shows the company cares about the problem and helping the customer solve it
4. To be offered recompense equivalent to the burden the customer has endured
5. To receive the recovery service promised rather than one that falls short[10]

Table 5-1

IMPACT OF STRONG VS. WEAK SERVICE RECOVERY

Company	Type of Service	Percent of Customers Willing to Recommend Company When Service Problems Were:		Customers' Overall Assessment of a Company's Service Quality When Service Problems Were:**	
		Not Resolved Satisfactorily*	Resolved Satisfactorily	Not Resolved Satisfactorily	Resolved Satisfactorily
1	Telephone Repair	13%	86%	−1.99	−0.74
2	Insurance	24%	82%	−2.24	−1.36
3	Insurance	31%	85%	−2.26	−1.06
4	Banking	21%	78%	−2.25	−1.33
5	Banking	54%	78%	−1.84	−0.90

* The 13% in the first row has the following interpretation: Of the Company 1 customers who perceived that their service problems were not resolved satisfactorily, 13% were willing to recommend the company to a friend. Other percentages have similar interpretations.

** Service quality scores measure customers' perceptions of the company relative to their expectations. If perceptions fall short of expectations, the company receives a minus score. The bigger the minus score, the worse the company's service quality.

Source: Leonard L. Berry and A. Parasuraman, *Marketing Services: Competing Through Quality* (New York: Free Press, 1991), p. 40.

These expectations encompass both the outcome and process dimensions of service discussed earlier in the chapter. Recovery requires both a pleasing process and a satisfying outcome. What the company does to restore the customer's confidence—and how it is done—are both important.

Three Possibilities

Three possibilities arise when a customer experiences a service problem: the customer complains and is satisfied with the company's recovery service; the customer complains but is not satisfied with the recovery service; or the customer does not complain to the company and remains dissatisfied. Unfortunately, the latter two possibilities are quite common.

Many companies do not encourage their customers to complain when displeased with the service, and they make it difficult for those who try to do so. They do not place sufficiently trained personnel, or enough of them, in problem-solving positions. They do not empower front-line servers to solve most problems immediately. And they do not invest in the systems and technology necessary to support recovery service.

To be sure, recovery service poses a special challenge. Complaining customers can be confrontational and unpleasant. Some service problems are beyond the control of the company or caused by customer error. Some customer complaints are ridiculous by any standard. The range of service problems varies so much that preparation is difficult. Still, most companies underachieve in recovery service. They are wasting funds invested in attracting new customers who defect because of unresolved service problems before becoming profitable. These companies also are losing the future revenue streams defecting customers would have provided had the recovery service satisfied them.

The root causes of recovery service underachievement are threefold. First, the costs of recovery service are immediate and visible while the benefits are long-term and indirect. Managers evaluated and compensated on short-term financial performance criteria may have little incentive to invest the necessary resources and mental energy into recovery service. Their priorities lie elsewhere.

Second, many executives are cynical about the purity of customer motives and purposely establish a proof-of-injury recovery approach. The net result is a service system that is difficult for both cheating and noncheating customers to use. John Goodman, president of Technical Assistance Research Programs (TARP), a research firm well known for its work in service recovery, states:

> Our research has found premeditated rip-offs [by complaining customers] represent 1 to 2 percent of the customer base in most organizations. However, most organizations defend themselves against unscrupulous customers by . . . treating the 98 percent of honest customers like crooks to catch the 2 percent who *are* crooks.[11]

Third, many dissatisfied customers do not complain to the company. They view complaining as a psychological burden because of potential unpleasantness, a logistics burden because it is unclear whom to contact or how, or just as a waste of time because they don't believe the company cares about service quality.[12] Moreover, many of the complaints customers do voice are registered with customer-contact personnel who don't pass the comments on to management for some of the same basic reasons customers don't complain in the first place, such as a perception that management doesn't care. Thus, even when customers do complain, managers in position to implement a recovery service may not learn about it.

Investing in Recovery Service

Firms that do not perform the service right the first time must be prepared to perform the service very right the second time. Recovery service is not "business as usual." The customer is dissatisfied, and a sense of urgency should prevail. Two broad purposes should influence the development of a recovery service strategy: to resolve the problem and restore the customer's confidence in the firm; to improve the service system so that the problem occurs less frequently in the future.

A four-step approach for designing a recovery service strategy is presented in Exhibit 5–2. Although the particulars will vary from company to company, the four steps are essential. Managers need to work hard to build cultural support for recovery, to identify and resolve service failures, and to use the experiences to improve future service.

Teach the Importance of Recovery Service. Like service reliability and surprise, service recovery is an attitude. Developing the attitude within the organization that an unhappy customer is bad business is no small task. Nor is it a one-time task. Teaching the virtues of recovery service as a customer-retaining profit strategy is an ongoing challenge. The natural temptation is to avoid customers carrying bad news; the opportunity, unrealized in so many companies, is to embrace them.

Language is a key to making recovery service a cultural imperative. Garrett Jamison, Executive Vice President of Bank One Texas Trust Division, teaches his associates to "run to the problem." Jamison explains:

Exhibit 5–2
ESSENTIAL STEPS IN RECOVERY SERVICE

```
┌─────────────────────────────────────────────┐
│    Teach the Importance of Recovery Service  │
└─────────────────────────────────────────────┘
                      │
                      ▼
┌─────────────────────────────────────────────┐
│          Identify Service Problems           │
└─────────────────────────────────────────────┘
                      │
                      ▼
┌─────────────────────────────────────────────┐
│        Resolve Problems Effectively          │
└─────────────────────────────────────────────┘
                      │
                      ▼
┌─────────────────────────────────────────────┐
│         Improve the Service System           │
└─────────────────────────────────────────────┘
```

If you can train yourself to call the rough customer, to run to the problem, you will not only make the customer feel better, you will feel better. I explain the run-to-the-problem philosophy during new employee orientation. Then, whenever we have a problem I use the phrase. Employees like to use the phrase. They say: "I ran to the problem." It has turned out to be a powerful phrase that gives guidance to our people.

Part of Harold's core culture is to make customers' merchandise exchanges even more pleasant than buying the items in the first place. Each salesperson is authorized to make exchanges. Management approval is unnecessary and the paperwork is minimal. Darryl Wiesenthal states: "By example, we teach our sales staff that when customers come into the store with a box you approach them even faster than if they are empty-handed."

Linda Lash, director of customer satisfaction for Avis Europe, suggests positioning the recovery service role as "getting customers back" rather than "resolving problems." She writes: "Instead of reluctantly allocating funds to a cost center to handle complaints, the successful companies . . . will . . . eagerly invest in customer assistance centers."[13]

Another culture-building key is regular group discussions about customer service problems. How managers spend their time symbolizes what is important in the organization. If they spend significant time discussing service problems that occurred and how to improve, then these matters must be important. Roberts Express managers meet every weekday morning to review service problems from the previous day. They focus on what should be done to resolve specific service problems and how to prevent reoccurrence. It is, according to Regional Service Manager Virginia Addicott, "a 'why' and 'what' type of meeting."

Dell Computers holds weekly customer advocate meetings. Dozens of personnel from sales, merchandising, finance, and manufacturing meet with senior executives to discuss customer complaints and employee suggestions. Solutions are found for unresolved problems. An open part of the agenda enables employees to raise additional customer satisfaction issues.[14]

Documenting the financial implications of effective recovery service is another cultural key. Roland Rust, Bala Subramanian, and Mark Wells suggest that organizations use a "Problem Impact Tree" (PIT) graphic to highlight the implications of effective versus weak recovery service. Illustrated in Exhibit 5–3, the PIT has been used successfully at Hampton Inns where managers can see at a glance information previously accessible only by detailed analysis of computer printouts.

The exhibit isolates the relationship between recovery service and customers' service quality scores. The same basic framework could be used to monitor other relationships, for example, recovery service and customers' repurchase intentions. The top of the tree represents all customers, who then are divided into those who have not and have experienced a recent service problem. The latter group is then divided into those who do and do not report the problem. The reporting group is further divided into those who are and are not satisfied with the recovery service. Data from our ongoing service quality research program are used to demonstrate the adverse consequences of ineffective recovery.[15]

The total market survey described in Chapter 3 can easily be designed to collect data needed to construct various PITs. The transactional survey also can be adapted for this use, although sufficient time must be allowed for customers to report problems and for recovery service to occur. This represents a tradeoff with the desirability of collecting transaction-specific data on a timely basis.

The PIT can be a powerful tool for teaching the importance of recovery service. It also can be an excellent diagnostic tool, especially when data are categorized by type of service problem. These more detailed analyses show the differential impact of weak recovery for various kinds of service problems.

Still another means of teaching the importance of recovery service is the performance evaluation and reward system. If customers' service quality scores and retention rates figure in the evaluation and reward system, recovery service will be better— probably much better—than if these criteria are omitted. Chapter 12 will develop this perspective.

Identify Service Problems. An essential element of recovery service is encouraging customers to complain by making it easy for them to do so. Managers cannot afford to sit back and wait for

Exhibit 5–3
USE OF PROBLEM IMPACT TREES
TO IMPROVE RECOVERY SERVICE

Recovery Service and Customer Service Quality Scores

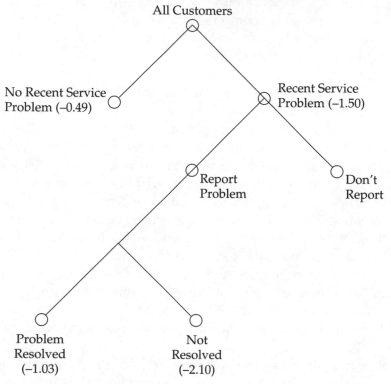

Service quality scores are determined by measuring customers' expectations and perceptions for the service. If perceptions fall short of expectations, the company receives a minus score. The bigger the minus score, the worse the company's service quality. The data reported in this exhibit are mean scores pooled from samples of customers of five major service companies. Based on the use of seven-point scales, the difference between the "no problem" score of –0.49 and the "not resolved" score of –2.10 is alarming. Customers whose service perceptions fall two scale points short of expectations on a seven-point scale possess little or no confidence in the company.

The PIT diagram is based on Roland T. Rust, Bala Subramanian, and Mark Wells, "Making Complaints a Management Tool," *Marketing Management*, Vol. 1, No. 3, 1992, pp. 41–45. The data are from research reported in Valarie A. Zeithaml, A. Parasuraman, and Leonard L. Berry, *Delivering Quality Service* (New York: Free Press, 1990).

unhappy customers to inform the company. Too many customers just won't do it for reasons enumerated earlier. Customer comment cards available in the service facility and toll-free telephone numbers for customers to call are useful strategies, but they do not go far enough. Dissatisfied customers who are unwilling to initiate contact with the firm to complain are precluded.

Proactive methods to uncover service problems also are needed. Whereas reactive methods rely on the customer to initiate contact (and then the company reacts), proactive methods involve the company making the initial contact. Customers checking out of the Harvey Hotel in Plano, Texas, during the morning rush may be approached by a "Lobby Lizard," a member of the management team who asks for feedback. This proactive approach prompts many more hotel guests to voice concerns or make suggestions than would otherwise be the case. General manager John Longstreet explains: "When we ask 'How was your stay?' the guest invariably says 'fine.' But when we ask 'Did you notice anything we could improve?' the response frequently is 'Well, now that you ask. . . .'" If the situation warrants, the Lobby Lizard can implement immediate recovery service. The hotel has made numerous service improvements as a result of the guest feedback.

As mentioned in Chapter 3, Longo Toyota and Lexus makes more than 40,000 customer telephone calls a year to follow up on automobile purchase and service transactions. Three days after the sale of a new car the salesperson calls the customer. Three days later, a customer relations follow-up manager telephones. The purpose of the calls is to make sure the buyer is satisfied and that the car is problem-free. If it is not, the customer is invited to bring it in, and a report is sent to the service manager indicating that the customer will be bringing in the car. If the customer is pleased with the car but not with the sales service received, he or she can comment to this effect in the second interview. When this occurs, the staff contacts the salesperson for his or her input and then recontacts the customer and attempts to resolve the problem.

Longo goes far beyond what most automobile dealers are willing to do to please the customer. One customer thought the smell from the leather in his Lexus wasn't right; it gave him hives. Longo replaced the leather. President Greg Penske states: "If you don't have customers, you don't have anything. You can't replace customers. We make sure that customers love this dealership."

Proactive recovery methods help overcome the common customer perception that companies don't care about customer problems and that complaining is fruitless. Companies pave the way for constructive feedback when they take the first step and ask for it.

Resolve Problems Effectively. The window of opportunity to make things right for the customer may be open only for a short time. The customer has been burdened, and the company is on the defensive. A complaint can come into an organization at different levels. An airline passenger, for example, may complain to a ticket counter agent, a departure gate agent, in-flight personnel, a reservations agent, a headquarters executive, or others in the organization.

Pages of detailed rules to guide servers are clearly not a good way to address the complexity of recovery. Nor is taking recovery completely out of the hands of customer-contact personnel and centralizing it with staff experts a workable solution for many businesses. Centralization has certain advantages, such as staff expertise, but in-the-field recovery also has advantages, such as the possibility of resolving the customer's problem while service delivery is still underway. For most companies, a sequential recovery system makes the most sense: solve the problem in the field if possible, solve it in headquarters if necessary.

To excel in recovery service, companies need a set of guiding principles that simply and powerfully communicate to *all* employees the importance and philosophy of recovery. Part corporate values, part strategy directives, this "service recovery manifesto" provides the guidance and inspiration to servers in the field who are interacting with distressed customers and who must respond to them thoughtfully despite little time to think.

Smith & Hawken is a successful California mail-order company that has created a service recovery manifesto. The company guides its employees with these ten principles:

1. Our goal as a company is to have customer service that is not just the best, but legendary.
2. You are the customer. If the customer is upset, you are upset. If the customer is satisfied, you are satisfied.
3. In relations with customers, act as if you own the company.
4. There is no such thing as taking too much time with a customer.
5. The phone is mightier than the pen.
6. If it doesn't feel right, make it right.
7. A job isn't done until it is checked over.
8. Do it once, and do it yourself.
9. When in doubt, ask. When not in doubt, ask.
10. A mistake is not a mistake. It is a chance to improve the company.

Are these ten principles right for every service company? The answer is "no." Each company must develop its own set of guiding principles that fit its corporate values, its overall service strategy, and the way it manages people. However, several central guidelines have emerged from research and experience. In one way or another, these guidelines should be reflected in a firm's service recovery manifesto.

First, *recovery should be personalized.* Responding to an unhappy customer with a form letter is unlikely to restore the customer's confidence in the company. By responding personally to the customer, while the customer still is in the service facility or with a follow-up visit or phone call, the company creates an opportunity for dialogue—an opportunity to listen, uncover additional information, explain, provide an appropriate remedy, and apologize. As Ron Zemke writes: "Never underestimate the power of apology. The importance of apologizing for unmet expectations can't be overstated."[16]

Kaye Lowe of West Point Market illustrates personalized recovery with this story:

A customer ordered 12 box lunches to be picked up at 2:00 P.M. She came in at 1:30 P.M. and they weren't ready. She came back in 15 minutes and then again 15 minutes later and they still weren't ready. Actually, the lunches were ready when the customer returned the first time, but the front-line staff didn't let the people in the back know she had returned. It was a communications foul-up. The incident took place on a Saturday. On Monday, Russ Vernon sent this customer a personal note of apology and a bouquet of flowers. He indicated in his note that the store would address what occurred in a training meeting.

This story illustrates a second guideline: *recovery should be quick.* A fast response to a service problem conveys a sense of urgency. The company shows that the customer's concern has become the company's concern, too. Some companies adhere to a "sundown policy" in which contact is to be made with a complaining customer before sundown on the day of the complaint. A response policy of 24 or 48 hours is a variation on the same theme.

When a Virgin Atlantic Airways departure from Newark to London was delayed, waiting passengers received the bad news in a letter from the airline's chairman, Richard Branson. Branson dictated a letter over the telephone that was quickly typed and handed to the inconvenienced passengers. The letter apologized for the delay, explained the cause, gave a new departure time, and offered to forward messages to friends and relatives.[17]

Quick recovery reinforces a third guideline: *recovery should be at the first point of contact whenever possible.* Recovery should be as simple as possible from the customer's perspective. The customer should not have to deal with multiple staff members or retell the story several times to get relief. Federal Express research revealed that 77 percent of complaining customers were satisfied with the recovery service if they dealt with only one employee, but only 61 percent were satisfied when they were sent to a second company representative. These findings led Federal Express to increase the level of compensation customer-service representatives could offer to satisfy a claim without secondary approval.[18]

Management and staff should collaborate in developing potential recovery actions that contact staff can use without further approval. Servers can then judge which recovery action best fits a specific situation and implement it on the spot.[19] Marketing executive Evelyn Capel and a colleague arrived in Washington, D.C. to attend a conference and instructed their cab driver to take them to "the Marriott." When they arrived, the front-desk server could not find the reservation, which led to the discovery that the travelers had come to the wrong Marriott.

The server asked Capel what the two had paid the taxi driver, had them sign a voucher, refunded the fare, and asked the doorman to hail a taxi. The travelers were at the correct hotel within ten minutes. Says Capel: "She never hesitated. She just took care of us."[20]

A fourth recovery concept is: *keep the customer informed.* Silence is not golden when a problem exists and the customer is waiting to hear a solution. The company must stay in touch. A progress report on a recovery service signals to the customer that the company is trying, even when a problem has not been resolved.

The First National Bank of Chicago identified through research the most important attributes consumers consider in evaluating bank services. A number of the top attributes directly concern *service recovery communications*; the customer wants to be told:

- how a problem happened
- when a problem is resolved
- how long it will take to solve a problem
- useful alternatives if a problem can't be solved
- ways to prevent a future problem
- what progress has been made if a problem can't be solved immediately[21]

A fifth guideline is: *emphasize a fair solution.* Fair play, the subject of the next section in this chapter, is critical in service recovery situations. The service failure has limited the value of the service and may have inconvenienced the customer. Companies need not provide a big payoff to solve a small problem. Sincerity of response, honest communications about what happened and what will be done, and tangible compensation that reflects the severity of the problem fulfill the fair play expectations of most customers.

Improve the Service System. A service failure is not only an opportunity to win back the customer's confidence but also an opportunity to perform better. As much as possible, service failures need to be captured and categorized for analysis and corrective action. Otherwise, the same problems will continue to occur with little or no improvement.

Management needs to know how the service system is breaking down most frequently. Managers can then conduct root-cause analyses of specific service problems and implement corrective measures. Project teams, an organizational approach to analyzing and solving specific service problems, are discussed in the next chapter.

Roberts Express codes the cause of all service failures and creates a daily summary report. A shipment not picked up or delivered within 15 minutes of the promised times is considered a service failure. Company executives scrutinize and discuss the failure reports at their daily service meeting. The managers look for trends or patterns in the data. For example, if the same driver appears several times in the "lost driver" category, it may mean the driver cannot read a map and would benefit from remedial training.

A service recovery strategy that focuses on solving the individual customer's problem but ignores the opportunity for systemic improvement is incomplete. An excellent service recovery strategy produces both immediate and long-term benefits.

SERVICE FAIRNESS

The service promise that companies sell includes the implicit promise of fair play. Customers expect service companies to treat them fairly; they become angry and mistrustful when they perceive otherwise. Fairness is not a separate dimension of service but, rather, touches all customer expectations. Customers expect service companies to keep their promises (reliability), to offer clean, comfortable facilities (tangibles), to give prompt service (responsiveness), to be competent and courteous (assurance), and to extend caring, individualized attention (empathy).

Interviews with customers concerning negative *service* experiences frequently bring forth comments about perceived *unfairness*:

- "They say in their advertising that they are the 'good driver' company and yet my premiums kept going up even though

I had no accidents. When I inquired they said it was the average number of accidents in my group" (an auto insurance customer).

- "You get charged when you don't show up but there is no reverse penalty when they don't have your guaranteed room" (a hotel customer).
- "When you are on a service contract, they usually send in a trainee. They are training their people on our equipment. A repair that should take two hours takes six or eight hours" (a business equipment repair customer).
- "Service departments are more interested in making a profit than in finding out what's wrong with your car" (an automobile repair customer).

To customers, fairness and service quality are inseparable issues. A company rated low in fairness will be a company rated low in service quality. The intangibility of services heightens customers' sensitivity to fairness. As performances, services are difficult for customers to evaluate prior to purchase. Customers cannot try on services for fit and feel; there are no tires to kick or test drives to take. Customers typically must buy the service to actually experience it. Thus, they must trust a service company to deliver on its promise and conduct itself honorably.

Some services are difficult for customers to judge fully even after they have been performed, and therefore trust plays an even bigger role. These "black box" services are usually technical services (such as automobile repair) or services performed away from the customer's presence (such as meal preparation in a restaurant kitchen). As important as fairness is for services in general, it is even more important for black box services because customers are more vulnerable.

Customers remember companies that violate the promise of fair play. They remember for a long time. Food Lion is a case in point. From 1983 to 1992, Food Lion was one of America's most successful food retailers, with sales and earnings growth averaging more than 20 percent. Then came a November 1992 national television report alleging that Food Lion was doctoring and repackaging out-of-date meat for sale. The "Prime Time Live" reporters, using hidden cameras, filmed Food Lion personnel in

multiple stores "in the act." It was riveting television, and the
Food Lion chain has not yet recovered—and may never recover.
Food Lion earned $178 million in 1992 and $3.85 million in 1993.
Expansion plans were curtailed. The company's debt rating was
lowered. Shareholders' suits were filed against the company.
Food Lion was caught delivering a black box service unfairly,
undermining stakeholder confidence in the company as a result.

Customers also remember those companies that operate with
integrity when other companies do not. In the aftermath of Hurri-
cane Andrew in the southeastern United States in 1992, many
retailers engaged in price gouging for urgently needed building
materials, such as plywood and roofing shingles. However, the
Home Depot chain of home-improvement stores took the opposite approach and sold these materials at cost, forsaking even normal profit margins. People were in trouble and Home Depot's
response was help, not take advantage. By giving up short-term
profits from the storm, Home Depot strengthened its long-term
bond with customers. As one Home Depot customer told *The
New York Times*: "If they had spent $50 million on advertising,
they couldn't have bought the goodwill they got by doing this."

Company fair play is a keystone of the customers' trust. And
trust is the basis for loyalty. Customers are most likely to form
lasting relationships with firms whose practices are beyond
reproach. The marketing research company, Yankelovich Partners, has documented an erosion of trust among American consumers in its annual Monitor study of consumer attitudes and
lifestyles. Barbara Caplan, a senior researcher at Yankelovich
Partners, writes:

> How people are feeling and thinking speaks to a national mood
> of skepticism. Distrust permeates the very fabric of American
> life. . . . There is a sense that integrity, credibility, and compe-
> tence are lacking. Consumers are wary of misrepresentation,
> exaggeration and hype and are determined to stamp deception
> out.[22]

Caplan believes that companies delivering genuine value to customers in a forthright, believable manner are benefiting from
this mood of skepticism. In effect, the lack of trust is an opening
for companies that can demonstrate they are trustworthy.

Legality Is Not the Standard

Service fairness is usually not a top-of-mind issue with customers unless they are given reason to make it an issue. Fairness becomes an issue when customers perceive a firm is being unfair. It also can become a positive issue when a firm surprises customers with its fairness. The Home Depot case is an example of the latter, the Food Lion case an example of the former.

Many managers pay insufficient attention to the issue of service fairness. This is a grave mistake because perceived unfairness or fairness affects the customer's emotional state like few other influences. A customer may not think of a service firm as either fair or unfair for years. Yet one perceived act of unfairness can destroy the company-customer relationship forever. And it is not only blatant ripoffs that produce these customer perceptions. As mentioned, fairness is embedded in the spectrum of customer service expectations.

The following episodes—taken from personal diaries that my students keep of service encounters—illustrate how customers can perceive rudeness, inattention, or lack of respect as unfair:

O.K. I'm in a hurry. I need one small item from "XYZ store" and figure I can run in, grab it, and be out in a flash. I went in and went to the general area where I thought my item could be found. I looked for a few minutes, but couldn't seem to locate it. I then began looking for a salesperson to help me. I didn't see anyone, so I quickly began scanning the store in search of help. After several minutes, I finally located what appeared to be all of the salespeople in the back chatting together. I actually had to stand there and wait for them to finish their conversation before one of them noticed that I was waiting!

You would think that the salesperson would have been really nice after realizing that I had been waiting for her, but she acted more like I had some nerve interrupting the group. She asked me if she could help me with no real conviction in her voice while the other salespeople looked on as if waiting to get back to their conversation. I told her what I was looking for and she got this perplexed look on her face. At that point, one of the other salespeople chimed in and said, "Oh, that's over in notions on that wall." She pointed in the general direction of the item.

I said thank you (for what, I'm not sure) and went in the direction she pointed. I got to the notions section and looked for a good five or six minutes without finding what I sought. Finally, I saw what I needed, grabbed it, and ran to the front to check out.

I entered "CDF" to buy a cable to lock up my bike. On the shelf, I find the display and all of the cables were packaged with a combination lock. I have a lock with a number I memorized in junior high school so why change? I only want the cable. Bingo, I found a package where someone else wanted just the lock apparently and slit the package open leaving only the cable. I brought the item to the salesman, and asked, "Can I buy this cable without the lock and if so, what will the price be?" The combination items were priced at $6.99. The salesman had to ask a co-worker who refused to make an "executive decision." He suggested that they call a manager. Three phone calls and one page later, there was still no manager. At this time, an older salesman returned from lunch and was informed of my desires. Immediately, the older salesman asked if they attempted to locate the missing lock around the display. I felt that I had just been accused of removing the lock for my own benefit! My blood pressure began rising as the two clerks began to dismantle the display looking for a lock that I did not want anyway! I said, "If locating the lock is necessary to make the sale, I do not have the time to wait." I hoped this would register that I was not going to stay much longer. "I must find the lock to know how much to charge you," the older salesman said. The price was on the package and we both knew it. That was insult number two. I said "Thank you for your lack of help!" and walked out of the store. $6.99 minus the lock price is a very small amount to lose a customer over!

On March 26, 1992, I received a leather daily planner as a birthday gift from my boyfriend. When I began to fill out the calendar in the planner, I realized that it was a 1991 calendar rather than 1992. I knew that it had been purchased at LMN Department Store in Waco, but since I live in College Station, I decided to go to the College Station LMN to inquire about the problem. I learned that all of the daily planners had 1991 calendars in them. I will point out that this item retails at $150; therefore it is supposed to be a very high quality product. The LMN salesperson did not offer to order a calendar for me; instead, she gave me an 800 number so that I could call the manufacturer myself.

Before calling the 800 number, I called the Waco LMN only to find out that all of their daily planners also had 1991 calendars in them. They mentioned that the item was supposed to have been marked down $8 since the calendar was out of date, but the salesperson must have forgotten. They offered to give me the $8 if I would bring in my receipt. I explained that the daily planner was a gift and I did not have the receipt. The salesperson replied by saying, "With such an expensive item, you will have to get the receipt. You will need to get it from whoever gave you the gift." I would never ask my boyfriend for the receipt for a gift, so I did not pursue the $8.

Next, I decided to call the manufacturer's 800 number. This was no easy task. The number was busy for an entire hour. I thought that there might have been a problem with the number, so I called the College Station LMN back and explained the problem. Very rudely I was told, "They are a busy company, you'll just have to keep trying." So, I did, and finally got through. After relating the whole story, the lady informed me that she really couldn't do anything and that she would have her supervisor, who was out for the afternoon, call me back tomorrow. The next day passed without a return phone call so I called them back. I told the entire story again, and was advised that my only option was to order a 1992 calendar from them for $8. I was not pleased with this solution, but I had already wasted so much time, and become so frustrated, that I was just ready to get my calendar and go on with my life.

The customers involved in these service encounters were not given any recompense for the personal resources they expended and the frustration they endured while trying to do business with these companies. Neither the outcomes (called "distributive justice" in the academic literature) or the processes to reach these outcomes (called "procedural justice") pass the fairness test, the common sense test, or any other test. In each episode, both customer and company were losers. This is the reality of service unfairness: the customer loses in the short term, the company in the long run.

The episodes also illustrate the differences between legality and fairness. Assuming a customer opened a package to buy a bicycle lock cable is not illegal. Nor is ignoring a customer while socializing with co-workers. But these acts are void of respect and basic courtesy, robbing customers of self-esteem and justice. The acts were legal, but the customers perceived them as unfair. One reason for the trust gap between customers and companies is that too many managers ask, "Is it legal?" but not, "Is it fair?" when making decisions.

Indirect Effects of Unfairness

Perceived unfairness affects service quality indirectly as well as directly. The indirect effect comes from employees demotivated in the service role by a firm that mistreats customers or themselves. Employee pride in the company is a prerequisite for excellent service. Excellent service is hard work; it requires high discretionary effort from servers; it requires a service mentality. None of this is possible without employee pride in the company and its management. And pride is a casualty of unfair treatment of company stakeholders. Employees ask themselves: "Why give my all to a company that lacks integrity?" "Why go the extra mile for a company in which I do not believe?"

A company that systematically misleads customers in sales presentations, that engages in phony pricing schemes, or that refuses to provide relief to customers with legitimate, post-sale grievances, cannot build a strong service-minded culture. The puzzle pieces do not fit together. Rhetoric from management about serving the customer—if it exists at all—rings hollow. Nor can employee pride be developed and sustained in an organization in which personnel are terminated without just cause, individuals are promoted regardless of merit, or employees are expected to defend indefensible company practices to customers.

Justice is a fundamental need of people.[23] Its absence undermines essentials of loyalty—pride, trust, respect, value.

Fairness Is an Attitude

Like the other service principles discussed in this chapter, fairness is an attitude. Memos from management do not produce fair treatment of customers or employees. Executives have to role model fairness, not write about it.

Service fairness permeates Tattered Cover Book Store's belief system and operations. It is a state of mind; it is part of the company's core culture, part of its reason for being. Tattered Cover employees are trained to be nonjudgmental about customers' purchases. "People buy sensitive books. It's the customer's right to read what he or she wants," says floor manager Sidney Jackson. This nonjudgmental attitude is reinforced by the wide variety of publications in stock—about 150,000 different books and approximately 1,300 newspapers and magazines. Materials on every conceivable topic are available at Tattered Cover.

Many customers feel a strong emotional bond to Tattered Cover. Business need not be done in a detached, arm's-length manner, and, when customers are invited to become "family members" as they are at Tattered Cover—when they feel trusted, respected, and valued—some decide to join. When Tattered Cover moved to a new store location in 1986, more than 200 customer volunteers reported at 8:00 A.M. to help with the move. They helped move more than 200,000 volumes in one day so the store could reopen for business the next day. A 1992 *Denver Post* survey asked shoppers what they liked best about the shopping district where Tattered Cover is located. The Tattered Cover Book Store was mentioned by 30 percent of the respondents. The runner-up store was mentioned by 3.5 percent.[24]

Fair play permeates Harold's culture just as it does Tattered Cover's. And customers are intensely loyal because of it. Harold's runs only two big sales per year. They are announced to regular customers first, then advertised once the regular customers have had four days to shop. Every item placed on sale is from the stock. Harold's does not buy lower quality, special-priced merchandise for a sales event. Michael Wiesenthal states: "We have one iron-clad rule for our store: 'Put yourself in the customer's place.' The most important factor in our success is integrity."

Most customers drive out of their way to get to Harold's. Operating from the same street corner location in Houston for 45 years, Harold's is no longer conveniently located. Nor does Harold's have an exclusive on the merchandise. Much of what Harold's sells is readily available at competing stores and frequently at a discounted price. The difference for Harold's—the reason it grows more than 10 percent a year—is superior service quality. Harold's is successful because it is exceptional on the four service quality principles—reliability, surprise, recovery, and fairness. Harold's tracks why new customers come to the store. Ten years ago, the number one reason was referrals from other customers; it still is today. Television advertising, which Harold's does aggressively, is number two.

Fairness Is Planned

Service fairness is too important to leave unplanned. Managers need to consider which business practices are most likely to create perceptions of unfairness and attempt to design the service system to prevent the problems from occurring. The potential for abuse can be limited through service system design. Few, if any, businesses better illustrate the potential for abusive practices than the used car business. Customers purchase an already-used, "black-box" product from a salesperson whose compensation probably depends on making the sale at the highest possible price. The car's price is negotiated, a practiced skill for the salesperson, an unpracticed skill for the customer. A trade-in car may be involved, further complicating the pricing issue.

Enter CarMax, a used car retailing format being tested by Circuit City Stores, America's largest consumer electronics chain. Faced with a mature consumer electronics market and fierce competition, Circuit City's management searched for an additional growth business. They wanted to apply the company's core competencies in selling high-ticket durable goods on credit. They settled on the used car business with an estimated $150 to $175 billion market potential, fragmented competition, and a reputation for shady selling tactics.

CarMax is designed to demonstrate tangibly to consumers and employees a commitment to fair play. The original store in Richmond, Virginia, sits on twelve acres. The inventory numbers about 500 cars, most less than five years old and all inspected prior to being put up for sale. The 33,000 square foot store houses a brightly lit showroom and a service operation. Only one car is featured in the showroom, and it's not for sale. It is on a pedestal, shiny and clean, to dramatize the appeal of a well-maintained used car.

The salesperson invites the customer to sit before a touch-screen computer and specify requirements, for example, type of vehicle and price range. The computer produces color pictures of the cars available that meet the specifications. Mileage, features, price, and location on the lot also are presented. The customer can print out sheets for cars of interest. The listed prices are nonnegotiable and trade-ins are decoupled from purchases. The customer can sell his or her existing car to CarMax, but the transaction is handled separately from the purchase of a car. CarMax used cars are backed by a 30-day warranty. Salespeople are paid commissions based on the number of transactions they make, not on the purchase prices.

Will CarMax become a successful chain and revolutionize the way used cars are sold in the United States? It is too early to say at this writing. CarMax does illustrate the concept of "planned fairness," however. Circuit City studied the root causes of unfair practices in used-car retailing and designed a service system specifically to circumvent these causes.

Fairness Is Standing Behind the Service

Perceptions of unfairness often result when the primary service goes awry and the company responds insufficiently. Fairness involves standing behind the service. A potentially powerful strategy for doing so is the service guarantee. Customers dissatisfied with the service can invoke the guarantee and receive consideration for the burden they have endured. When executed well, service guarantees can symbolize a company's commitment to fair play with customers and facilitate competitive dif-

Table 5–2
AN EFFECTIVE SERVICE GUARANTEE

- focuses on elements of the service the company can control
- is specific and simple
- is easy for the customer to invoke
- focuses on what is important to the customer
- is worthwhile for the customer to invoke
- provides a quick payout

Note: This exhibit is based on ideas first presented in Christopher W. L. Hart, "The Power of Unconditional Guarantees," *Harvard Business Review,* July–August 1988, pp. 54–62.

ferentiation. Guarantees also force the organization to improve service quality to avoid the cost and embarrassment of frequent payouts. Table 5–2 presents the characteristics of an effective guarantee.

A service guarantee is a bold step. A company should never take this step without a thorough analysis of its reasons for doing so and the risks. Guaranteeing a poor service is always a mistake. Firms delivering poor service should first significantly improve their service quality. Then they can consider guarantees that will help them to improve service further.

When Bank One acquired a failed Texas bank in 1989, it found itself in the unusual situation of needing to start a trust banking division because the failed bank's trust department had been sold. Bank One brought a veteran Dallas trust banker by the name of Richard Hart out of retirement to head up the new trust company. Hart in turn hired another Texas banker, Garrett Jamison, as the number two executive. The two men believed that only superior service quality would give their fledgling operation a chance to compete, and they recruited staff accordingly. They decided to guarantee service unconditionally— apparently the first trust bank in the United States ever to take such a step.

The guarantee is simple. Clients dissatisfied with the service need not pay the fee. Given to all new clients, the written guarantee reads: "If you are not satisfied with our service quality in any given year, we will return to you the fees paid, or any portion thereof you feel is fair." Customers wishing to invoke the guarantee must inform the bank in writing within 90 days of the end of the account year.

Four clients invoked the guarantee during the first four years of operation. According to Garrett Jamison, all the claims were justified and were for the same reason: overpromising. Jamison states: "Many companies won't guarantee their service because they don't trust their customers. Thus far, not one client out of 4,500 accounts has tried to take advantage of us. In fact, I am embarrassed our number of claims is so low. We need to do a better job communicating to our clients that we have the guarantee." Jamison adds: "Our guarantee has had minimal impact on sales. It has had a dramatic, positive impact on internal service quality. Our employees talk about it constantly. They are proud of it."

Customers buy a promise when they buy a service. They expect the company to deliver on its promise and to do so honorably. Fairness is fundamentally linked to customers' expectations for service. Executives interested in service quality must go beyond the legal standard in making decisions and ask: "Is this decision just?" They need to consider ways to reinforce fairness in the company's belief system and design it into the service system. And they need to stand behind the service after the sale.

SUMMARY

Customers are most likely to do business with companies that are reliable, excellent in interactive service, prepared to recover if the service fails, and eminently fair. These principles are the essence of service excellence. Reliability, recovery, and fairness are the basics of service; surprising service makes customers say "wow." Service quality is integral to value creation and thus must be emphasized in the service strategy.

The exploration of the service quality principles suggests the following checklist for management discussions:

1. *Do we make special efforts to nurture an attitude of service reliability in this organization?* Do we stress accuracy and dependability in our training? In performance measurement and reviews? In our reward system?
2. *Do we make special efforts to design reliability into the service system?* Do we map new and mature services? Do we thoroughly test new services prior to marketing them? Do we monitor the performance of our services? Do we have a sense of urgency about solving reliability problems?
3. *Do our services ever make our customers say "wow"?* Do we strive to create emotional bonds with our customers through superlative serving?
4. *Do we "major in minors" in this firm?* Do we purposely use details to be different from our competitors?
5. *Do our service providers have the incentive, authority, and confidence to give extra effort in serving customers?* Do they understand the opportunity to exceed customers' expectations when interacting with them? Does our management understand this opportunity?
6. *Do we view recovery service as a strategic opportunity?* Do we view it as an investment in our company's future? Do we view it as a way to retain customers?
7. *Are we proactive in recovery service?* Do we take the initiative in contacting customers or must they always take the first step?
8. *Are we using our recovery system to improve service?* Do we seek long-term solutions to frequently occurring problems?
9. *Do we make special efforts to demonstrate a commitment to fair play to customers?* Do we make special efforts to demonstrate this commitment to employees? Is fair play part of our company's belief system?
10. *Do we know which practices in our industry are most likely to create perceptions of unfairness?* Have we been systematic and thorough in addressing these issues? Have we been bold?

CHAPTER 6

ORGANIZE FOR
GREAT SERVICE

How to organize to implement the service strategy is among the most crucial of decisions. The wrong answer will defeat even the most brilliant of service strategies. Service companies often are organized in ways that block strategy implementation. The strategy calls for speed, but the structure insures slowness. The strategy calls for cross-functional teamwork, but the structure encourages isolated specialism. The strategy calls for service flexibility, but the structure delivers inflexibility.

Strategy dictates structure. No one structure is right for every company. Again, the proper question is not "what is the best structure?" but, rather, "what is the best structure for our strategy?" In this chapter, we examine structural forms that top performing organizations are using to improve service quality. Although the specifics of these structural arrangements vary from company to company, the basic concepts are widely applicable, for they address common organizing requirements for service improvement.

Regardless of its service strategy, a company intent on delivering excellent service needs a structure that will facilitate the following:

- cultural leadership for continuous service improvement
- guidance and coordination of service improvement initiatives
- technical expertise and resources to support service improvement
- solutions or recommendations concerning specific service quality issues

- service delivery that meets or exceeds customers' expectations day in and day out
- excellent recovery when the original service fails customers

Structure that offers these benefits and is in sync with a company's overall service strategy is part of the foundation for great service. Such a structure probably would include one or more of the following: steering group, support department, project teams, and service-delivery teams. These structural forms each serve a different purpose and thus are independent of one another. Increasingly they are being used in combination, however, sustaining the energy required for service improvement. The four forms are not for every firm, but there is something for every reader in the following discussions.

SERVICE QUALITY STEERING GROUP

A service quality steering group, if well executed, gives organizations large and small a focal point for service improvement and a cultural change force. Many organizations fail to realize their service quality ambitions because they do not formalize service improvement; no credible mechanism exists for keeping service quality on the front burner, for expanding a sense of ownership in the service quality journey, for getting things done.

A service quality steering group can be this mechanism, especially when coupled with an effective service quality department (to be discussed in the next section). The steering group's charge is to provide strategic direction, coordination, and impetus to service improvement. It constructs an overall plan of action and establishes funding priorities. It guides the development of company-wide service initiatives, such as the design of a service quality information system. It sponsors or encourages more narrowly focused service-improvement efforts, such as forming project teams to redesign services vulnerable to failure. It serves as a clearinghouse for service-improvement ideas that come up through the organization, seeking coherence and alignment in initiatives that are proposed. It monitors the firm's overall service performance, tracks the effects of various initiatives, and takes the appropriate actions. It reports internally on the firm's service performance, issuing progress reports, listing priorities, summarizing activities and plans. It recognizes outstanding service achievements in the organization, applauding excellence while encouraging continuous improvement.

Of course, few service quality steering groups will function so well as to deliver all of the above. But the above listing does reflect the mandate; it represents what is possible. Selecting the right people for the group is critical. Primarily it should be composed of senior executives who are "can-do" achievers, highly respected within the organization, thus bringing the group credibility and influence, and varied in their respective skills and experiences. Although a "service mentality" (as discussed in Chapter 2) is desirable, joining the service quality steering group may also be an opportunity for a key executive to develop such a mentality.

Key staff executives (for example, marketing, human resources, and service quality department heads) normally would belong to the steering group, but the group essentially should be line-driven. The operating units of organizations are typically centers of influence. Service improvement is most likely when line managers are personally and centrally involved in the improvement journey. The staff can play a valuable role but they alone cannot change a company's culture or implement its service strategy. Recall the Ritz-Carlton example from Chapter 4 in which the top 14 executives serve as the company's service quality steering group, meeting weekly to review service performance, progress, and plans. The importance of the service quality mission and the wherewithal to pursue it aggressively are not in doubt within the Ritz-Carlton organization. Service improvement is not delegated to professional staff who are buried in the middle of the organization chart; service improvement is a principal responsibility of the people who run the company.

The steering group is not a temporary form, hence a label such as *task force* is inappropriate. The term *committee* sounds weak. Terms such as *group, council,* or *board* are better. Language, as stressed earlier, is important.

Executives appointed to the steering group do not leave their respective positions, but, rather, incorporate their steering group duties into their work schedules. This is important for reasons other than just the obvious expense issue. Group members should continue experiencing directly the realities of the service system they are charged to improve; in effect, they would become "staff" were they to leave their positions. Any structural form, including a steering group, carries the risk of actually impeding service improvement due to bureaucracy or politics. This risk becomes greater if the steering group operates more like a "department" than a steering group.

SERVICE QUALITY SUPPORT DEPARTMENT

A staff department devoted full-time to service quality support can make a valuable contribution in a company aspiring to excellent service. The positioning and leadership of the department is critical to its success, however. The wrong positioning or leadership can imperil the service-improvement cause. Thus, the decision to create a service support department must be approached carefully and strategically.

The service support department is not an alternative to a service steering group; rather, it provides vital staff support to the steering group by giving information, following up on issues, and carrying out steering group initiatives.

The fundamental role of a service support department is to facilitate the service-improvement process. The department's role is not directly to improve the firm's service but to help everyone else in the company to improve service. This is a vital distinction—one that can mean the difference between success and failure. Top management must understand this distinction. Steering group members must understand it. The director and staff of the service support department must understand it. And so must the rest of the organization.

Lynn Shemmer, who served as Quality Improvement Officer for Maritz Motivation Company in St. Louis from 1990 to 1992, once listed her department's top three priorities as facilitating ownership for quality improvement in the line organization, removing obstacles to progress, and providing needed tools.[1] Shemmer understood perfectly the distinction between improving the firm's service quality and helping everyone else to improve it.

Positioning service improvement as "everybody's job" and the service support department's role as facilitative is important from the outset. This is one reason to keep the service support department small—even in large companies. The symbolism of a small department conveys better the message of "support unit" than a 20- or 30-person department. Moreover, a small department insures (out of necessity) that most of the service-improvement work will be done in the line organization, which is where it should be done. A small department also diminishes the opportunity for bureaucracy to strangle service initiative and innovation. The formal departmental name—Service Quality Support Department, or something similar—communicates the desired positioning better than more common labels, such as the Customer Service Department.

If small is better than big, is nothing better than something? Except for the smallest of companies, the answer is usually "no." A service support department assures full-time attention within the organization to service improvement. A service quality staff may bring to the company a core of expertise in specialized areas such as service research and training that wouldn't exist otherwise. An excellent department should make the steering group more effective for reasons noted.

In addition, the department can play an important role in educating all employees on the meaning, importance, and application of service quality within the company. The department can provide technical support needed to plan and implement various initiatives, such as a new employee orientation program or a service guarantee program. The department can advise service providers in the field who require specialized assistance. The department can also handle customer complaints, although this function should be split off to another unit if the work volume dominates the department's central role of supporting service improvement.

Ideally, a service support department head should be someone from the upper reaches of management who has broad experience in the company, including line management experience, and who knows how to get things done. The department head should possess a leader's vision and entrepreneurial instincts and a manager's organizational skills. Credibility within the organization and a personal passion for quality service are indispensable. Expertise in the service quality field is desirable but not essential because it can be acquired with dedicated study and experience in the role. The other attributes listed are essential, however. Successfully leading a service support department requires a special person; it is not an easy job.

SERVICE QUALITY PROJECT TEAMS

Service quality steering groups and support departments inevitably will unearth problems and issues that must be resolved for quality to improve. Frequently, the best way to tackle such matters is with project teams. These teams are groups of employees brought together temporarily to analyze a specific problem or issue and recommend a course of action. The team disbands once its work is done.

Assigning an ad hoc team rather than an existing work unit to a project is indicated when the work unit does not have the time, talent, knowledge, or motivation to address the project successfully. Also, many service-improvement projects transcend functional departments and require cross-functional inputs.

Project teams offer the flexibility of assigning the best people to work on a specific project. If members are selected from throughout the organization, the team can bring a holistic perspective to the task. Project teams enable employees to become more personally involved in service improvement; project team participation is a way to learn and grow. Team members benefit from unusually high motivation levels deriving from the elixir created by teamwork, peer pressure, and a special assignment.

Mary Kay Cosmetics uses project teams extensively, calling them Creative Action Teams. The purposes of the teams at Mary Kay Cosmetics are shown in Table 6–1, which succinctly summarizes the principal benefits of service quality project teams.

Several years ago, Federal Express formed a project team to develop a new performance appraisal system. The conventional

Table 6–1
PURPOSES OF CREATIVE ACTION TEAMS
AT MARY KAY COSMETICS

- To encourage kaleidoscopic thinking, to "stir up" creative juices and incorporate this process and new way of thinking into day-to-day tasks.

- To generate fresh ideas, new perspectives, and enthusiasm.

- To allow people to cross functional boundaries and learn more about our Company, our co-workers and their responsibilities.

- To resolve crisis problems where input from various functional areas is needed.

- To allow leaders to emerge by creating leadership opportunities.

- To enhance teamwork between functional areas.

- To offer opportunities to better understand new technologies and/or to become more technically proficient.

- To challenge people to contribute beyond day-to-day tasks and problem solving.

way of designing a new system may have taken about two years. The team took just six months. The team conducted focus group interviews with couriers and with managers to determine their likes and dislikes about the existing appraisal system. It learned that both couriers and management disliked the system's checklist approach because it made the process too quantitative, simplistic, and impersonal. Armed with field input, the team designed a new, more flexible appraisal approach. It then piloted the new system before turning it over to the company for implementation.[2]

AT&T Credit used a project team to overhaul its organizational structure. In 1985, when AT&T Credit was formed, management created two organizations, a national accounts group to handle complex financing for large companies, and another group to serve smaller companies with standard credit packages. The structure proved to be unwieldy, error-prone, and unresponsive. Small customers wanted more flexible financing and personal service; big customers wanted faster turnaround.

To address the problem, management selected ten employees to serve on the project team out of sixty employees who applied. Management provided team-building and organizational design training; they told team members to devote 50 percent of their work time to the project. The team first interviewed customers and salespeople about their needs, then surveyed AT&T Credit employees. They met with employees each month to keep communication lines open and received comments through voice mail. The team did a work-flow analysis, tracing each step in the service system from the original customer order to the final credit payment. This process revealed numerous opportunities to reduce costs and improve productivity and quality. Next, the team went off-site for five days to redraw the organization structure and rewrite job descriptions. After the team's work was completed, all employees were invited to apply for the newly designed jobs. Then another project team was formed to serve as a transition team that would select people for the positions.[3]

Project teams should be used to resolve important issues, as they were in the Federal Express and AT&T examples. Success is a function of a clear mandate and timetable, careful selection of team members, team leadership, appropriate training, and visible support from superiors. Too many teams in motion at one time can drain necessary resources and management attention from teams working on top priority projects. Richard Chang advises: ". . . dispense quality-improvement teams sparingly. . . . Teams that are formed to improve the identified top-priority processes generally have the greatest potential for implementing changes that can benefit the organization."[4]

SERVICE DELIVERY TEAMS

Of all the structural forms discussed in this chapter, service delivery teams hold the most potential for service improvement—and pose the most difficult implementation challenge. Whereas service quality steering groups, departments, and project teams involve facilitating service improvement, service delivery teams are an alternative means of actually delivering service.

The service a customer receives typically results from a chain of related services. Some of these services occur behind the scenes, removed from the customer's direct experience. Other services the customer experiences directly. Deficiencies anywhere in the service chain can affect the customer's perception of service quality.

The traditional organizational form to deliver a chain of services is the functional structure. Service providers are organized by the particular function they perform in the service chain. The rationale is the efficiency and quality that specialism should provide. For example, an automobile fleet management company organized functionally would have departments such as automobile procurement, title administration, billing, and used vehicle sales. These are complex functions, and the functional structure seems appropriate.

But is the functional structure really the best model for great service delivery? For many companies, the increasingly clear answer is "no." Such a structure can be problematic for both service providers and customers.

For many services, the functional structure obscures the focus on satisfying the end customer and constrains the customer-serving talent and energy potentially available within the organization. By limiting customer contact to employees at the end of the service chain, functionalism discourages internal servers from claiming end customers as their own. The system of functional "handoffs" from one department to another diminishes internal commitment to the end customer.

Although functional specialization can mean greater efficiency and quality *within* a given function, it also can mean poorer teamwork, slower service, and more errors *between* functions. Geary Rummler and Alan Brache discussed these vulnerabilities in an article entitled "Managing the White Space":

> . . . managers of individual departments tend to perceive other functions as enemies rather than as partners in the battle against the competition. "Silos" are built around departments: tall, thick, windowless structures that keep each department's affairs inside and everyone else's affairs out.[5]

From Interunit to Intraunit Service Delivery

More and more companies are responding to the vulnerabilities of functionalism by placing people with different specialties into the same unit and saying, "Work together as a team, take ownership of the customer, and improve the way we do things."[6] In effect, these companies are restructuring from interunit service delivery that requires departmental "handoffs" to intraunit delivery that does not. The entire service chain, or much of it, is brought together in a cross-functional unit that serves a specific group of customers (or even one customer in the case of a large account). The unit is charged with becoming a *service delivery team*.

Katzenbach and Smith define a team as "a small number of people with complementary skills who are committed to a common purpose, set of performance goals, and approach for which they hold themselves mutually accountable."[7] These authors clearly distinguish between a team and a work group. Departments or field offices are work groups but are not necessarily teams. A work group's performance reflects what its members accomplish as individuals. A team's performance reflects both individual and collaborative achievement. Work group members are primarily responsible for their individual work product. Team members also are accountable for the team's work product.[8]

Service delivery teams, if executed well under the appropriate conditions, offer multiple benefits: service continuity, structural clarity and service control, teamwork, and employee growth. By serving a designated group of customers, such as those within a specific geographic area or industry, teams become familiar with individual customers and can personalize and tailor service delivery. Customers deal with essentially the same service providers for all or most of their needs over time. Service delivery teams enable large companies to operate like small companies because the team, in effect, becomes a "company."

Although teams are difficult to implement, the team structure is conceptually simpler than the functional structure. Customers need only contact the team regardless of their need. Because managers must authorize teams to serve customers creatively and responsively to make the system work, organizational layers often can be reduced. Excessive supervision gets in the way. Taco Bell's successful experience in reducing middle management layers and expanding spans of control, as discussed in Chapter 4, illustrates the organizational flattening potential of service delivery teams.

Teams foster structural clarity. The team either does the job for the customer or it doesn't. In functional structures, control over service quality is dispersed among various organizational units; in team structures, service control lies within the team, potentially improving service flexibility and speed and minimizing handoff problems between functions. The team structure prepares service organizations to play rugby. "Rugby is a flow sport," says Professor Noel Tichy. "It looks chaotic, but it requires tremendous communication, continuous adjustment to an uncertain environment, and problem solving without using a hierarchy."[9]

Teamwork is possible without teams, but teams are not possible without teamwork. If companies can improve teamwork by restructuring into service delivery teams, they will also improve service quality. Service team members usually work in close proximity and have considerable contact with one another, facilitating communication and the sharing of knowledge. Members learn teammates' strengths, limitations, and habits and can adjust their own behavior accordingly.

Team membership can be rejuvenating, inspirational, and motivational. Teams often set higher performance goals for themselves than their superiors would set. Pressure to perform is strong within a true team that offers more than the sum of its parts.

Team membership promotes employee growth. By operating like a small company, service delivery teams assume more responsibility with less supervision than is likely in a functional organization. Although employees initially may join teams as specialists, the demands of intraunit service delivery require that they broaden their skills and capabilities. Cross-training is a fact of life for service delivery teams. For employees joining teams from internal service departments, the team structure may provide their first experience working with external customers. Team membership can offer the challenge learning opportunity described in Chapter 2.

Aid Association for Lutherans (AAL), one of the nation's largest insurers, recognized the potential of restructuring early, reorganizing its insurance product services group (about 30 percent of the home office employees) into service delivery teams in 1987. Before the restructuring, the 2,000-plus AAL field agents had to contact various functional units for the support services they needed, a cumbersome and impersonal process. The team structure gave each field agent one contact point for all support services required. The service delivery teams could perform more than 150 services formerly dispersed in functional departments.

The roots of AAL's decision to restructure were in an internal study that revealed serious concerns with the existing organization. These concerns will hit close to home for many readers:

- The functional structure was not truly customer oriented.
- Decisions were made high in the organizational hierarchy, often far removed from the point of service delivery, negatively affecting both the quality and timeliness of the decisions.
- Employees' skills and abilities were underutilized, and many jobs were boring because of their narrow scope.
- Productivity was viewed from a functional perspective rather than from an integrated whole.
- Staff and related expenses were growing excessively.[10]

Not an Easy Transition

A 1992 *Training* magazine study shows that at least 80 percent of the organizations that have used team structures report improved quality, productivity, and profits.[11] These improvements are not easily gained.

For most organizations, restructuring into service delivery teams involves a major cultural change from the accustomed ways of operating. Restructuring will surely cause a significant disruption in the work flow during the transition period. Some, perhaps many, middle managers and first-line supervisors will be threatened—unable or unwilling to change from boss to coach and worried about fewer management slots. Not all non-managerial employees will relish the added responsibilities and higher performance expectations that come with team member-ship. Many employees will resent the breakup of social net-works that accompany the elimination of functional depart-ments. Companies that restructure only part of the organization create the potential for antagonism between the old and new groups. Organizing into teams requires systemic operating changes, from how employee performance is measured and rewarded to facility design and furnishings (teams need space for individual and group work).

Unless management is fully committed to the long-term potential of service delivery teams, it is best not to proceed. Training consultant William Byham states:

> Top managers must be clear about the positive advantages they expect, because they are going to have to pay for the change. There will be costs in training. There will be disruptions of com-munication and coordination as control and leadership migrate downward. They will have to deal with the problem of too many supervisors and middle managers. So, they must not lose sight of the payoffs they're striving for or they will give up in midstream.[12]

When Teams Make Sense

Service delivery teams make the most sense when the service chain is complex and interdependent. Multiple skills are required to deliver the service, and the need for cooperation among service providers is high. Uncertainty in the service task environment also favors the team structure. When the nature and pattern of customers' service demands more closely resem-ble a hospital emergency room than a production line, teams that can respond quickly and flexibly are probably needed.

Teams may even be indicated in more stable task environ-ments if specialist workers become less productive due to bore-dom or a sense of isolation. CRST, a trucking company, uses two-driver teams on long runs to help combat loneliness and reduce driver turnover, an industry-wide problem. Maids International, a housecleaning service, uses four-person maid teams to decrease boredom and fatigue and increase productivity. The teams rotate tasks as they move from one house to another and have the opportunity to socialize.[13]

Teams also should be considered when an organization supplies a variety of services to the same customer, requiring the customer to deal with multiple units if the firm is structured functionally. The need to reorganize at Rank Xerox in England was apparent the day a field representative was waiting in a customer's reception area. To his surprise, another individual present responded when the receptionist announced "Rank Xerox." The two representatives didn't know each other even though they worked at the same office—one in customer service, the other in sales. Rank Xerox restructured into regional units, each incorporating sales people, service technicians, and administrative staff.[14]

Service work in many organizations meets *all* of the tests enumerated above: the service is complex and interdependent, the task environment is turbulent, the potential for burnout induced by boredom or isolation is high, *and* customers must deal with multiple contact points. Under these conditions, team structures will almost always be better suited to a quality service strategy.

Care Teams at Lakeland Regional Medical Center

Patient-focused restructuring at Lakeland Regional Medical Center in Lakeland, Florida, provides an excellent example of the benefits and challenges of service delivery teams. Lakeland is engaged in a multiyear process of changing from a traditional functional structure (the "classical" model) to a team structure (the "patient-focused" model). Lakeland's first pilot test of the new model was in 1989. It did not reorganize a second unit until it had good results from the first unit. Proceeding cautiously and systematically, about 25 percent of Lakeland's beds were in the restructured environment by early 1994. With part of the hospital organized functionally and part organized with teams, Lakeland has had an ongoing opportunity to compare the two structures and has done so with striking results.

The basic organizational unit in the team structure is the "care pair"—a registered nurse and a multiskilled caregiver. A care pair works with several other care pairs across shifts on a care team. The care team provides up to 90 percent of the hospital's services to four to six patients for the duration of their stay. One member of each care team serves as the team leader, which is essentially a "player-coach" role.

The care team not only serves the same patients but also the same doctor. More than 90 percent of the time, physicians work with their primary or secondary care teams. Pharmacists, social workers, dieticians, physical therapists, and other specialists are part of the extended care team. Care team members must complete a six- to eight-week course at Lakeland's Patient-Focused University. The course teaches the broad range of skills required for the hospital unit being restructured, plus team-building skills. Among the services care teams provide their patients are preadmission testing, charting, X rays, respiratory therapy, physical therapy, EKG exams, environmental services (changing linens, vacuuming, dusting), in-hospital transportation, and charging. Care teams use a computer terminal in the patient's room for functions such as charging.

Lakeland's restructuring has been a difficult process. As Chief Executive Jack Stephens comments: "It is much more than a change in organizational structure; it is a whole new way of thinking about things." Phyllis Watson, senior vice president, Patient-Focused Development and chief nurse executive, adds: "Major cultural change just takes time. It requires constant reinforcement and training. It is hard on people and consumes a lot of energy. We used to think it would get easier but it doesn't."

The pain has led to gain, however. For 71 of 72 patient satisfaction measures, patients in the restructured environment ranked their experiences equal to or better than patients in the classical environment. For 49 of the 72 measures, the results were statistically significant.[15]

Survey research with the 44 staff members involved in the original pilot project show improvements in job stress, quality of work life, perceptions of care quality, and overall job satisfaction. Satisfaction with teamwork contributed to perceptions of reduced job stress.[16]

Improved continuity of care is a key to these results. In a classical setting, the average Lakeland patient sees 53 different personnel in a four-day stay. Phyllis Watson refers to these 53 people as "faces in a parade." In the patient-focused setting, the average patient sees 13 personnel.

Laticia Baily, a radiologic technologist, and Andy Thomas, a registered nurse, are a care pair. Laticia states: "You really get to know your patients. I've never been as happy with a job and I've never seen patients as happy. We can spend more time with the patients than doctors. The doctors don't have time to explain in detail. We step in and spend the needed time with the patients." Andy adds: "We get to know the doctor real well and if we have a complication with a patient, we know what the doctor would want us to do."

The patient-focused structure also gives the care team more control over the service. Wanda McManus and Marge Richardson, both RNs and multiskilled professionals, are a care pair. Marge says the new structure definitely leads to better nursing care: "It helps you to be a better patient advocate. We have a lot more input on what goes on with the patient. If the prescribed therapy isn't right, we intervene." Wanda states: "We can be more proactive and plan the patient's day; in the classical world you don't have control. The lab calls and you have to react." Ted Anderson, a respiratory technician and multiskilled professional, states: "In the old world, the patient would ask for a glass of water and I tried to help, but I didn't know if the patient could have a glass of water. It would take 15 minutes while I checked. Now, I know. And while I get the glass of water, I can do six other things in the room." Ted comments also on another benefit of the patient-focused model: team members' personal development. "I am a respiratory therapist. But I have been cross-trained to do so many things. I haven't paid for any of this training, but instead get paid for the new skills I develop."

Lakeland started down the path of a radically new structure to achieve four objectives: improve medical care, service quality, and quality of work life, and decrease costs. It is achieving the first three objectives and projects cost reductions once the transition period ends, and it no longer is operating with two structures. Because hospital services are complex, interdependent, and unpredictable, a team structure holds much promise for facilitating great service. Through its patient-focused approach, Lakeland, a big hospital with approximately 900 beds, can deliver a level of personalized, customized service that might be more expected from a small hospital. As Andy Thomas puts it: "We are delivering personalized care in a technological age."

Customer Assistance Teams at Roberts Express

Roberts Express, the expedited freight company in Akron, Ohio, provides another example of the effective use of service delivery teams. Roberts Express Customer Assistance Teams, known as CATs, have seven or nine members. The odd number is to avoid ties when the team votes on operational or policy decisions. Each CAT serves customers in a specific geographic area; there were 17 teams in early 1994.

Before Roberts Express restructured, the customer service department would take a shipper's order and hand it off to the operations department, which would secure a driver and truck and dispatch the job. Customer service representatives spoke only with customers, operations only with drivers. Communications between the split functions was a challenge. A customer could be frantic but the customer's mood state might not be conveyed to operations.

In the team structure, a CAT member "owns" the service from start to finish. The representative takes the shipper's order over the telephone, inputing data needed to set up the run (such as pickup and delivery location, number of pieces and weight) into a state-of-the-art computer system called C-Link (for Customer Link). C-Link identifies the available drivers most appropriate for the run in terms of location, truck size, and other criteria. Every truck is equipped with a computer and the driver at the top of the list will receive a C-Link message offering the run, which the driver as an independent contractor can accept or reject. If the driver accepts, he or she touches the "yes" code, automatically receives routing information and special instructions and begins the trip. If the driver rejects the offer, the process is repeated for the next driver on the list. Drivers located within

25 miles of one of Roberts Express's 52 Express Centers normally will pick up the load within 90 minutes of the shipper's call.

The CAT representative uses C-Link to track the run's progress and communicate with the driver as necessary. If delays occur, the representative can alert the shipper and recipient. The CAT representative remains involved until the delivery is made and unloaded, and the driver receives a computer message concerning where to lay over for the next load.

Members of a CAT work in adjoining cubicles. They share information, cover for one another during breaks, and help out during crises. They meet once a week for an hour to discuss service issues and needed actions. Team members rotate in running these meetings.

Quarterly bonuses for team members are determined strictly by the team's performance against goals in areas such as customer satisfaction, on-time pickup and delivery, and telephone response time. Each team rises or falls together, encouraging members to help each other and to teach newcomers the ropes.

The teams share facilitators for supervisory, coaching, and problem-solving purposes but, by and large, they operate as self-managed teams. The more time that passes, the less the facilitators are needed.

Roberts Express piloted its first CAT in 1989; nearly two years later it launched the second team. Fifteen more CATs were added in 1992, and the restructuring was completed. The rollout of the new structure occurred when the C-Link system was ready.

The pilot CAT, known as CAT #14, invented many of the procedures the CATs use today. One of the team's creations was the "7-Star" system in which each team member was responsible for developing expertise in one of seven specialties, such as safety and contract relations, human resources, and driver issues. The idea was to bring added expertise to the team in a balanced way.

Service delivery teams are bringing to Roberts Express the same benefits Lakeland Regional Medical Center is reaping: improved control of the service chain, more speed and flexibility, personalized customer service, employee skill and knowledge development, and better teamwork. CAT #14 member Joyce Compati says: "I get more satisfaction out of my job now. The team approach broadened and expanded my job. I was used to just taking orders but now I dispatch too, which is more interesting. And I have star duties." Sue Zordich states: "We just hear a voice on the phone and we know who it is and why he is calling. We know it is Bernie and what he needs. We try to make the customer feel like our only customer." John Suich says: "You never say it's not your job when you are on a team like ours." Charlene Donato, a newcomer to CAT #14 when she was interviewed, adds: "When I went through three weeks of pre-training, it was overwhelming. There was so much to learn. However, my team encouraged me and it became easier. Now, I can contribute to the group."

Roberts Express's CATs work under enormous pressure on busy days to get critical shipments dispatched and on the road. CAT #14 normally handles between 45 and 50 loads a day, but has handled as many as 70 runs a day. The company's technology is exceptional; Roberts Express depends on it to implement its service strategy of personalized, reliable, time-efficient shipping. But it is not just technology that supports the strategy. It also is pride, spirit, communication, and sharing nurtured by membership on a team.

Implementing Service Delivery Teams

The potential benefits of service delivery teams are clear. So are the difficulties in making the transition. Much can be learned from the experiences of others in implementing service delivery teams. What follows are some "rules for the road" in team restructuring.

1. *Demonstrate management support.* Restructuring into service delivery teams fundamentally changes how the firm does business. Operating policies and practices necessarily will change, as will social networks within and between departmental units. The inevitable realities of undoing and uprooting require that senior management lead the charge. Uncertain senior management commitment to the restructuring will fuel the resistance movement within the organization (and resistance is inevitable).

Top management must communicate clearly that the change will occur, why it will occur, how it will occur, and how it will affect employees. Top management must educate and persuade—and continue to do so throughout the transformation process. Lakeland's Phyllis Watson states: "Strong organizational leadership is required because [the restructuring] shakes every ounce of glue that holds the organization together. You can't communicate enough. Everyone wants to hear it from top management personally."

2. *Start with a pilot team.* That both Lakeland and Roberts Express initiated the restructuring process with pilot teams is instructive. Piloting enables management to learn much about team service delivery prior to rollout and even to change its mind about restructuring. A pilot team can work through issues and problems that arise, greatly refining the new system. The experience with the pilot team may persuade skeptics within the organization on the merits of teams. Lakeland's and Roberts Express's managements both used pilot team data to help sell the restructuring internally. Roberts Express pilot team surveys, for example, showed increased customer, employee, and driver satisfaction.

3. *Keep the teams small—and together.* The qualities that contribute to team effectiveness, such as continuous communication, teamwork, and response flexibility, are in part a function of team size. Small teams, generally fewer than ten members, are best. Team members should also work in close physical proximity, as do the teams at both Lakeland and Roberts Express. Physical separation inhibits the same qualities of team effectiveness as unwieldy team size.

4. *Link the teams to the strategy.* The teams' mandate to implement the service strategy must be clear. Without a common purpose, there is no team. Short-term performance goals—which the teams should help set—should be both specific and challenging. Teams on a mission will be more successful.

5. *Seek complementary skills for the team—and look for potential.* Service delivery teams need a complementary mix of technical

skills and backgrounds to bring so much of the service chain through one point of contact. Team members also need to be able to solve problems, make decisions, and work constructively with others.[17] Although teams require a reasonable mix of skills at the outset, team members will develop and enhance their skills through participation on the team. Katzenbach and Smith write:

> . . . in all the successful teams we've encountered, not one had all the needed skills at the outset . . . teams are powerful vehicles for developing the skills needed to meet the teams' performance challenge. Accordingly, team member selection ought to ride as much on skill potential as on skills already proven.[18]

6. *Educate and train.* Education and training are critical success factors for the teams. For service delivery teams to work, service providers skilled in function A must also learn to perform functions B, C, and D. They must learn new skills and acquire new knowledge. They must learn how to make decisions not required in the old structure. Supervisors must learn how to be a coach instead of a boss, a facilitator instead of a decision maker. Education and training are necessary to give participants in the restructuring the confidence to proceed and the capability to succeed.

7. *Address the issue of team leadership.* Teams need leadership from above and leadership from within. Part of the restructuring decision concerns the nature of the team's leadership. At least three sets of questions should be addressed:

- What is senior management's role in leading the teams and how should they perform it?
- What is middle management's role and how should they perform it?
- What is the team's role in leading itself and how should the team be structured for leadership?

Clarity of the leadership role is particularly crucial for middle management. The transition for middle managers can be especially difficult because of the anticipated loss of middle-manager jobs and power. Lakeland's Phyllis Watson underscores the latter point: "The bottom line is that when you empower, managers give up power and people grieve giving up power. It is what makes real hard something that sounds wonderful."

In broad terms, top management must establish the service strategy, make the case for a team structure, and keep the restructuring process moving forward. Senior managers also must establish the context for performance, such as measures and rewards. Middle managers must remove obstacles in the teams' path, coach and teach, and help the teams solve problems that cannot be solved from within. The teams should function as small businesses, assuming responsibility to manage themselves, doing what needs doing to be successful. Teams cannot be completely self-managing. As part of a larger organization, the teams' mission is to support the organization's. Within this framework, the more the teams can function as self-managing units that can creatively satisfy customers' needs, the greater the potential for significant service improvement.

8. *Measure and reward team performance, not just individual performance.* True teams produce a collective work product and should be judged and rewarded accordingly. Individual recognitions are not inappropriate, but team accomplishment should be central in judging and rewarding performance. The quarterly bonuses of CAT members at Roberts Express are based on team performance. Individual's performance appraisals are influenced by team performance. Few if any actions in an organization carry more symbolic weight than what an organization measures and rewards. If management wishes to reinforce the salience of a team structure, it must measure and reward a team's collective work product.

SUMMARY

The wrong organizational structure will defeat an excellent service strategy. Strategy precedes structure. No one structure is right for all companies. This chapter presents structural forms that many top-performing companies are using to clarify leadership roles, formalize responsibilities, solve problems, and provide coordination, expertise, and resources for ongoing service improvement. Service quality steering groups, support departments, and project teams are structural forms to facilitate service improvement in the company; service delivery teams are an alternative means of actually delivering the service.

Although the steering group, support department, project team, and service delivery team forms can be used independently, increasingly they are being used in combination. If quality service is a central part of the service strategy, the first three should all be considered. If the service chain is complex and interdependent, and demand for the service unpredictable and varied, service delivery teams should definitely be considered as well.

Service improvement is hard to sustain; structure is a key to continuous improvement. Executives can use the following action checklist to discuss the company's structural needs for service improvement:

1. *Does our structure reflect our service strategy?* Have we asked and answered the question: what is the best structure to implement our strategy?
2. *Do we have a service quality steering group?* If not, why not? If so, is it effective? How can we improve its effectiveness?
3. *Do we have a service quality support department?* If not, why not? If so, have we successfully positioned the department's role as facilitative and service improvement as everyone's responsibility? What have we done to improve the department's effectiveness?
4. *Do we use service quality project teams?* If not, why not? If so, do we use them on top-priority assignments? Do we give them the resources and attention they need to be successful? How can we improve project team effectiveness?
5. *Have we thoroughly considered the possibilities of team service delivery?* If not, why not? If so, is the team structure superior to what it replaced? What can we do to improve effectiveness?
6. *Viewing our organization as a whole, have we done enough to institutionalize and sustain the service-improvement process?* Do the appropriate structural forms exist to keep service improvement on the front burner in our company? Are service leadership roles to be played at different levels of the organization clear?
7. *Do the different parts of our organization work in unison on service improvement?* Do we have structural synergy?

CHAPTER 7

EMBRACE
TECHNOLOGY

Just as the service strategy should dictate organizational structure, so should it dictate the use of technology. Technology is a tool, a means to accomplish the desired strategy. Technology investments not linked to strategy are doomed to failure. Thus, the proper question is never "what is the best technology?" but, rather, "what is the best technology for our strategy?"

Companies featured in Chapter 4 for their clear, compelling service strategies all are creatively implementing them through technology. Taco Bell is using information technology to reduce management layers and empower store personnel; off-site food preparation and taco-making machines to improve productivity, product freshness, and speed of service; and mobile units to expand distribution beyond fixed sites. All De Mar service trucks are equipped with two-way radios and each service advisor wears a portable radio on his belt. This communications system enables a service advisor to promptly request backup support or advice on a tough job. It allows dispatch to operate like a 911 center, reassigning service advisors to the highest priorities. And, because several of the radio channels are reserved for service advisors to schmooze with one another and with dispatch personnel, the technology fosters the teamwork and bonding so critical to the company's "do what it takes to solve the customer's problem" strategy. Roberts Express's C-Link computerized information and communications system is so central to implementing its time-sensitive shipment strategy that it did not roll out the Customer Assistance Team (CAT) structure until C-Link was ready. With C-Link, a CAT member has quick access to

Exhibit 7–1
THREE FORMS OF TECHNOLOGY

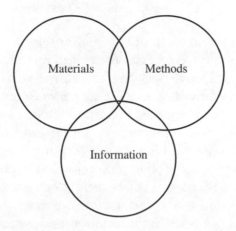

Source: Adapted from James L. Heskett, W. Earl Sasser, Jr., and Christopher W. L. Hart, *Service Breakthroughs—Changing the Rules of the Game* (New York: Free Press, 1990), p. 182.

necessary information for dispatching an order and monitoring the progress of the job until it is completed. Roberts Express simply could not be in the express delivery business with low technology systems.

As shown in Exhibit 7–1, technology can be applied to materials, methods, and information.[1] Service firms that combine technologies to simultaneously improve the materials, methods, and information supporting the service often experience the greatest gains. ServiceMaster has built a highly successful business providing janitorial, laundry, and other institutional services to hospitals, schools, and companies. Heskett, Sasser, and Hart credit much of ServiceMaster's success to its innovations in materials, methods, and information technology:

> Through the years, this company has built competitive advantage not only by assembling information about cleaning tasks and developing information systems for staffing and work allocation on individual jobs, but also by developing superior methods and materials in its laboratories. For washing windows, the company replaces ladders with specially designed,

light-weight, long-handled squeegees using easy-to-remove
velcro-backed, washable cleaning cloths soaked between uses
in fluids developed in Service Master's laboratories.[2]

Service-sector investment in technology has exploded in
recent years as service companies seek to lower costs, raise productivity, and improve service. An estimated 80 percent of all
technology investments are made by service companies.[3] However, much of the anticipated payoff, whether measured by productivity gains, cost reductions, or service improvement, is yet
to be realized. The problem is not impotent technology. One
needs only to observe Roberts Express CAT members working
magic with C-Link to appreciate technology's vast possibilities.
To scorn the promise of technology in service is to overlook the
American Airlines SABRE information and reservation system,
Federal Express's COSMOS package-tracking system, and Mer-
rill-Lynch's Cash Management Account—each a profit-pumping
breakthrough that forced competitors to play catch-up.

No, the problem is not technology per se but the management of technology. Edward Johnson, CEO of Fidelity Investments, a technology and market share leader in mutual funds,
makes the point:

> Technology's success depends on the hand that guides the tool.
> If you put a Stradivarius violin in the hands of an average six-
> year-old, you don't expect beautiful music. It's not much differ-
> ent with a technology tool. It may be able to do wonderful
> things. But in the hands of an unskilled user, it's worthless.[4]

Using the technology tool to improve service is the subject of
this chapter.

USING TECHNOLOGY TO IMPROVE SERVICE

Great service companies continually strive to increase productivity *and* improve service, to be more efficient and more effective. Technology's role in these quests is salient, but successful
application is elusive. Within organizations, technology is particularly susceptible to panacea-like hype and, eventually, bitter

disappointment. Managers can raise the probability of success by following six guidelines for technology-based service improvement:

- Take a holistic approach
- Automate efficient systems
- Solve a genuine problem
- Offer more—not less—control
- Optimize basic technologies
- Combine high tech with high touch

Take a Holistic Approach

Technology, as already stressed, is a tool to help deliver the service strategy. Thus, any good technology investment, as a means to an end, always starts with a clear explication of the end. Wisely investing in technology requires that management think strategically on at least four levels:

- What is our service strategy? What do we want to be famous for in the eyes of our customers? What is our "reason for being?"
- What is preventing our company from fully implementing this strategy today? What are the principal barriers, the key obstacles?
- What are the best ways to overcome these barriers? Is technology part of the solution—or does it just seem this way on the surface? If new technology is needed, what kind and at what level of the organization? What are the specific roles the new technology will play? What is the cost justification? And how will the new technology work with the old?
- What is our strategy for encouraging prospective users to adopt the new technology? How will we sell the concept of change? How will we teach the users to apply the technology? How will we make technology a friend?

Technology is a slow fix. Technological innovations are more social than technical. Nothing is automatic with automation. If management is looking for light-switch results when applying new technology, they will be disappointed.

Technology investments are strategic. Management not only needs a technology strategy to facilitate the service strategy, it needs a behavior-changing strategy to implement the technology.

Senior executives cannot stay on the technology sidelines and hope to win with technology. The top leaders of the business must articulate the technology strategy, monitor its design and implementation, and champion its role in delivering the service strategy. Management must tell the technologists what the technology must do; management, not the technologists, must be in charge of the technology strategy.

Automate Efficient Systems

Technology is not the solution for poorly designed service systems. Superimposing new technology on inefficient, outmoded systems will almost always lead to disappointing results. Operations must be redesigned first for efficiency and effectiveness and then be integrated with technology as the following story illustrates:

> . . . a major West Coast savings and loan association was originating $3 billion annually in mortgages using twenty-year-old operating strategies. First, an account executive took a customer's application. The executive then transferred the application to a processing center, where someone collected information about the customer's credit history and ability to repay the loan, and about the collateral's security. This information was forwarded to an underwriter, who typically requested additional data from the customer before making a decision. This process of cycling back to the customer could occur three or four more times—substantially stretching out the decision period—before the underwriter was satisfied. The entire process usually took thirty days or longer to complete. Almost one-third of the applicants were eventually turned down.
>
> The thrift's competitive environment had evolved over time, leaving the institution at a disadvantage. Quick decisions had become a competitive imperative—final decisions needed to be rendered in as few as ten to fifteen calendar days. In addition,

unsuitable applicants had to be notified very early in the process so they could seek alternate financing. And traditional application fees, which offset processing costs, were being waived to attract new customers.

Management's initial approach to meeting the new requirements was to computerize the processing and tracking systems. Upon investigation, it was determined that the process itself was ineffective; automating the approach that had been used for the past twenty years would not change the thrift's competitive advantage.[5]

It is tempting to expect miraculous breakthroughs from technology, but what really is needed is clear-headed management. Steps in the service process that do not add value commensurate with their cost, that add needless delay or complexity to the service, should be redesigned or eliminated, not automated.

Solve a Genuine Problem

All technology should have a customer. Sensibly investing in technology requires identifying this customer, probing the customer's needs, and eliciting the customer's feedback. Like any new product, technology must be market driven.

Regardless of whether the customer for new technology is inside the company or outside, success hinges on the technology's potential to benefit that customer. Otherwise, why should the prospective user change behavior? Why should the customer change from the accustomed methods? Why should the customer undergo the effort of learning to use the new technology, plus risk the possibility of poor results—without the promise of tangible benefit?

Investing in technology strictly to lower operating costs rarely produces optimum results. Users need to benefit, not just the investors. The technology should help service providers perform more effectively, with more authority, confidence, creativity, quickness and/or knowledge. Or the technology should offer external customers more convenience, increased reliability, greater control, lower prices, or some other value-adding property.

Ideally, new technology should benefit both internal *and* external customers. It should benefit service performers *and* service performance. The United Services Automobile Association (USAA), a San Antonio-based insurer primarily serving a military clientele, is a classic example of an organization that uses technology strategically to help representatives serve customers* better. Among the fastest-growing, most profitable insurance companies in America, USAA is first and foremost a service quality leader.

The heart of USAA's technology strategy is its concept of an automated insurance environment (AIE). USAA has invested heavily in automating insurance policy writing, member inquiries, claims, and billing, among other processes. Building a computerized, integrated member database was a pivotal step. By 1994, USAA had information on more than 2.6 million members and associate members (members' children and grandchildren) in its database. Although USAA's military clients are spread throughout the world and change locations frequently, policy changes are a simple matter. In one brief phone call, a member can insure a new car, add a driver, change an address, or effect any number of other changes. The member's file is all together. No handoffs to other departments are necessary. It is a one-stop process. The transaction is completed and the new or changed policy is mailed the next morning. "In one five-minute phone call, you and our service representative have done all the work that used to take 55 steps, umpteen people, two weeks, and a lot of money,"[6] explains former chief executive Robert McDermott, who retired in 1993.

USAA's aggressive technology strategy requires trained and empowered service providers. Otherwise the technology's potential remains unrealized; it becomes the Stradivarius in the hands of an unskilled user. USAA service representatives—who receive a minimum of 16 weeks of initial training, are empowered to make policy changes as necessary, and can offer callers a quick, seamless service experience—clearly benefit from the

---

*As an association, USAA refers to its customers as members. Hereafter, we will use the term "member" in referring to USAA's customers to be consistent with USAA's terminology.

technology strategy. And so do the members whose entire files, having been image processed, are immediately available to the service representative who answers their calls. USAA's member retention rate for auto insurance is a stunning 98 percent.[7] Technology solves genuine problems at USAA; it is a competitive weapon, not just a cost weapon.

Offer More—Not Less—Control

Technology should be the servant, not the master. Accordingly, technology should give its users more control in accomplishing what they wish to accomplish, not less. Technology that restricts the users' options, that strips users of authority and freedom of action, that leaves users helpless if it fails—such technology will hardly be greeted with enthusiasm.

Consider the huge success in recent years of videocassette recorders (VCRs), cable television, facsimile machines, pagers, compact discs, personal computers, portable telephones, and microwave ovens. These technologies have in common at least three characteristics. First, they solve a genuine problem; they are useful. Second, they are easy to use or easy to learn to use. Third, they give users greater control.

These technologies are all divisible. Divisibility means that a technology can be tried on a limited basis without complete adoption required. Users can control the timing and extent of the transition from old to new technology. They do not have to completely abandon the old technologies to adopt the new technologies and thus are not without alternatives if the latter prove unsatisfactory.

Divisibility extends users' control. So does choice. Pennsylvania's Meridian Bancorp's technology strategy is to let customers choose their preferred mode of service delivery. Customers can do their banking over the telephone, through the television set or ATM, or at the branch office. A Meridian branch serving Amish customers even has hitching posts for horse-drawn buggies. In contrast, Meridian's full-service "bank of the future" features advanced service delivery technologies including two-way video remote terminals that allow bank representatives and customers to interact.[8] As Faye Rice writes in *Fortune*: "Remember some customers will want to be chauffeured, others will want the wheel themselves. Some will speed, and others will take it slow. One way or another, all will be in the driver's seat. It's just a question of which companies they pay for the ride."[9]

Optimize Basic Technologies

Advanced technologies are not always the answer, and even when they are they need to be effectively combined with basic technologies. Advanced technologies can be intoxicating with their incredible new applications. It is easy to get caught up in the hype of advanced technology and lose sight of the fact that service providers and customers use basic technology most of the time. Executives aspiring to use technology to improve service quality need to make sure that the low tech materials, methods, and machines work and that they are well integrated with the newer, more advanced technologies.

Service quality consultant Linda Cooper surveyed employees of several retail chains to determine what management could do to improve service. One of the survey questions was: "Does the equipment work properly? If no, please explain." Responses included the following:

- ". . . front express cash drawer needs fixing."
- "The safe. Almost every time I put it on day lock I have to redo the whole combination to open it."
- "Deli slicers are almost unworkable. One of the sinks has had retained water for a month. No gloves for taking chickens out. The equipment for cleaning the fryer/warmer doesn't keep at the right temperature."
- "Conveyor belt guides are broken. The keyboard stands are broken and the keyboards slide onto the counter."
- "Power jacks not working right."

Quality service is not only a function of service providers' motivation to perform well but also their ability to perform well. Technology that doesn't work adversely affects ability to serve directly and motivation to serve indirectly. Many companies could improve service quality by monitoring more closely service providers' use of and satisfaction with technology, encouraging them to request assistance when problems occur (through an employee hotline, for example), and developing a quick-response capability for breakdowns.

Integrating basic technologies with advanced technologies is critical. Christopher Lovelock, a services management educator and consultant, illustrates the importance of synergy in this story:

> Consider my experience while checking out of a hotel. The receptionist quickly computed my bill on the monitor in front of her, transformed it into a paper copy on the adjacent printer, and asked me to sign the credit card slip; but then she walked off, papers in hand, to the far end of the long reception desk. There she remained several minutes, standing beside a couple of her colleagues. I began to fear that something horrible had happened to my credit line. Other customers behind me muttered restlessly. Finally the receptionist returned. "You're all set!" she said. "What was the problem?" I asked. She gave me a tired smile. "Oh, we've only got one stapler on the desk, so I had to wait my turn to staple your bill and credit card slip together." For want of a low-tech, $3 stapler, was lost a sizable chunk of the potential gains in employee productivity and customer satisfaction to be derived from a computer system that probably cost ten thousand times as much! (Of course, assuming that a paper receipt is needed in the first place, a better solution would be to integrate bill and card receipt into a single document.)[10]

Sophistication is not the appropriate measure of technology's effectiveness in service businesses. The appropriate measure is whether the technology helps service providers perform more effectively for their customers. Service companies need a technology strategy to help implement their service strategy. The technology strategy should integrate technologies—basic and advanced—and allow assessment and improved effectiveness.

Combine High Tech with High Touch

A principal marketing opportunity for most services firms is to "act small." This is true for both large and small companies. Acting small is not an automatic result of being a small organization. Rather, it comes from the organization's willingness and ability to personalize and customize the service, and to deliver it promptly and seamlessly with a minimum of bureaucratic fumbling. Acting small means "purposely treating customers personally."[11]

Technology supports a service firm's ability to act small as the earlier example from USAA illustrates. But service providers—and their managers—must want to personalize service, for acting small is as much attitude as information, as much commitment as tools.

Combining the powers of technology and personal service is usually superior to emphasizing one over the other. Technology-supported processes can reduce to seconds service functions requiring hours or days to perform manually. The application of technology also provides more consistency and accuracy than the most conscientious and skilled human beings. Technology decoupled from the personal touch, however, is not nearly the quality service weapon of technology and personal service combined.

Service providers can add warmth, sensitivity, advice, and a smile to the service. They can lead the customer through technology-based steps in the service process and then close the loop on the transaction. They can perform many services more suited to human than machine delivery—a medical doctor's counseling of a patient after the test results are in, a financial advisor's interpretation of a computerized financial plan for a pre-retirement couple. They can back up the technology when it falls short, for example, when the ATM swallows the customer's bank card. They can serve those customers who are technology-averse (such as bank customers who always use human tellers for routine transactions) or technology-cautious (such as the customers who use ATMs to withdraw funds but never to deposit funds).

Service companies must be prepared to serve customers situationally, with technology-driven speed and precision in some situations, with personalized bonding and expertise in other circumstances, and with a balanced blend of technology and personal service in still other situations. Moreover, firms must be ready to serve effectively customers who differ in their receptivity to automated service delivery. Managers should view technology and personal service as mutually supportive, interconnected keys to excellent service. Technology and personal service are critical pieces to the same puzzle. The potency of each to deliver quality service is influenced by the other.

TECHNOLOGY ROLES IN SERVICE IMPROVEMENT

In developing a technology strategy to support the service strategy, managers should be clear on the specific roles of a given technology. Integrating appropriate technologies into a cohesive strategy partially depends upon awareness of technology's service-improvement roles. Among the most important roles are:

- Multiplying knowledge
- Streamlining service
- Customizing and personalizing service
- Increasing reliability
- Facilitating communications
- Augmenting the service

Multiplying Knowledge

Service providers unaided by information technology are limited in the service they can offer by their personal knowledge. Human memory and notebooks storing information about individual customers, specific services, prices, and company policies have obvious inherent limitations. Information technology ranging from computerized customer files to artificial intelligence dramatically multiplies the knowledge processing power of individual servers.

Information technology provides vast amounts of intelligence to first-line service providers—and to their customers—minimizing the need for supervisors to answer questions, approve exceptions, and solve problems. Well-selected, carefully trained, service-minded providers can combine their personal knowledge, judgment, and values with the intelligence embedded in the information system to effectively serve their customers. Managers whose primary service is to supply such intelligence manually are redundant. Information technology, when used wisely, is an empowering and de-layering force in organizations—a lesson that companies as different as Taco Bell and USAA are teaching today.

The USAA story illustrates how multiplying knowledge improves service quality. This is how Robert McDermott remembers USAA in the late 1960s:

> There was paper everywhere. . . . Every desk in the building was covered with stacks of paper—files, claim forms, applications, correspondence. You can't imagine how much paper. Stacks and piles and trays and baskets of it. And of course a lot of it got lost. On any given day, the chances were only 50–50 that we'd be able to put our hands on any particular file.
>
> In fact, so much of it got lost that, depending on the season, we had from 200 to 300 young people from local colleges who worked here at night finding files, just going around searching people's desks until they found the ones they were looking for. Every night.[12]

One of USAA's most important technology investments is an electronic imaging system. The more than 30,000 pieces of mail that arrive daily never leave the mailroom. Instead, the correspondence is scanned onto optical disk and inserted in the member's policy service file, accessible electronically to 2,500 service representatives. Knowledge has been multiplied effectively.

Streamlining Service

Technology can streamline service by automating or eliminating manual processes that slow delivery and cause errors. Streamlining service means removing obstacles to delivery at a more effective state—obstacles to a more timely, reliable, productive, or valuable service, for example. Streamlining service through technology often lowers costs as well as improves quality.

Walgreens Intercom system, the heart of the company's efforts to gain competitive advantage through superior pharmacy service, illustrates the service streamlining concept. Intercom is a satellite-based computer system that links all Walgreens stores—1,879 of them in early 1994. The system maintains customers' prescription records for timely use in emergencies. Where state law allows, Walgreens customers can obtain a refill at another Walgreens store. Thus, a Walgreen customer living in Texas who forgets her medicine on a trip to Arizona need only visit an Arizona Walgreens store for a refill. Walgreens' customers can reach a pharmacist 24 hours a day via a toll-free 800 number, and the company will send the prescription by overnight mail. Through Intercom, Walgreens can provide a patient's prescription records to hospital emergency rooms 24 hours a day, 7 days a week.

Intercom saves pharmacists' and customers' time. Once the customer's name, address, and prescription information are put into the system, a label and receipt are printed automatically. Refills, if permitted by the original prescription, require no new information. Intercom can supply customers a printout of prescription purchases for their tax and insurance records.

Walgreens, the nation's largest drugstore chain filling 7 percent of all prescriptions in the United States, is a high-performance retailer. Its stores average nearly $450 in sales per square foot, well above the drugstore industry average of less than $300. Walgreens' technology strategy supporting its service strategy of superlative pharmacy service is keying the company's success. In 1993, Walgreens' pharmacy sales were 37 percent of total sales, up from 25 percent five years earlier. The company expects the pharmacy to produce 50 percent of sales by the end of the decade.[13]

The use of technology to streamline service is expanding rapidly. United Airlines has been testing electronic gate readers at airports to streamline the flight check-in and boarding process. A magnetic strip on the back of the airline ticket is coded with the passenger's name, seat, and flight number. Rather than queue up at the check-in desk, passengers swipe their ticket through the electronic reader and board the plane.

Lakeland Regional Medical Center is using computers in patients' rooms to move toward a computerized patient record (CPR) system. Initially, the in-room computers were used to enter charges as services were performed and products were used, creating a more efficient charging process. However, in October 1993, Lakeland began using the computers on a test basis for point-of-care documentation, that is, creating electronic medical charts. Lakeland's goals are for no one to have to write down anything twice and for patient-care information to be available wherever it is needed—at the bedside, in dictating rooms, in examination rooms, in the radiology department.

The Aurora, Colorado, police department is one of a growing number of police departments in the country to use information technology to streamline the 911 emergency service. In the Aurora system, the caller's telephone number and address are displayed on the operator's computer screen within one second after the call is answered. The operator can display recent police calls to that address with one keystroke, the patrol cars closest to the address with another keystroke.

Customizing and Personalizing Service

The complexity and pace of modern life sometimes induce a yearning for the "good, old days" when life was supposedly simpler and slower, and relationships were more personal. Of course, this familiar refrain is a product of selective memory. The doctor in times past may have known all of his patients by name and family history, but he didn't have antibiotics to treat infectious disease. Nonetheless, with technological progress came more standardized, less personalized service, which Ives and Mason call "the standardized cornucopia." They write:

> The town diner was replaced by a McDonalds, the village doctor by a health maintenance organization, the bank teller by networks of automated teller machines, and the neighborhood garage by dealers, muffler specialists, and Jiffy Lube. . . . In this, the 1980's edition of the standardized cornucopia, regular customers were treated the same as occasional purchasers.[14]

One of the most important technology roles in service improvement is to reverse the standardized cornucopia—to use automation to customize and personalize. If the first service era was high touch and the second high tech, the third era has arrived: high touch through high tech.

Customization and personalization are related, but different, concepts. USAA has designed its member database so that a member's propensity to buy each USAA service can be estimated on a scale of one to 1,000. Thus, the marketing department of USAA's Investment Company can identify the individuals most likely to be interested in a specific mutual fund and mail brochures only to them. This is customization but not personalization. However, USAA's electronic imaging technology enables service representatives to personalize service to each of the 2.6 million members in the database. Colonel Smith's correspondence from last week, plus the rest of his file, have been image-processed, and 2,500 policy service representatives have access to his entire file on an IMAGE terminal. Colonel Smith will receive customized *and* personalized service.

The effective use of technology offers the potential of transforming customers into clients—a powerful strategy for building durable, multiservice relationships. Clients are served individually, not as part of the mass. Their demographics, services in use, past transactions, and need profile are captured in a database. They are referred to by name when they interact with the company. They are sent customized communications. Clients, in effect, are marketed to as a segment of one.

Brady's, a San Diego chain of men's clothing stores, illustrates the concept of segment-of-one marketing. Brady's uses a personal computer system to capture client-specific information such as demographics, clothing size and style preferences, purchasing history, and hobbies. The company uses this database to customize and personalize service. For example, Brady's mails personalized letters at the start of each month to clients having birthdays that month. A 15 percent discount coupon is included for any merchandise in the store. Regular customers are notified a week before a sale is publicly announced, allowing them the first look at the sale merchandise. If overstocked in certain sizes, Brady's writes and calls clients to invite them to the store for discounts on their sizes.[15] Practicing client marketing, Brady's competes with many clothing retailers still practicing customer marketing.

Increasing Reliability

Reliability is the core of quality service. No substitutes exist for dependable, accurate service. Unreliable service is often caused by insufficient information available to the service provider. The service provider may not have the personal knowledge or skill necessary to perform the service reliably—or the time to acquire the knowledge or skill from another source. Information necessary to maximize service reliability may not be accessible at all on a manual basis. Data manipulation crucial to accuracy may be so intricate that it is beyond human capability. Technology offers an answer; it is service reliability's friend.

Since 1988, Xerox has been marketing copiers with built-in diagnostics to monitor the performance of various functions. Any indication of potential failure triggers a transmission of perfomance data over a standard telephone line to Xerox's central computer. An expert system quickly evaluates over 1,000 indicators. If a potential problem is predicted, a call is automatically placed to the appropriate Xerox Service District, which in turn contacts the customer to make an appointment.[16] A Xerox official explains:

> Nine of 10 times [when] a customer has an interaction with Xerox, it's because a machine is down and we have to send a technician into a hostile environment. Now if a threshold is exceeded—if the timing of paper moving through the system is off, for example—that information is sent back to an expert system which evaluates the problem, and electronically communicates to our work support dispatch team that within 24 to 48 hours they will have a problem with that machine. Our goal is to have 50 percent of customer interactions with Xerox involve a technician coming out to fix a problem *before* a customer knows it's there.[17]

Auto Source, a fast-growing midwestern chain marketing automobile parts, tires, and service, has computerized virtually every facet of its operation. The service system is completely paperless until the customer receives a receipt. Auto Source's technology strategy emphasizes service reliability and productivity in an industry noted for neither.

Technicians handle maintenance and repair services ranging from oil changes to engine exchanges. Each service bay includes a computer that can be used to diagnose 99 percent of all problems. A computerized *Mitchell Manual*, which identifies the appropriate parts for all automobiles, is located at each service bay for technician use and on the sales floor for customer use. A skid pad is at the entrance to the service department. Driving over the pad indicates the car's front-end alignment. Point-of-sale scanning facilitates inventory monitoring to prevent stock-outs.[18]

Facilitating Communications

Communication between service providers and customers is clearly central to quality service—and particularly vulnerable to mishap. A company advertises a toll-free 800 number, but the line is frequently busy, the service representative lacks the requested information, or the caller encounters an answering machine, leaves a message but receives no answer.

Consumers often view technology as the villain in botched communications ("I called the company, but they put me on hold and played elevator music for ten minutes until I finally hung up.") Technology per se is not the villain, however. The blame should be directed to those who designed and approved a communications system that leaves callers helpless without an estimated wait time or any option other than to disconnect.

The potential for companies to improve communications with customers through technology (as well as to improve internal communications) is striking. In particular, managers should consider the possibilities of using communications technologies to expand access to needed information, provide more relevant information, reduce the time and effort necessary to obtain information, and deliver information in a more pleasing form.

Communication technologies need not be exotic to be effective. Outback Steakhouse, a fast-growing restaurant chain, gives a beeper to customers waiting for a table. Customers are then free to shop in a nearby store until their beeper vibrates, signaling an available table. This technology could be used in many businesses that involve customer waiting, for example, doctors' offices and automobile service firms.

Roadway Express, one of America's largest trucking companies and the sister company of Roberts Express, uses an interactive voice response system to handle many of the more than 250,000 customer calls it receives each month. By dialing 1–800-ROADWAY, customers can use their telephone keypad to access Roadway's computerized database 24 hours a day. The system uses voice prompts to enable customers to determine the cost of a shipment or track a shipment, among other applications. Customers calling can get the information they need quickly during and outside of business hours and eliminate the problem of telephone tag.[19]

Zanussi, a European kitchen-goods manufacturer, places interactive video units in retail stores to provide customers with comprehensive information about the appliance products of interest to them. The system uses video-disk technology to ask customers about their needs and to help them progressively narrow their choice. Through this technology, Zanussi can control the quality of information provided customers at the point of sale and compensate for the wide variation in product knowledge among retail salespeople.[20]

Continental Cablevision, a cable television system in St. Paul, Minnesota, has programmed a channel called "TV House Calls" in which a representative demonstrates—live—the solution to a subscriber's problem while that customer is watching. Customer reaction has been extremely positive, as a company spokesman attests: "People are absolutely astounded. You can almost see jaws dropping at the other end of the phone when they experience this.[21]

Augmenting the Service

Another potential role for technology in service improvement is service augmentation. Service augmentation involves supplementing the primary service with features that are beneficial to customers, not easily copied by competitors, and financially and operationally feasible. The purpose of service augmentation is to attract new customers who want the supplementary features and to retain existing customers who don't want to give up the augmented service. State-of-the-art technology is usually a centerpiece of the service augmentation strategy.

Federal Express's Powership program, which involves installing computer terminals in the offices of high-volume customers, illustrates service augmentation at its best. Powership is actually a series of automated shipping and invoicing systems that save customers time and money while solidifying their loyalty to Federal Express. Customers receive free an electronic weighing scale, microcomputer terminal with modem, bar-code scanner, and laser printer. Powership rates packages with the correct charges, combines package weights by destination to provide volume discounts, and prints address labels from the customer's own database. The program allows users to automatically prepare their own invoices, analyze their shipping expenses, and trace their packages through Federal Express's tracking system.[22] By 1994, Federal Express had deployed more than 60,000 Powership systems.[23]

McKesson Corporation has built a huge pharmacy supply distribution company by helping drugstore retailers, many of them smaller independents, operate their businesses more efficiently. Investing millions of dollars over the years in electronic data interchange capability, McKesson assists its customers in inventory management, merchandise pricing, and credit, among other functions. Retail customers, for example, can automatically replenish stock by swiping a laser scanner supplied by McKesson over the shelf label bar-coded with the product's name and the normal order quantity. The order first goes to McKesson's central warehouse computer. It is then transmitted to an order filler in the warehouse who has a two-way radio and computer on the forearm and a laser scanner strapped to the hand. The order is displayed on a three-square-inch computer screen, indicating where the items are and the most efficient route to retrieve them.[24] Myron Magnet writes in *Fortune*:

> Dick Tracy would gasp with astonishment. . . . As the employee chooses each item, he points a finger, like some lethal space invader, at the bar-coded shelf label beneath it, shooting a laser

beam that scans the label and confirms that he has picked the right product. When the order is complete, his arm-borne computer radios the warehouse's main computer, updating inventory numbers and the bill. The result: a 70 percent reduction in order errors and a hefty rise in the productivity of order takers.[25]

What the Federal Express and McKesson examples demonstrate is the deployment of technology-based solutions to customers' problems that increase the value of the service. In effect, service augmentation, practiced effectively, raises the customers' switching costs. Customers are given disincentives to switch to a competitor.

SUMMARY

Companies need a technology strategy to help implement their service strategy. Technology is a primary tool for strategy implementation in general and for service improvement in particular.

It is easy to go off track with technology, wasting money and turning off service providers and customers alike. However, the problem is not technology-based but management-based. Technology's success depends on the managerial hand that guides its use. Used wisely, its possibilities for helping service providers perform better are vast, as the USAA, Walgreens, Federal Express, and other examples from the chapter illustrate. Technology, used effectively, can be a service provider's and customer's best friend.

This chapter was organized in two main sections. The first section discussed six guidelines for managers to follow when investing in technology for service improvement. These guidelines involved the necessity of viewing technology holistically, automating efficient rather than inefficient service systems, focusing technology on genuine problems, giving users more control rather than less control, effectively combining basic and advanced technologies, and creating synergy between technology and personal service.

The second section stressed important service-improvement roles that technology can play. These roles are: multiplying knowledge, streamlining service, customizing and personalizing service, increasing reliability, facilitating communications, and augmenting the service.

Senior executives who aspire to great service for their companies cannot sit on technology's sidelines. They must articulate the roles for technology in the company, insuring its linkage to the service strategy. They must monitor the design of new technology and facilitate its successful implementation. Senior executives must be in charge of the company's technology strategy. The following action checklist may be helpful.

1. *Do we have a technology strategy in this company?* Are our technology investments integrated or are they more or less independent? Are they assigned specific roles that fit a cohesive pattern? Are we taking a holistic approach to technology?
2. *Does our technology strategy support our service strategy?* Do we make a conscious effort to link our discussions of technology to our service strategy?
3. *Is our technology strategy market-driven?* Are we investing in technology that genuinely benefits its users, technology that gives them a good reason to change from the old to the new?
4. *Do we think of technology as social innovation?* Do we do a good job preparing people to use new technology? Do we provide the necessary training (how) and education (why)? Do we invest sufficiently in the human side of technology?
5. *Do we monitor employees' use of and satisfaction with technology?* Do we know when technology hinders rather than helps service providers? Do we know what tools they need to perform their work more effectively? Do we have a quick-response capability when the technology breaks down?
6. *Do we consider technology and personal service as interdependent keys to excellent service?* Do we fully recognize the potential of technology to support personal service and the potential of personal service to support technology? Do we seek to combine the powers of high tech and high touch?

CHAPTER 8

COMPETE
FOR TALENT

————— ...⌒○⌒... —————

Structure and technology are critical to implementing the service strategy. But they won't get a company very far unless the company has personnel with the attitude, knowledge, and skills to turn the strategy into reality. This chapter begins a five-chapter sequence on implementing the service strategy through people. We focus first on bringing the right people into the company because input shapes output. Subsequent chapters concern skill and knowledge development, empowerment, teamwork, performance measurement, and rewards. The essential issues in linking human resources strategy to service strategy are: recruiting and selecting the performers, developing their performance capabilities, nurturing their freedom in performing, leading them to perform in concert, creating a climate of achievement.

Service Providers Are the Company

Who should a company hire? It depends on the service strategy. Just as strategy dictates structure and technology decisions, so should it dictate human resources decisions. Marriott Corporation's Fairfield Inn's service strategy is to offer its target market of frequent business travelers ("road warriors") clean rooms, a friendly atmosphere, and budget prices. The simplicity of this service strategy requires just two categories of front-line employees: front desk and housekeeping personnel. Personnel able and willing to deliver consistent cleanliness and genuine friendliness are needed at reasonable wage rates to make the strategy work. Fairfield Inns created a pay-for-performance system called Scorecard, which is a computer that guests use at checkout to evaluate their stay. Guests touch the screen to answer questions such as "How would you evaluate the cleanliness of your room?" and "How personable was the hotel inn personnel at the time of check-in?" The data are linked to the appropriate employees and used to award monthly bonuses of up to 10 percent of base pay.[1]

Who should Fairfield Inn hire? Clearly, the company needs conscientious individuals with a strong work ethic. It also needs pleasant, outgoing people. And it needs people who will be motivated by a pay-for-performance evaluation system.

Why title this chapter "Compete for Talent?" Why not stick to words like "recruiting" and "hiring?" Because great service requires talented people with the desire to excel. Services are performances and people are the performers. From the customers' perspective, the people performing the service *are* the company. An incompetent insurance agent is an incompetent insurance company. A careless bank teller is a careless bank. An arrogant waiter is an arrogant restaurant. Service companies need the right people carrying the company's flag in front of customers. They need to compete aggressively and imaginatively for the best people to implement the service strategy. They need to compete for talent market share as hard as they compete for customer market share. After all, when the product is a performance, talent wins customers.

Ben Schneider and David Bowen interviewed 97 groups of three or four employees from three different financial services companies. The groups were asked only one question: "Would you describe the climate or culture of your organization and the role of service in it?" From these interviews, the researchers created a service passion index based on the amount of time respondents spent talking about service and the favorability of their comments. Employees who spoke extensively and favorably about service were deemed to have a passion for service. Schneider and Bowen found strong correlations between service passion and various human resources practices such as performance feedback (.46), internal equity of compensation (.43), and training (.40). Their strongest correlation, however, involved hiring practices. The research revealed a correlation of .64 between service passion and favorable/lengthy discussions about hiring procedures—who gets hired and how the hiring is done.[2] These results are consistent with research my colleagues and I have conducted indicating that poor hiring practices are a principal cause of poor service quality. Customer-contact employees who believe their units are *not* meeting service standards *disagree* with this statement: My company hires people who are qualified to do their job.[3]

Service employees pay close attention to who and how management hires. Few, if any, management acts are more symbolic of executives' true beliefs about the importance of service quality than the care and resources they invest in recruiting and hiring. For the same reasons, job promotion decisions also are powerfully symbolic, as discussed in Chapter 2.

Managers who receive many applications in response to job openings may question the need to compete for talent. "Why the sense of urgency when so many people apply?" they may ask. It is a matter of standards and tenacity. Companies with clear, stringent hiring standards frequently find that the vast majority of applicants do not pass muster. Indeed, some companies reject shockingly high numbers of applicants for entry-level positions who cannot pass a basic literacy or drug test, or admit stealing from a previous employer. Positions requiring much-in-demand specialized skills and training are all the more challenging to fill with excellent candidates. As this book is being written, some hospitals have shut down wings and some long-distance trucking companies have idled rigs and canceled truck orders because they could not attract sufficient numbers of nurses and drivers.

Hiring the wrong people contributes to excessive turnover for which companies pay dearly. People who don't fit the job—in temperament or skills—are likely to quit or be fired. The costs of high turnover are both direct (hiring and training replacements) and indirect (lower productivity and service capability as replacements learn the job, potential broken relationships with customers). Leonard Schlesinger and James Heskett view high employee turnover as a critical factor in what they term "the cycle of failure." High turnover leads to management's

unwillingness to invest much in hiring, training, and other commitment-building activities because people are going to quit
anyway. And many employees do quit, in part because of the
minimal investments made toward their success in the job. High
employee turnover negatively affects service quality, which
hurts profitability which reduces further the means to invest in
employees' success.[4]

False Assumptions

The mediocre results that so many service companies obtain
from their recruiting and hiring efforts are rooted in false
assumptions, including:

- High employee turnover is a fact of life that cannot be
  altered. The work ethic in America is dead or dying, and
  you just can't find hard workers like in the "old days."
- A sophisticated recruiting and hiring system for lower-level,
  nonmanagement positions is neither necessary nor practical.
- Money talks; pay 30 cents an hour more than the market and
  you will have all the candidates you need.
- All essential service skills can be taught in training and thus
  selection is not critical.
- Entry-level jobs are only for young people.
- The more part-timers the better because of benefit cost savings.

Great service companies recognize these false assumptions
and find wisdom in their opposites. One of the most damaging
assumptions is that price equals value for customers. It does
not. To customers, value is the benefits received for the burdens
endured. Monetary cost or price is one kind of burden. Non-
monetary costs, such as incompetence, slowness, or inconvenience, are another kind. Outstanding service employees help a
company maximize benefits and minimize burdens for customers. Yes, some customers select the lowest-priced supplier
almost all the time. However, most customers who choose the
lowest-priced supplier do so because they perceive service parity in the market and see no reason to pay more. But give them a

Harold's, Roberts Express, Tattered Cover Book Store, West Point Market, De Mar Plumbing, USAA, or Ritz-Carlton to consider, and they have a reason to factor nonprice criteria into their patronage decisions. Only a few of the dozens of companies featured in this book have a lowest-in-the-market pricing strategy. Yet, all of them rely on superior employees to deliver their extraordinary service.

The price-equals-value assumption is damaging because it leads companies to the goal of "saving money" rather than "serving customers" in formulating their recruiting and hiring approaches. The model is low wages equals low prices equals more value equals more business. The best-performing service companies follow a different model: great people equals great service equals great value equals great business.

HOW TO COMPETE FOR TALENT

Great service is a pipe dream when a mismatch exists between the type of people a company actually hires and the type of people customers want serving them. Competing for talent market share requires that firms seek to be an employer of choice, aim high, use multiple recruiting methods, span and segment the market, and use multiple selection methods. Competing for talent market share requires thinking like a marketer.

Be an Employer of Choice

The best way to attract great employees is to offer them great jobs. Word gets around concerning which companies are excellent employers and which are not. Competing for talent centers on marketing jobs worth buying—jobs that enrich the spirit, not just the wallet, that challenge people to be at their best and to keep growing, that bring people together to create and achieve superior performance. Dead-end jobs come from their creators' lack of imagination and commitment to make them into something different. There are no dead-end jobs at De Mar Plumbing. None at West Point Market. Nor any at Mary Kay Cosmetics.

Employers of choice hire people for the long term. Recruiting and hiring are seen as first steps in a stream of investments that enable employees to progress in their careers and contribute increasingly to the company's success. Some employees leave early in the process, and the investment made in their behalf is lost. But this is viewed as a necessary cost of building a great service business. The mentality is: *recruit and hire well, offer a viable, expandable job, and expect most people to be productive, long-term employees. Invest in these people rather than save on those who leave.*

Russ Vernon, the owner of West Point Market, pointed out in an interview that his head cashier, Kim Kowalski, "has only been with us a couple of years." Now, it is plausible that Vernon's competitors have very few employees with as much as two years' tenure. Yet Vernon views Kim Kowalski as a relatively new employee. Russ Vernon hires people for the long term; because he does so, he is willing to invest in their success. West Point Market is one of Akron's most preferred employers. Here is how some West Point Market employees describe their jobs:

Terri Freiman, wine consultant: "The people who work here don't necessarily make the big bucks, but you gain so much knowledge here."

Kaye Lowe, director of public relations: "It's never, ever boring."

Carol Moore, director of food services: "Russ is there to help us. He tries to give us the tools we need. He knows us as individuals."

Kim Kowalski, head cashier: "Russ will let us do anything that we have to do to provide the best customer service. Russ will back you up 100 percent."

Wendy Woods, courtesy associate (carryout): "It's a lot more fun and interesting than I thought before starting to work here. I mean packing bags doesn't sound too exciting. Yet, everyone here makes you feel important. We are not ordered to do things; people ask. Mr. Vernon knows all of our names and tells us we are part of the team. You feel appreciated and it makes you work harder."

When asked what he is most proud of, Russ Vernon replied: "Our people. We've really worked hard to make this a nice place to work."

Many readers will be familiar with the strategy of relationship marketing—attracting, developing, and retaining customer relationships. The fundamental tenet of relationship marketing is the creation of "true customers": customers who are glad they selected a company, who perceive they are receiving genuine value from the relationship, who feel valued by the company and are unlikely to defect to a competitor.[5] Great service companies practice relationship marketing with employees, too. They focus on developing and retaining employees, not just attracting them. Their top managers understand that employee longevity contributes to customer longevity, that building internal relationships paves the way for building external relationships. As Frederick Reichheld writes: "The longer employees stay with the company, the more familiar they become with the business, the more they learn, and the more valuable they can be. Those employees who deal directly with customers day after day have a powerful effect on customer loyalty."[6]

Starbucks Coffee Company, a Seattle-based coffee retailer, was featured on a 1993 cover of *Fortune*[7] as one of America's 100 fastest growing companies. Its annual sales growth rate during the early 1990s was in the 70 to 80 percent range. The centerpiece of Starbucks growth strategy is an innovative, comprehensive employee benefits package that includes health care, stock options, in-depth training, career counseling, and product discounts for all employees, full-time *and* part-time. Chief Executive Officer and President Howard Schultz explains:

> Our only sustainable competitive advantage is the quality of our work force. We're building a national retail company by creating pride in—and a stake in—the outcome of our labor.
>
> . . . No one can afford to not provide these kinds of benefits. The desire to scrimp on these essentials helps reinforce the sense of mediocrity that seeps into many companies. Without them, people don't feel financially or spiritually tied to their jobs.[8]

Starbucks' inclusion of part-time workers in its benefits program is especially instructive. Many companies hire part-time employees to minimize benefit payments. Starbucks takes the opposite approach and grants part-time employees full citizenship status in the company. Shultz's rationale is that more than half of the company's retail sales force work part-time. The part-timers serve the majority of customers and are a key to the company's success.

Starbucks' stock option plan, called Bean Stock, also is noteworthy. The plan is designed to reduce employee turnover and instill the pride of ownership. The plan is structured on a five-year vesting period. It starts one year after the option is granted, then vests the employee at 20 percent each year. Every employee also receives a new stock-option grant each year, initiating a new vesting period. The percentage of the grant is linked to the company's profitability.[9]

Companies such as Starbucks Coffee and West Point Market enjoy a competitive advantage with customers in part because they enjoy a competitive advantage with employees. By taking a long-term investment approach to attracting, developing, and retaining employees, companies become employers of choice.

Aim High

Competing for talent involves setting high standards for potential employees—and sticking to the standards. The pressures to relax hiring standards can be powerful: the urgency of filling open positions, the dearth of candidates who meet all criteria, the desire to control labor costs, the time and costs of assessing many candidates to find just the right one. Yet holding out for the very best candidates is precisely the strategy of excellent service companies. Given that their product is performance, they are determined to hire the best performer. Mark Day, head of Bank One Texas Trust's Houston office, comments:

> We interview a lot of people. We may interview 10 to 15 people who already have passed the personnel department screen. We drive the personnel department crazy. We want to find the right person for our culture.

Day's reference to cultural alignment is significant. Service companies should seek people who, in addition to having the appropriate skills and knowledge, possess attitudes and values that fit the desired culture and support the strategy. This means searching for intangible qualities that may not be evident on a resume and probably cannot be taught in training. Experienced employees who embody the desired traits know what to look for in applicants. Mary Kay Cosmetics sales director Nancy Moser says: "We look for the inside. The integrity. I can train the person on technique. I look for that kindness, that smile, that willingness to learn." Another sales director, Jessie Logan, adds: "You can't fake the heart. It has to be there. This is a relationship-building company." And from sales director Mona Holte Butters comes this thought: "This does become a business of the heart. At most companies, it is profit and loss, at Mary Kay it is people and love."

Joyce Meskis, owner of the Tattered Cover Book Store, believes the strength of the store is its people. While the business grew from two to 320 employees in its first 20 years, Tattered Cover's basic service strategy of putting books and people together and the values propelling it have not changed. Meskis knows what kind of people she wants to hire:

- "Our people must have a passion for books."
- "Diligence and doggedness are what we do best."
- "We look at ego issues. With 800,000 books in print in the English language and 50,000 new books each year, people who work in a bookstore can't possibly know all of the answers. We actively look for people who are comfortable not knowing and who can work with others to find the answers."

Service companies should create written ideal candidate profiles to guide the recruiting and hiring process. Service quality project teams, as discussed in Chapter 6, can be formed to develop profiles for different types of positions. Bank One Texas Trust Division used a project team to create such a document. The team analyzed the strengths and weaknesses of the division's service and identified common traits of employees who had not performed well. The team then identified necessary service traits, placing each in one of three categories: essential, nice to have, least important.

Each company must create its own ideal candidate profiles. Much can be learned from analyzing the traits of employees who have been most and least successful in the firm. Moreover, an ideal candidate profile must reflect the company's values and service strategy as well as position-specific requirements. It is beneficial, however, to consider the experiences of other companies in identifying essential service traits. Table 8–1 presents listings of critical service traits from two sources: a Learning International study of 14 top service companies and a study of critical skills for telemarketing service agents in a large communications company. Strong similarities appear in the two lists, suggesting that some service traits transcend specific industries and can be used as a starting point in developing ideal candidate profiles.

Companies that aspire to deliver excellent service must make a concerted effort to recruit and attract people who can perform the service excellently. Developing employees' skills and knowledge once they are on the job is critical, but not all necessary service traits can be taught. Managers need to identify the personal qualities that distinguish the most effective service providers in the company and that best fit the company's service strategy. These qualities—skills, abilities, knowledge, attitudes, values— form the guidelines for successful recruiting and hiring. Companies that aim high in the talent market, that know what they want and insist on getting it, develop over time a far greater potential for service excellence than companies with unclear or relaxed standards.

Use Multiple Recruiting Methods

The better the applicant pool, the better the new hires. Many service firms are weak and unimaginative in their approach to employee recruiting. Read the look-alike employment advertisements in the local newspaper. The advertisers rarely discuss career path opportunities, the chance to learn new skills, or other distinctive features that could position them as preferred employers. Few bother even to present their logos. Is this any way to compete for talent market share? The same firms that

Table 8-1

CRITICAL SERVICE COMPETENCIES

Universal Competencies for Front-Line Service Providers at 14 Top-Service Companies		Critical Skills Differentiating Excellent Service Agents at a Large Communications Company	
Builds customer loyalty and confidence	Takes proactive approach to meeting customer needs. Establishes "partner" relationships to help customers achieve goals. Does what is feasible and sensible to maintain customers' goodwill.	**Speech clarity**	Ability to communicate orally in a clear, understandable fashion
Empathizes	Displays sensitivity to feelings of customers and others. Recognizes different personality types and responds appropriately to each. Interacts with customers and others in a manner that shows genuine concern and respect for life.	**Oral fact finding**	Ability to uncover the important and relevant information about a problem through conversation or questioning.
Communicates effectively	Expresses self in an articulate, easy-to-understand manner. Demonstrates ability to sell to and/or influence others when appropriate. Asks appropriate questions. Makes appropriate use of written communication. Demonstrates diplomacy. Responds to customers and others in a way that helps build positive relationships.	**Resilience**	Ability to recover normal energy and enthusiasm rapidly following a discouraging situation.

Table 8-1 (*Continued*)
CRITICAL SERVICE COMPETENCIES

Universal Competencies for Front-Line Service Providers at 14 Top-Service Companies		Critical Skills Differentiating Excellent Service Agents at a Large Communications Company	
Handles stress	Stays organized, calm, and constructive when handling stressful situations. Demonstrates tolerance, appropriate humor, and patience with customers who are irate or difficult. Controls emotions.	**Persistence**	Ability to keep trying despite such factors as fatigue, distractions, boredom or resistance. It includes being able to continue working toward goals that are difficult to attain.
Listens actively	Hears not only customers' words but also their meaning.	**Stress tolerance**	Ability to withstand high pressure and rapid job pace. This includes the ability to perform at a consistently high level over time.
Demonstrates mental alertness	Processes information quickly. Learns and understands readily.	**Empathy**	Ability to put yourself mentally in another person's situation and understand how that person feels.

Source: "Lessons from Top Service Providers," Learning International, 1991, pp. 12–19.

Source: Philip E. Varca, "Power, Policy, and the New Service Worker," *Marketing Management,* Spring 1992, p. 19.

compete intensely and creatively for customers compete meekly and mundanely for the employees who will represent them to their hard-won customers.

Just as companies use multiple marketing methods to attract customers, they would be wise to use multiple methods for attracting employees. Companies recruiting new employees need not rely only on classified advertising in the newspapers, or only on newspaper advertising, or only on advertising. Company-sponsored career "open houses," tuition assistance for students who work part-time while attending college, college internship programs, and employee-recruit-an-employee programs are just a few of the possibilities.

Companies such as Wal-Mart Stores and J. C. Penney hire college student interns to work in their stores or headquarters during the summer months with the objective of attracting at least half of them to career employment upon graduation. Internships give students the opportunity to experience the company's culture prior to making a career commitment. Likewise, the company can assess students' capabilities and "fit" without making a full-time employment commitment. Each party has the chance for an extended test-drive. Internships enable companies to establish an inside track in competing for the most talented college students.

West Point Market no longer relies on newspaper advertising to recruit job applicants. Instead, it is using an employee referral program and achieving excellent results. Employees (called "Associates" at West Point Market) receive $5 if someone they recommend receives an interview, $20 if the candidate is hired. The program works because the associates understand the personal qualities and work habits necessary to be successful in the store. Debbie Lautenbach, West Point Market's director of human resources states: "We are hiring a special breed of people here. You have to be up. You clock in and it's show time. The newspaper ads were not selective enough for us. We were handing out so many applications and wasting a lot of time." Naomi Baker, a high school student working part-time at the store in 1993 as a courtesy associate, clearly understood that not all of her friends would be right for West Point Market: "Not everyone could work here. Not everyone has the patience. Not everyone can smile all the time. The minute you walk in the door, you have to put your personal problems aside."

West Point Market also encourages families to work in the store. Mike Vernon, director of special projects, comments:

> It's great. Mom might be working in the bakery, the daughter in the cheese department, and the son in the front-end. We have at least 15 associates who have family members working here. It brings in even more of a family atmosphere in the store.

Recruiting success stems from having the right attitude. The idea of using multiple recruiting methods is a natural, comfortable idea when competing for talent has genuine priority for the company. To be timid, unaggressive, or ordinary in recruiting makes no sense at all. Scott Bruner, manager of merchandise operations at Hard Rock Cafe Orlando says: "We are very selective. We bring top-notch people on board. We look for people with the right attitude and a willingness to learn. If I am out shopping and I am impressed, I'll give them my card." Mary Kay Cosmetics has a "three-foot" rule: everyone within three feet is either a prospective customer, a recruit, or a hostess.

Span and Segment the Market

Aiming high does *not* mean limiting the search to a specific demographic group. Talented people come in different ages and skin colors and both sexes. Competing for talent involves searching far and wide for it. Companies need to cast a wide net to find the people who best fit the ideal candidate profile. Tattered Cover's Joyce Meskis states: "We deliberately seek a diverse staff—talented, creative, sometimes rebellious. We want to provide an environment that will mirror the society that we serve."

In 1994, Wal-Mart employed more than 17,000 people aged 65 or older. Pizza Hut has a history of hiring hundreds of disabled people each year, tapping into a large pool of prospective employees who want to be in the labor force and who have the skills to be effective.

Many auto service companies in America are limiting their

growth because they cannot hire and retain enough qualified mechanics. One problem is an old-fashioned—and needlessly restrictive—view of the labor pool. These companies should consider creating technician training schools—and aggressively recruiting women to enroll. A different view of the world could double the size of the market.

The greater the heterogeneity of the labor pool, the greater the need to segment it. The same "job-product" will not fit all employees. Research in the fast-food industry reveals several employee market segments, including people who work mostly for the money, people whose priority is a consistent work schedule, and people who want to advance and make a career in the industry. Fast-food companies offering one employment package for all are clearly missing the mark.[10]

The growing popularity of human resource practices such as flexible benefits and flexible work hours ("flextime") is indicative of the heterogeneity of the labor force and the need for managers to be responsive. Rigid thinking is passé. Flexibility is in.

Connecticut's Union Trust Bank has been able to hire more mothers as tellers by accommodating their desire not to work when their children are home from school.

Faneuil Research, a Chicago telephone research company, successfully employs full-time college students to work part-time as interviewers. One effective management practice is allowing the students to redesign their work schedules every two weeks. The company pays bonuses to meet staffing requirements at unpopular times like Saturday.[11]

Toys 'R' Us captures employees' locational preferences in its on-line human resources information system. Jeffrey Wells, vice president of human resources for Toys 'R' Us, reports that when the company decided to open stores in Germany, his department immediately provided a list of 42 employees who wanted to work in Germany.

Seeking candidates from diverse sources enlarges the pool of prospective employees who meet hiring criteria. A small net results in a small catch. Accommodating the individual differences of employees with "job-products" tailored to their needs helps a company become a preferred employer and a more effective competitor for talent.

Use Multiple Selection Methods

Recruiting effectively generates a pool of qualified applicants. Managers still face the task of choosing the best people from the pool. They will make better choices if they heed consultant Ron Zemke's advice and think of hiring as casting a Broadway show. It needs to be done slowly.[12]

It is tempting to rely on instinct when hiring employees. Instinct should not be forsaken, but selection decisions are too important to depend on it. A combination of approaches is far better. Soliciting the input of existing employees provides valuable insight and reinforces their worth in the firm. Selecting the best people is a process, not an event.

Identifying job applicants who match ideal candidate criteria is difficult. Traits such as resilience, persistence, and patience usually do not surface in a standard personal interview. True attitudes about serving customers may not surface either. Some candidates will be more polished or practiced interviewees than others, but these skills may have little to do with which candidates can best solve complicated customer problems or be team players.

A combination of three selection approaches sharpens the hiring process: reality dosing, multi-perspective interviewing, and simulations.

Reality Dosing. Portraying the job as it actually is prior to the hiring decision gives candidates a chance to "try on the job" and better assess whether it's a fit. And interviewers can observe how candidates respond to the job's realities.

The Tattered Cover Book Store makes it a point to present job applicants with the reasons they may not want to work in a bookstore. Joyce Meskis explains:

> People on the outside observe all the reasons to work in a bookstore, but they don't see the negatives—the detail is daunting, the pay is bad, and not everyone is suited to be in a service profession. We do all the talking in the first half-hour of a one-hour interview. We talk about the negatives. We learn something while we are doing the talking and they do too. After having heard what we said, we ask candidates: "How does this fit with you?"

Disney shows theme park job applicants a video even before they fill out an application. The video describes what is necessary for the candidate to be successful on the job. This step culls between 10 and 15 percent of the candidates who decide not to pursue the job.[13] West Point Market's Kim Kowalski has candidates for cashier and carryout positions read the job description before they are interviewed. She says: "You can get an idea about candidates just from their reaction to the job description." Au Bon Pain, a chain of French bakery cafes, has applicants participate in a paid two-day work experience in a cafe prior to final selection interviews. Managers observe candidates in action and the candidates can better assess their fit with the company.[14]

De Mar practices reality dosing by inviting candidates to spend some time on the truck before making the hiring decision. Don McCann, service coordinator for plumbing, explains:

> I spend more time visiting than interviewing so I get a feel about how someone will be with customers. Is he caring? Will he have our best interests at heart? I then have the candidate ride along in a truck for a day or two so he can see what it is really like. We show him the way it is. It scares off some people, especially the hours. But I would much rather scare them off than to have to fire them later. We try pretty hard to find people who will fit because you just don't want to go through firing very often.

Multiperspective Interviewing. When used imaginatively, the interview process reveals much about a candidate's current skills, career aspirations, service philosophy, motivation level, work habits, and self-image. The opportunity for generating information germane to the selection decision, including information a candidate wants to hide, is greatest when multiple interviews, interviewers, and interview methods are used.

A sequential process of screening interviews and follow-up, in-depth interviews for candidates surviving the screen enables a company to devote the most attention to the most promising candidates. The general manager and new and used car managers at Longo Lexus conduct a joint interview in hiring new salespeople. The joint interview gets the senior management team involved in the process and produces multiple perspectives on a candidate. If the three managers are positive on the candidate, a second interview is scheduled with the president of Longo Toyota and Lexus, Greg Penske. West Point Market hires only after three and sometimes four interviews with multiple associates participating. Hard Rock Cafe's Scott Bruner insists on two interviews before making a hiring decision. Bruner conducts the first interview and his floor manager the second, or vice versa. A sequential interviewing process allows a company additional contact with candidates and generates more input from existing staff.

Nonpersonal interview methods can supplement personal interviewing. West Point Market conducts in effect a written interview with its four-page job application that may take up to one hour to complete. The application includes a series of open-ended questions, such as:

- What kinds of people irritate you?
- What motivates you to get your job done?
- How do you feel about doing more than one activity at a time?
- What is the hardest job you have ever had and why?
- What was the easiest job you have ever had and why?
- Describe your greatest accomplishment from any previous position you have held?

As part of its interviewing process for managers, First of America Bank in Libertyville, Illinois, asks candidates to write a statement explaining what quality means to them. "We don't give them detailed instructions or ask for a certain number of words," says quality service officer, Bonnie Pickering. "We want their perspective in their own words . . . we want to know how the candidate makes it a way of life."[15]

Service firms are increasingly using computer-assisted interviewing to screen candidates and inform the personal interview process. Applicants respond on a keyboard to a series of computer-generated questions. "Expert" software can select questions based on a candidate's responses to previous questions. The computerized questioning enables the company to ask numerous questions efficiently. Sensitive questions often yield more accurate answers. In the Greentree system marketed by Aspen Tree Software, employers receive a concise summary of an applicant's responses that identifies contradictions, major concerns, and time-delayed responses. Suggested questions for use in a personal interview are also supplied.

Simulations. "Watch them behave, don't just talk to them," thunders Ben Schneider at a management conference in London. Schneider proceeds to advise his audience to go beyond interviews and create situations that allow candidates to demonstrate knowledge, skills, and abilities vital to the job. Schneider mentions his extensive knowledge about tennis. If he were interviewed about tennis, he might qualify for the tour. No one who watched him play would select him for the tour, however.[16]

Schneider advocates simulated job activity that forces candidates to respond as though they were on the job. Consider, for example, the hiring of telecommunications staff for a credit card operations center. Customers phone in with numerous problems and questions. Some problems are easy to solve but some are not. Some customers are pleasant and understanding, some gruff and impatient—or worse. Who should be hired for these positions? Giving candidates time to study some basic policies and procedures, and then having them interact with a "customer" over the telephone in role playing situations helps the employer decide. Normally, several assessors would evaluate a candidate's performance. This approach supplements interviewing by compensating for its limitations. As Varca writes:

> Simulated activities are critical in testing for the interpersonal and intrapersonal skills central to people-contact jobs. Those characteristics are difficult to measure through interviews or paper-and-pencil instruments. Simulations put ambiguous skills, such as empathy, into behavioral terms that can be observed directly.[17]

Some researchers distinguish between high- and low-fidelity simulations. Fidelity decreases as a simulation becomes less like the actual job conditions. At the lower end of the fidelity continuum are simulations presenting a verbal description of a work situation and asking candidates to describe how they would respond. High-fidelity simulations require candidates to demonstrate behaviors, low-fidelity simulations ask them to tell how they would respond. Because "show" simulations can be costly, managers may want to test the effectiveness of "tell" simulations. For example, candidates can be asked how they would handle an argumentative customer shown on a videotape. If implemented properly, low-fidelity simulations can reveal a candidate's behavioral inclinations and practical intelligence—their "street smarts."[18]

Selecting people most likely to be great service providers is an uncertain, risk-prone process. Service companies that do the best job selecting talent use multiple approaches to increase the probability of making good decisions. Incorporating realism into the process through reality dosing and simulations can be particularly valuable adjuncts to interviewing. In selecting service workers, haste begets waste.

SUMMARY

Just as a company's structure and technology must be linked to its service strategy, so must its human resources strategy. This chapter focuses on the crucial issues of who to hire and how to recruit the best applicants. Service employees are the product to customers; companies must compete as aggressively for talent market share as they do for customer market share. Indeed, competing for talent helps a service company compete for customers.

Competing for talent involves being a preferred employer, aiming high, spanning and segmenting the market, and using multiple, creative recruiting and selection methods. Executives can consider their companies' talent competitiveness by discussing the following questions:

1. *How do our employees describe the company's hiring standards and practices?* Do they think the company is committed to hiring excellent employees?
2. *What are the turnover rates in various job categories in the company?* How do these rates compare to industry averages? How do they compare to the rates at leading companies in our industry and similar industries? What are the root causes of our employee turnover?

What would be the financial impact of reducing our turnover rates by 10, 30, and 50 percent?

3. *Are we an employer of choice?* What are our competitive advantages in attracting talented employees? What can we do to improve our recruiting competitiveness?

4. *Have we specifically linked our recruiting and selection efforts to our service strategy?* Do we use ideal candidate profiles to guide recruiting and selection? Is our aim high enough?

5. *Are we bold and creative in the ways we recruit employees?* Do we do anything different from the other companies in our industry? Do we involve existing employees in finding new employees?

6. *Do we seek talent from diverse sources?* Do we look in unconventional places for excellent people?

7. *Do we segment employment markets?* Do we accommodate individual employee differences with jobs tailored to their needs?

8. *Do we use multiple selection methods?* Do we practice reality dosing? Do we use multiple interviews, interviewers, and interview methods? Do we assess candidates' responses to simulated job conditions?

CHAPTER 9

DEVELOP SERVICE SKILLS
AND KNOWLEDGE

C ompeting for talent and developing people's service skills and knowledge are mutually reinforcing. Companies with a reputation for investing in employees' development will have a competitive edge in recruiting. And companies recruiting able, motivated people should receive a greater return on their training and education investment than companies less successful in recruiting.

Delivering great service involves putting service skills and knowledge to work for customers. Service providers must possess the requisite skills and knowledge—and must have the desire to use them on behalf of customers. Preparing people to perform the service role contributes to both ends: it builds skills and knowledge and nurtures the desire to serve.

Service providers' ability and willingness to perform the service role effectively are linked. Confidence is a powerful motivator. People naturally gravitate to those roles for which they feel most competent—and avoid those for which they feel ill-equipped. It is difficult to be enthusiastic about doing something that you do not know how to do. Service providers who appear unmotivated to customers may actually be ill-prepared and unconfident. Like effective hiring practices, preparing people to serve helps a company reduce high employee turnover that is so destructive to service quality. Well-prepared servers are less likely to quit or be fired than servers failing on the job because of skill and knowledge deficiencies.

A job rich in learning opportunities is a job worth doing. Personal growth is stimulating and rejuvenating. It is fun. It breeds enthusiasm. It paves the way to the future. Consider the feeling that went into these words spoken by service providers interviewed for this book:

Debbie Smith, multiskilled support professional, Lakeland Regional Medical Center: "The best part of working here is the variety. The chances to learn other things. Before [the restructuring], I was hooked up to a telephone all day talking to insurance companies. Now, I can do so much for the patient. We can do it all."

Jackie Salazar, administrative assistant, Bank One Texas Trust Division: "Working here, I learned that I am better than I thought I was."

Gail Weston, sales director, Mary Kay Cosmetics: "I can now teach a class with 500 women, but I used to fear speaking to even a small group. At Mary Kay, you start small and develop your skills step-by-step."

Cindy Yost, specialty foods buyer, West Point Market: "What is most fun for me is learning the new things. I like to spend most of my time in Aisle 13—that is where the mustards and condiments are. I enjoy teaching the customer."

Sidney Jackson, floor manager, Tattered Cover Book Store: "You just keep growing."

Training Is Insufficient

"Training" is too limiting a term for the task at hand. The delivery of great service requires education, too. Service providers must learn about the company's values, strategies, products (goods and services), and practices. They must learn about customers' expectations, competitors, industry developments, and the business environment.

Training helps servers build their skills, education helps them to build their knowledge. Training supports the "how" of service delivery, education supports the "why." Education provides context for skill building. As Federal Express human resources executive Larry McMahon states: "We found people are much more apt to get involved in quality improvement and have a sense of ownership if they have a better understanding of it."[1]

Developing employees' service skills *and* service knowledge is part of the investment required of companies aspiring to great service. Skills without knowledge, or knowledge without skills, is insufficient.

A Never-Ending Journey

Service skill and knowledge development is a journey, not a destination, much like service improvement itself. Learning is an unending road with many stops to refresh skills that may have grown stale; to learn new skills required by changing customer expectations, strategies, structures, and technologies; to reinforce knowledge about the service role, company, customer, and business environment; to add new knowledge, awareness, and insights; to renew the spirit of serving, to keep the flame lit, to keep the energy level high.

Executives err when they put employees through a specific training program and consider them to be "trained." Skill and knowledge development is a process, not an event. Sporadic learning leads to sporadic improvement; continuous learning leads to continuous improvement. Job-relevant learning is a good tonic that helps human beings overcome the repetitiousness, fatigue, "onstage" pressures, and sense of powerlessness that accompany many service roles. Personal growth is a source of self-esteem for people in jobs that can burn up esteem as though it were jet fuel.

The theme for this chapter is *continuous service skills and knowledge development for all employees*. No one should be denied the path of personal growth. Every employee has a "customer" either inside or outside the company; every employee is a service provider. Each needs to partake in the good tonic of learning. A central idea at companies like USAA, Bank One Texas Trust Division, the Tattered Cover Book Store, Ritz-Carlton, and De Mar Plumbing is that *all* employees, regardless of their job, must keep learning and growing. The alternative is staleness, boredom, burnout, and ineffectiveness.

The case of ServiceMaster is instructive. ServiceMaster provides janitorial, laundry, grounds maintenance, plant operations, and other unglamorous support services for hospitals,
schools, and corporations. It manages more than 150,000 workers, some on its own payroll, others on the payrolls of its clients.
ServiceMaster invests heavily in the personal growth of all, living by this principle: "Before asking someone to do something,
you have to help them be something."[2] The Downers Grove, Illinois, company provides intensive skills training on an ongoing
basis. Service providers learn not only technical skills but also
communication and customer service skills. And they learn
about the contribution their work makes to the end customer.
Workers are cross-trained so they can become more versatile.
Career-pathing provides employees the opportunity for
advancement. ServiceMaster offers personal finance, stress management, and other "life-skills" classes that employees can
attend on company time. Advanced educational opportunities
are available for first-line managers in an MBA-like program
taught by professors from local universities. The program takes
four years to complete.[3]

Does investing in the personal growth of people performing
basic support services make good business sense? Dave
Aldridge, vice president for people services and educational
development at ServiceMaster, answers the question:

> Providing an environment which promotes the development of
> the whole person (from orientation and initial job skill training
> to personal development), enhances the dignity and worth of
> the individual service provider. In honoring the dignity of ser-
> vice through people development and people-focused manage-
> ment, we increase the motivation of the 'service partner' and
> thus can provide service that exceeds customer expectations.

HOW TO DEVELOP SERVICE SKILLS
AND KNOWLEDGE

Continuous service skills and knowledge development for all
employees sounds good, but how does a company do it? How
can a company meld objectives for employee development with

its own quantitative and qualitative performance objectives? How can a service firm use training and education to become a better firm? We turn now to some answers:

- Focus on critical skills and knowledge
- Start strong, teach the big picture
- Formalize learning as a process
- Use multiple learning approaches
- Seek continuous improvement

Focus on Critical Skills and Knowledge

Companies can spend impressive sums of money on training and education and receive little in return. The investment made in low-payoff training and education—if measured—would be astonishingly high in many companies. Too often, skill and knowledge development monies are spent without cohesion and focus. Strategic guideposts are lacking. The spending goes in too many directions, accomplishing too little as a result.

The purpose of skill and knowledge development is to help a company effectively implement its service strategy. Thus, the service strategy should provide the guideposts for skill and knowledge investment. Just as structural, technology, and hiring decisions should be linked to the service strategy, so should skill and knowledge development decisions. Senior executives must ask: what service skills and knowledge are *critical* to implementing our service strategy? Generic answers to this question are not sufficient. Management must determine specifically the skills and knowledge that are essential for the company to be what it wants to be with customers.

The critical skills and knowledge development chart that a company should complete to guide programming and funding decisions is presented in Exhibit 9–1. The blank chart illustrates the need to capture in writing the crucial service skills and knowledge necessary for different categories of service providers to implement the service strategy. A company may choose categories different from those shown for both the vertical and horizontal axes. The significance is to create a road map that aligns development of skill and knowledge with the service strategy.

The task of filling the blank spaces in the Exhibit may appear simple. It is not. Companies should consider the following steps to create a critical service skills and knowledge chart and revise it as necessary:

- Form a team to organize and complete the project. Large organizations may wish to use several teams focusing on different strategic business units or different employee categories. If multiple teams are used, their work should be coordinated. The team(s) should include line personnel who perform the service roles of interest.
- Hold focus group interviews with service providers to brainstorm critical skills and knowledge for the company's strategy.
- Conduct an anonymous employee survey (or include questions on an existing employee survey) to identify learning priorities. Ask questions such as: "What one skill would you most like to improve to better serve your customers?" "If you could learn more about any subject to enable you to do your job more effectively, what subject would you choose?"
- Consult existing company research for insight about service skills and knowledge that should be stressed because of their importance to customers, perceived deficiencies, or both. Sponsor a new study, if necessary.
- Identify the company's most outstanding service providers and analyze why they are so outstanding. Consider how their service traits can be incorporated into the critical skills and knowledge chart.

Focusing on the development of critical service skills and knowledge is one of the most important steps an organization can take in the service-improvement journey. The up-front investment required to identify learning priorities for implementing the service strategy will pay for itself many times in better quality, more loyal customers, lower employee turnover, and less waste in training and education. Documenting learning priorities in writing (Exhibit 9–1) provides tangible direction for skill and knowledge development programming and funding.

Exhibit 9–1
ALIGNING SKILLS AND KNOWLEDGE DEVELOPMENT
AND THE SERVICE STRATEGY—
A BLANK CHART THAT COMPANIES SHOULD COMPLETE

Service Strategy: _____

_____

_____

_____

	Customer Contact Personnel	Noncontact Personnel	Middle Managers	Senior Managers
Critical Service Skills				
Critical Service Knowledge				

Start Strong, Teach the Big Picture

Those who perform a firm's service need to know about the firm. They need to know the company's central beliefs, strategy, history, traditions, policies, and procedures. They need to know how the firm works, how things get done, who is who, and what is what. Service providers need to know how they fit into the overall system, why what they do is important, and why what the firm does is important. They need to know about the products, the customers, the competitors, the industry.

Like actors on a stage, service performers need to know the play, the setting, the context; they need to understand the "big picture" so they will be able and eager to perform their parts.

The best time to begin teaching the big picture—and to underscore a company's commitment to the development and success of its employees—is during the initial stages of employment. New employee orientation offers a prime opportunity to socialize newcomers in the organization's culture and to set the stage of high expectations. To limit orientation sessions to explaining operational procedures is a lost opportunity. As human resources consultant Jeannie Meister notes: "When people learn about the big picture first, the specifics of their own jobs will have greater meaning for them and they will usually become more productive."[4]

The Tattered Cover Book Store conducts a two-week training and education program for all new employees. They refer to it as "boot camp" within the organization. New hires spend the first day with owner Joyce Meskis who teaches the philosophical foundation of the company. Employees understand clearly that Tattered Cover is no ordinary bookstore after that first day. They learn the specifics of how to apply the philosophy for the remainder of boot camp. Then they start working at the cash register. Floor manager Sidney Jackson comments: "You get a wonderful overview when you are 'thrown to the wolves' at the register. You get to meet a lot of customers who ask a lot of questions."

Childress Buick in Phoenix, listed by *Inc.* magazine as one of the best small companies to work for in America, has new employees spend one day a week for the first six weeks with a different department in the dealership. The rotation introduces new hires to the whole company and helps break down departmental communication barriers.[5]

Bank One Texas Trust Division gives a "Service Quality Culture Pack" to all new employees at their orientation. The pack includes copies of the Division's mission statement, unconditional service quality guarantee, service determinants and standards, and organizational chart. A service quality book used throughout the Division is also included as is a map of the service improvement process. The pack also contains an "I Am a Service Animal" lapel pin, a gold Bank One lapel pin, a Bank One tee-shirt, quarterly and annual shareholders' reports, and descriptions of three service quality awards given to employees. A statement on the history of the Division's service quality journey is also included.

New merchandise operations employees at Hard Rock Cafe in Orlando begin their orientation with a day of "product show and tell." Juli Powers, regional director of merchandise operations, explains:

> We do "product show and tell." We have 35 products and our staff have to be comfortable with them before they can sell them. We line up the products and discuss them one at a time. We want everyone to see the products, touch them, discuss them. Everyone goes through product show and tell.

The company's orientation also includes discussion of the company's beliefs and values, its history, "fun facts" about the company, and a memorabilia tour. Powers adds: "I have to make sure they learn all about the company before they get near the store, and I have to make sure they like the company because they will serve customers better if they do."

New employees are invariably eager students. The first day and weeks of employment offer a wide-open window for learning. Companies build their belief system, skills, and knowledge through individual employees. Starting strong in skills and knowledge development by teaching the big picture is a one-time opportunity to be seized.

Formalize Learning

Companies that benefit the most from employees' personal development are those that formalize the learning process; they establish systems that build learning into the work life, that make learning a mandatory part of the job, that institutionalize it.

Unless skills and knowledge development is formalized, unless time and resources are explicitly set aside for it on an ongoing basis, unless it becomes nonnegotiable in the company's belief system, the realities of day-to-day business pressures will defeat it in most companies. Learning will become a luxury, a sidebar, and its pace will slow and become spasmodic.

In a study of hotel managers, customer-contact employees, and customers, Michael Hartline and O. C. Ferrell found that role conflict and role ambiguity perceived by contact employees had strong, negative effects on service quality and value. Formal learning opportunities that allowed employees to focus directly on acquiring job-related skills and knowledge were found to be particularly effective in reducing role ambiguity. Providing employees positive on-the-job feedback to reinforce their confidence in their skills had the strongest effect in decreasing role conflict.[6]

Learning at Dawn. De Mar conducts training and education sessions three times a week. The sessions start promptly at 6:00 A.M. and last about an hour. Monday morning's subject is customer relations. Wednesday's subjects are customer relations and sales. Friday morning is reserved for technical training with the air conditioning and plumbing groups meeting separately.

Here is what happened at one recent customer relations and sales session. Larry Harmon, who presides, reads aloud a customer's letter praising Cecilia who had been the customer's first point of contact on the telephone. Then Cecilia is invited to the front of the room to make a little speech. Harmon then reads a second complimentary letter about Darrin, and Darrin responds. Cecilia and Darrin are presented valued De Mar pens for exemplary service. Next, Harmon asks a member of the staff to read a detailed customer complaint letter. Harmon uses the customer's experience to do some teaching: "Don't ever let a few bucks, or even a lot of bucks stand in the way of a satisfied customer." Harmon passes out the prior month's sales figures, which include each service advisor's results, and reviews them aloud. "It was a dynamite month," he proclaims. He asks the assembled group: "What is it that people pay for?" and then listens for the collective response, loud and in unison: "Solving the problem and leaving the customer with good feelings." The group clearly has done this exercise before.

Next comes an excerpt from a Tom Peters video that features a German manufacturer's obsession with high quality. Following the video, Harmon asks, "What did you get out of the tape?" and calls on individuals to answer. Harmon then distributes De Mar's "shared values" test, which contains 27 questions. The group answers each question aloud, with Harmon adding commentary to reinforce and emphasize the correct answers. Question 15: "Should we get every job we bid?" The answer: "No. It means we are too low. Don't be slashing prices. Sell value." Question 21: "Who does a customer call if they don't call De Mar Company when they need plumbing, heating, air conditioning, refrigeration services?" The answer: "A competitor." Question 21A: "How does this affect everyone at De Mar Company?" The answer: "No money." Question 23: "When we say we have 'Value Added Service,' what does this mean?" The answer: "Giving people more for their money." The meeting ends with the company cheer: "Give me a D, give me an E . . ." The service advisors then move to their trucks to start the second phase of their day. It is a little after 7:00 A.M.

Creating a Curriculum. The number of companies establishing their own internal "colleges" seems to be increasing. Ukrop's, a highly successful Richmond, Virginia, supermarket chain, has established a Center for Retail Food Studies to support its corporate value of lifelong learning. The Center offers a wide range of core curriculum and elective courses. Core courses are linked directly to the company's strategy, and employees (called *associates* at Ukrop's) take them during paid work hours. New associates attend five specific core classes during their first year and a half of work. The core courses focus on subjects such as company values, customer service, teamwork, safety and sanitation, and industry trends. Many of the elective courses are skill based.

Associates take electives during their time off. Elective courses include stress management, business math, business writing, coaching and counseling, and a variety of computer software courses. Ukrop's Center also offers leadership education through a four-module "Emerging Leaders" course, an eight-module "Leadership Development" course, and other courses.

PHH US Mortgage, one of America's fastest growing mortgage banking companies in recent years, has formalized the learning process into a series of modules based on where employees are in the employment cycle, their specific positions, and their interests. Courses are offered on a weekly, monthly, quarterly, and as-needed basis. The curriculum is categorized into initial core modules (for example, quality service, telephone skills), mortgage banking modules (for example, selling mortgages, new product reviews), and career development and specialty modules (for example, supervising skills, presentation skills). The company offers an in-depth orientation course for new employees each month and maintains a library of videotapes and audiotapes on various subjects.

At De Mar, Ukrop's, PHH US Mortgage, and many of the other companies discussed in this book, continuous learning is expected behavior. These firms have formalized learning. They have made learning a central part of work life in the company. They approach learning as an ongoing process, not an event. One can never learn enough to stop.

Use Multiple Approaches

People learn by multiple means, including listening, reading, observing, and practicing. No one method is appropriate for all learning situations, nor best for all people. Organizations are far more likely to realize their training and education objectives by using a combination of learning methods.

Listening. People can learn by listening to others who possess useful knowledge—presenters at a conference, corporate role models in a classroom, on-the-job mentors, customers in a videotaped focus group. Listening is hard work and some individuals are much better at it than others. Much of what is heard is soon forgotten. Yet when information is presented effectively and perceived as relevant, active listening contributes to sustained skill and knowledge development and increased confidence and motivation. These effects are most likely when listening is reinforced by other learning methods.

Corporations rely on classroom-based training and education more than any other approach and with good reason. The classroom environment facilitates multiple learning methods, creates the opportunity for dialogue among the participants, and offers the efficiency of group learning.

When classroom experiences are supplemented and reinforced by managers and mentors on the job, the effect can be powerful. Kathleen Alexander, a senior human resources executive at Marriott Corporation, recalled such a learning experience in an essay:

> I owe a lot of my business success to Mrs. Rosenblum. She captained the boys' department at Hahne & Co. the summer I started as a rookie salesclerk. Mrs. Rosenblum was tough—she made us sit through 15-minute meetings on underwear, forced us to know the why and where of every piece of inventory, made us learn how shirts were constructed and showed us how to calculate size in the absence of a boy. We did ticketing and markdowns, set up displays and dressed mannequins (I hated that). We learned what happened on buying trips and what types of people shop in the boys' department. She taught us how to be a good customer.
>
> I didn't understand everything at the time, but I do know that at the end of the summer, if someone came in for a pair of socks, I could sell them the trousers, shirt, tie, belt, sweater and jacket to go with it. Knowing how to do that made me feel good. I felt smart and "in charge." And I sold a lot of clothes.[7]

Among the most positive actions companies can take to foster learning are to promote effective teachers into middle management and to help existing managers improve their teaching capability. Service providers typically are exposed daily to the managers to whom they report. The opportunity for teaching is great—and often wasted because the wrong people are in charge. As discussed in Chapter 2, people frequently are promoted to managerial positions because of their success in nonmanagerial positions. Their service attitude, personal commitment to helping others learn, and interpersonal skills may not have been considered. One of the principal criteria that should be used when selecting middle managers—teaching capability—often is neglected.

Managers should take the courses designed for front-line servers before the front-line servers take them. It is demoralizing for employees to return from learning experiences enthusiastic about applying new skills or knowledge only to confront insecure managers threatened by change. It also is wasteful because new learning requires repetition and reinforcement to take hold. Just as learning boosts the confidence of servers, so does it boost the confidence (and openness) of the managers to whom they report.[8] As David Bennett, Carter Brown, and I wrote in an earlier book: "Training and education for managers is truly pivotal—for the example it sets, for the understanding it builds, and for the leadership and coaching skills it nurtures."[9]

Reading. Reading is another way people learn. People can read at their own pace, slowing down when necessary, stopping to reread difficult or important material, resting when tired. Reading also is an efficient and practical way to share with employees the knowledge and wisdom of experts from outside the company. It may be impractical to hire a renowned author to conduct in-company seminars, but it is practical to distribute the author's books or articles to employees.

Employees vary widely in reading proficiency. Many companies are finding it necessary to invest in basic literacy training for large numbers of employees to boost productivity. The problem is not just employees who cannot read, or who do not read English; it also is the poor reader with a high school or college degree. Confidence and motivation are linked. People who know they are poor readers are probably not going to sign up to read the new book circulating through the office. Reading is such a potent way to learn that midsize and larger companies should consider including reading skills in training offerings if they are not already providing it.

In general, companies can do much more to stimulate learning through reading. Every reader of this book should pause for a moment and ask these two questions: What percentage of the reading material distributed within the company to service providers is likely to be inspiring and uplifting? What percentage offers new knowledge that helps service providers solve problems they confront in their work?

Bigger companies should consider publishing internal newsletters for people in specific job categories. For example, a regional bank with 500 offices might have separate newsletters for tellers, customer service representatives, lenders, operations personnel, and branch managers, among others. People holding these positions could contribute much of the copy, sharing customer service tips, motivational messages, and advice on how to deal with recurring problems. The newsletters also could be a forum for management to communicate with people in a specific job classification.

Book reports or book clubs also are worthy of consideration. Employees who work together can read the same book and then discuss how to apply it to their jobs. Chapter 2 contained examples of companies using this method to encourage employees to become more personally involved in service improvement.

Distributing monthly reading packets of relevant articles and book summaries widely within the company is another possibility. A readers' panel can be formed to nominate materials for the monthly packets.

Managers who are sending front-line servers only policy and procedures memoranda to read are missing a grand opportunity to spread knowledge and wisdom that is available but not necessarily easily accessible to all employees. Many managers read widely for their own growth and intellectual development. A manager invigorated by exciting ideas and innovative concepts can communicate both personal response and pertinent information to employees. Brief evaluative summaries or restatements created by an energized manager send a powerful double message to employees. The overt message is the specific information and the manager's purpose for sending it. The underlying message is: "My manager is *alive and interested* in me and my job performance; therefore, I am a valuable person, and my manager takes time to tell me things that will help me do my job." Managers and employees alike will find truth in the statement, "A student who learns from a teacher who is also learning drinks from a running brook rather than a stagnant pool."[10]

Participative Observing. People also learn through demonstration and vicarious experience. Visual and other sensory stimuli can evoke powerful emotions, leave lasting images, and reinforce written and oral information. When investing in skills and knowledge development, managers should consider the possibilities of experiential learning. The possibilities are limited only by the imagination.

Meridian Banking Group has had customer contact personnel complete deposit slips with Vaseline smeared on their glasses and count money with three fingers taped together to help them learn to empathize with elderly customers having poor eyesight or arthritis.[11] Experiencing this sensory simulation heightens their awareness of their role in providing service to customers with special needs.

When De Mar botched a maintenance job on an air-conditioning unit, failing to thoroughly clean it, Larry Harmon personally went to the site and videotaped the unit. The videotape he played (and commented on) at the next training and education session clearly demonstrated how dirty the technician had left the burners. Through the videotape, employees "visited" the scene rather than just hearing about it.

Rob Perez, general manager of the Hard Rock Cafe restaurant in Orlando, faced a problem of slipping mystery shopper ratings. He responded by having every member of his staff assume the role of a customer and shop the restaurant. They went through the entire customer experience, including standing in line waiting for a table. Then they had to write a shoppers report with recommendations for improving service. The process motivated a number of operational changes.

The Walt Disney World Company in Orlando has all employees (cast members) in its parks group (Disney World, EPCOT, and MGM Studio) attend *Disney Traditions*, the company-wide orientation program. Part of the program is devoted to the demonstration of appropriate and inappropriate verbal and nonverbal communications. Through role-playing scenarios, cast members have the opportunity to use performance skills such as posture, gestures, eye contact, facial expressions, vocal image, and humor. These skills are reinforced through an on-site field experience. After observing their peers on the job, cast members discuss and reflect on the impact of their behavior on the total customer (guest) experience.

Practicing. In sports, even grizzled veterans and superstars are expected to practice. Playing the game isn't sufficient. To hone their skills, to work on weaknesses, to stay sharp, athletes practice. Practice is no less important for developing and maintaining nonathletic skills and knowledge. A few years back, Coca-Cola mounted a massive training program for 1,300 employees. It was initially judged successful, but follow-up research three years later showed that employees had forgotten almost everything because they did not have the opportunity to use most of what they were taught. This finding prompted the company to emphasize "just-in-time" training. Skills such as brainstorming and consensus building are taught to employees moving into positions where they need them.[12]

The sports analogy of playing games and practicing to play games is a helpful one for business. Many companies don't provide much practice time for employees who mostly just play the game. Although employees can practice on the job, they also need off-stage opportunities to prepare without the risk of failing in front of customers.

Off-stage practicing allows for repetition, self-paced learning, and coaching. Consider De Mar's approach to training and education discussed earlier. Much of the information provided in the weekly sessions is purposely *old* information. De Mar's training room is actually its practice field. And Larry Harmon is the head coach. When asked in an interview why training is so important at De Mar, Harmon answered: "I can't believe how important it is to reinforce. You need constant reinforcement."

Ritz-Carlton's practice habits include daily departmental lineups in its hotels in which employees review one of the company's twenty service basics presented in Chapter 4. The daily practice sessions make it virtually impossible for servers to forget or ignore the twenty ideas.

One of the best ways to practice is to teach. Teaching requires probing the material, thinking it through, developing examples to illustrate the points, and rehearsing before going in front of the group.

Employees who attend conferences outside the company should be asked to teach other employees what they learned. Company training and education sessions should not be led solely by full-time trainers, but also by managerial and nonmanagerial personnel who possess or can develop expertise on a certain subject and can teach it to others.

People develop their skills and knowledge by listening to others, reading, participatively observing, and practicing. These learning methods are most effective when combined. Without listening, reading, and/or active observation, for example, employees may have nothing to practice. Firms that invest in multiple learning approaches—and do so with practicality, relevance, and imagination—have the best chance of creating a culture of continuous learning.

Seek Continuous Improvement

Training and education services are highly vulnerable to waste, dependent as they are on the skill and motivation levels of both teachers and students, and the need for follow-up reinforcement. Firms frequently receive a low return on their training and education investments. Even worse, managers may not know they are receiving a poor return.

Measuring the effectiveness of employee training and education is an essential step in service improvement. To know is to improve. To not know is to waste. Firms should measure their efforts on both the specific course (or project) and overall programming. They should seek feedback not only from participants in the programs but also from their managers—and indirectly from customer research. They should obtain not only immediate feedback following a learning exercise but also later feedback (one, three, or six months later, for example) to assess attitudinal and behavioral changes.

Questions for participants immediately following a specific session normally include the usefulness of the subject matter, the effectiveness of the instructor(s), and suggestions for improvement. Follow-up surveys focus on what was taught that is being used on the job, what isn't being used and why. Participants might be asked again to suggest how to improve the course as their ideas may change with time. Managers of the participants also should be queried in follow-up surveys concerning their perceptions of how a learning experience helped—or didn't help—job performance.

Course-specific evaluations help to improve those offerings, but they don't answer the more fundamental questions of whether a company is receiving a good return on its training and education investment and what it should do differently? For these purposes, an annual learning review is in order. Among the survey questions that front-line service providers might be asked are:

- What are the most useful skills you have developed since coming to work for the company?
- Are you learning what you need to deliver high quality service to your customers?
- What is the most valuable learning experience you have had in the company?
- What is the least valuable learning experience you have had in the company?
- What should the company do to improve the training and education of employees in your job?

Managers should be asked these same questions about their own learning experiences. In addition, they should respond to questions about the people they manage, including:

- Are the people reporting to you learning what they need to deliver high quality service to customers?
- What is the most valuable learning experience the company offers to your direct reports?
- What is the least valuable learning experience they receive?
- What are the most important actions the company could take to improve the training and education of your direct reports?

The annual learning review should also include cost-benefit assessments of specific training and education programs and priority objectives and plans for the next year. The results of the review should be reported to top management. The company also may wish to distribute a report summary to all employees. A summary report would underscore the company's commitment to continuous learning and improvement.

Management measures what is important. Every employee knows this truth about organizations. The skill and knowledge development of those who perform services—and those who lead them—is crucial to service improvement. Ongoing, rigorous evaluation of training and education gives a company the opportunity to continuously improve its learning initiatives and realize increasing returns on its investments.

SUMMARY

The last chapter focused on recruiting and hiring people with the most potential for implementing a company's service strategy. The present chapter focuses on developing the potential for excellence that people bring to a job. Job-relevant learning is a competence builder and a confidence enhancer; it is a motivator, a source of self-esteem, a tonic to prevent burnout. A job rich in learning is a job worth having.

Training alone is insufficient. Service providers need to know the what and why of service delivery (knowledge) as well as learn the how (skills). Learning is a process, not an event; the continuous learning of service providers contributes to the continuous improvement of service. Skill and knowledge development is a never-ending journey. It is a journey for all employees because all employees are service providers. All employees have a "customer" either inside or outside the company.

To best prepare people to deliver the service strategy, firms should (1) focus on identifying and developing critical skills and knowledge; (2) create a strong orientation experience that teaches the big picture; (3) formalize the learning process so that it cannot be shunted aside; (4) use multiple learning approaches;

and (5) rigorously evaluate skill and knowledge development efforts in the spirit of continuous improvement.

The ideas presented in this chapter can be discussed in a company using the following checklist:

1. *Do we give sufficient attention to both skill and knowledge development in this company?* Do we teach the what, why, and how of service delivery?
2. *Do we invest in the skill and knowledge development of all employees regardless of their rank or position?* Do we think of every employee as a service provider?
3. *Do we view skill and knowledge development as a continuous process?* Is continuous learning part of our company's belief system?
4. *Have we made a conscious effort to align skill and knowledge development with our service strategy?* Are we focusing on developing skills and knowledge that are critical to the execution of our strategy?
5. *Do we view new employee orientation as an important learning opportunity?* Do we use this opportunity to introduce the company's culture, teach them the service strategy, convey the importance of their roles, and establish high performance expectations? Do we use this opportunity to underscore our commitment to investing in employees' skill and knowledge development?
6. *Have we formalized skill and knowledge development sufficiently so that it cannot be put on hold?* Have we made learning an expected, necessary part of work life in this company?
7. *Are we purposefully using multiple learning methods?* Are we innovative in our use of learning methods? Do we provide sufficient off-stage opportunities for employees to practice skills and reinforce knowledge?
8. *Do we seek to continually improve the effectiveness of our training and education efforts?* Do we assess our current programming in terms of attitudinal and behavioral changes? Do we attempt to identify what employees are not learning that they need to learn?

CHAPTER 10

EMPOWER SERVERS
TO SERVE

Hiring talented service providers, investing in their training
and education, and then stifling their flexibility and creativity in serving customers makes little sense. Human beings
are not meant to be robots. They are not meant to put their ability to think on hold during work hours.

Empowering servers to serve is a necessary condition for
delivering great service. In developing this theme, we may
define empowerment differently from many readers' accustomed understanding of the concept, however. Empowerment
does not mean the elimination of hierarchy, direction, or personal accountability. Nor does empowerment mean simply
granting servers more freedom and discretion to do their jobs;
this is too narrow a view of empowerment's essential meaning—and potential benefits.

Empowerment is a *state of mind*. An employee with an
empowered state of mind experiences feelings of (1) *control* over
how the job shall be performed; (2) *awareness* of the context in
which the work is performed and where it fits in the "big picture"; (3) *accountability* for personal work output; (4) *shared
responsibility* for unit and organizational performance; and (5)
equity in the distribution of rewards based on individual and
collective performance.[1]

Management creates an empowered state of mind in the
organization by treating employees as part-owners of the business and expecting them to behave like owners. Employees
have not only the authority but also the responsibility to use
their skills, knowledge, judgment, and creativity to serve their

customers effectively and contribute to their company's success. The firm's central values and strategy—its "reason for being"— provide the guidance rather than thick policies and procedures manuals. Employees are knowledgeable about the firm's performance, progress, problems, and prospects. They share in the fruits of their labor; the company's success is their success.

In the empowerment model, top management sets direction and establishes a culture of achievement; middle management coaches achievement and removes obstacles in its path; and front-line servers manage themselves to a significant degree in creating value for their internal or external customers. Everyone is supposed to think on the job. Everyone exercises some control over how he or she performs a job. Everyone is accountable for his or her own performance and shares responsibility for the organization's performance. Everyone is on the team.

Listen to the words of service providers with an empowered state of mind:

Bellman, San Antonio Marriott: "I like working here. The managers let you do what you gotta do."[2]

Andy Thomas, registered nurse and care pair member, Lakeland Regional Medical Center: "This is the first time in 15 years I have been totally satisfied with my job. We have the freedom of running our small business. Patients remember who you are."

Randy Oates-Woodberry, pharmacist, Lakeland Regional Medical Center: "The patient-focused concept gives us accountability and authority. When you are accountable, you put more into it. You're all working to serve the patient and your co-workers."

Jackie Salazar, administrative assistant, Bank One Texas Trust Division, Houston Office: "I have worked for Mark [Day] for ten years. He lets you work. He wants you to take charge."

Judy Frow, personal trust administrator, Bank One Texas Trust Division, Houston Office: "I know when I tell the customer something, my two managers will back me up. I know my limits, but most of the time I try to help the customer right then and there."

Anne Semrick, credit and receivables manager, De Mar: "You are given the opportunity to make decisions and follow through without committee approval. Everyone in this firm is given this privilege to make the decision."

Neil Strandberg, floor manager, Tattered Cover Book Store: "This store just suits my nature. I don't feel like I have to put on my work face. I can be myself and be paid for it. You have latitude. Standards are high, but you have flexibility in how you reach them."

Jessie Logan, sales director, Mary Kay Cosmetics: "There is no ceiling in this company. You can promote yourself by working hard."

Nancy Moser, sales director, Mary Kay Cosmetics: "We are building a business."

Cindy Yost, specialty foods buyer, West Point Market: "Russ [Vernon] has always put us in the position to take care of things on our own. It is humiliating to have to say 'I have to ask my manager.'"

Empowering Managers

An empowered state of mind is beneficial at all levels of an organization, not just at the first level. Managers need to be empowered to manage, just as servers need to be empowered to serve. Timothy Firnstahl is the founder and chief executive of Satisfaction Guaranteed Eateries, a Seattle company operating five restaurants. Profitable in the 1980s, the company experienced declining income, rising expenses, and operating losses in the early 1990s. Firnstahl knew he had to cut costs dramatically or the company would fail.

During the late 1980s, Firnstahl had empowered front-line employees with a program and company credo called WAGS—We Always Guarantee Satisfaction. Food servers had the authority to do what was necessary to satisfy the customer. Slow service could bring a complimentary dessert; an overcooked meal might be free. After a halting start described by Firnstahl in a 1989 *Harvard Business Review* article,[3] the empowerment approach worked well. However, Firnstahl realized later that he had not gone far enough. The crisis of impending failure spurred the realization that he must empower his managers, too. Here is what he wrote in a follow-up 1993 article:

> Now it suddenly occurred to me that I had failed to extend this same kind of power and responsibility to my local managers. WAGS had done wonders to increase repeat business and employee commitment and, by proactively identifying problems before customers even had a chance to complain about them, to help us find and correct the causes of each system failure.
>
> But where food servers had the power to take action on their own initiative, my line managers—bar managers, restaurant managers, kitchen managers, general managers—were still firmly subordinate to corporate headquarters when it came to payroll, menus, marketing, product development, accounting, training, hiring, and general decision making, just about every-thing except reservations and breathing. We were still operating under an antiquated line-staff system as obsolete as the central-ized communist approach. What a revelation. How could I have missed such an obvious connection?[4]

Firnstahl decided to transfer virtually all power and respon-sibility to the line managers. A 4,000-square-foot corporate headquarters with 17 people became an 800-square-foot "work-room" with just a few staff. Planning, problem solving, and decision making became the province of the line managers who convened weekly in "ally management" meetings. The line managers brainstorm new products, ways to cut costs, and decor improvement, among other decision areas. Most of the bill paying was moved to the restaurants to give the managers a better sense of how their revenue dollars were being used.

Creating an empowered state of mind among the managers resulted in significant cost savings and revenue increases within a year. The company is making money again. The lesson from this case is not that every CEO should eliminate the corporate headquarters as Firnstahl essentially did for his restaurants. With a money-losing, five-store operation, Firnstahl needed to take drastic action. The action he chose, though extreme, illus-trates a fundamental lesson valuable to any service company: *The line organization must be a source of innovation and inspiration.*

The line must have the authority to act; the skills, knowledge, and tools to do so; and the accountability for results. The staff should be lean; its role is to help the line organization be successful.

Not a Quick Fix

An empowered state of mind cannot simply be turned on like a light switch. Senior management's words will not transform an unempowered work force into an empowered one. People must directly experience being in charge of themselves and their destiny to develop an empowered state of mind. They need time to process how an empowered state feels and to try out empowered behavior. They need time to develop confidence in their ability to perform based on the internal authority of empowerment.

Empowerment works only in a climate of trust. An atmosphere of mistrust does not nurture or sustain empowered employees. Managers will not push authority downwards in the organization without trust. Recipients will not embrace it without trusting management's intentions.

Effective empowerment comes from *shared leadership*. Shared leadership disperses power and loosens reins. The middle manager who empowers direct reports must trust their judgment, capabilities, and goodwill. The middle manager also must trust higher management to continue to recognize his or her worth and to perceive giving up power as positive. Organizational power, after all, is a precious commodity. Making the change from boss to coach may be quite a difficult adjustment for one who has worked hard to become a boss. Lakeland Regional Medical Center's Senior Vice President of Administration, Phyllis Watson states: "Empowerment is real hard. We've taught empowerment 150 ways. The bottom line is that when you empower, you give up power and people grieve giving up power. It is what makes something that sounds wonderful so hard."

Being empowered can be unwelcome for front-line servers as well; receiving power will be as difficult for some employees as giving it up is for others. Some employees will prefer a narrow solution space with the appropriate behaviors spelled out. The risks of making mistakes, the burdens of acquiring knowledge, and the pressures of creative problem solving are less in an unempowered environment. Being treated as a "part-owner" and behaving like one is no walk on the beach.

Linda Cooper, a service-quality consultant based in Evanston, Illinois, was head of the consumer affairs department at the First National Bank of Chicago from 1989 to 1993. In this role, she was intimately involved in service improvement within the retail part of the bank. Empowering customer-contact personnel was a key goal. It proved to be harder than expected. Existing mindsets were tough to change, as Cooper explains:

> It's not that our front-line people aren't smart, or that they don't want to take care of customers. Over a period of time, though, we had so demotivated them that they quit trying. It took us quite a while to get empowerment going, even though senior management had long ago agreed to the concept. We found that it meant bringing our employees up to speed on our business, the competitive environment, our market identity and strategy, and where they fit into all of that. If we really wanted them to act more like owners with a vested interest in each customer encounter, we had to treat them that way.
>
> When we tried to determine why empowerment wasn't catching on, we found it also involved our expecting too large a leap from the employees. For example, tellers found it frightening to suddenly make decisions involving large sums of money. Through discussions with supervisors, we established decision-making guideposts, settling on transaction and dollar limits determined by tellers' tenure. The process functions as training wheels for the empowerment vehicle, providing a comfort level for all.[5]

Empowerment is not for every manager, nor every server. Ideal candidate profiles will be different in an organization using an empowerment approach from one that isn't. Senior executives seeking to empower the organization must be prepared for some attrition—forced and voluntary. Many employees, however, will flourish in an empowered environment. They may resist at first or they may falter, but they will discover that the freedom to act, to be innovative and smart, to choreograph instead of being choreographed adds richness and dignity to their work. Being an owner can be fun.

Platform for Excellence

Creating an ownership feeling within a company provides a platform for service excellence. Sustained service excellence requires high discretionary effort from servers; it requires preparation, ingenuity, persistence, discipline, risk taking, and continuous improvement. Those with an empowered state of mind are most likely to exhibit these traits. Most service providers will work harder, smarter, and faster for *their* company than someone else's company. An Ohio company, Marketing Services by Vectra, has signs throughout its facilities that say: "Go hard or go home."[6] Empowerment offers the cultural support to "go hard."

De Mar employees begin their day early and frequently finish it late. They command top wages for themselves and top prices from their customers because they bring a genuine sense of urgency to the job. They do what it takes to solve the customer's problem when the customer needs it solved. An ownership feeling permeates this company. Randy Newman, service coordinator for air conditioning and heating, says: "The technician's truck is his own little business. He needs to make it profitable. My job is to provide the support." Don McCann, service coordinator for plumbing, adds:

> You have to have that one driving force and Larry [Harmon] has been that. He has never wavered from what he knows this company can do. He's consistent. He doesn't waver. He allows people to do the job. If they have a different way of doing it, that's fine as long as it meets our goal. And the people get the credit—Larry doesn't take the credit. I've heard Larry say hundreds of times: 'Well, if you think that will work, let's try it.' Larry always has been willing to try new things. And he has a heck of a memory. If you tell Larry you're going to do something, you better do it. He doesn't like excuses. Talk is cheap, show me. This show-me attitude alleviates a lot of politics. Either you can or can't do the job.

De Mar could not implement its service strategy without empowerment. Nor could Roberts Express, USAA, Harold's, Lakeland Regional Medical Center, Mary Kay Cosmetics, Taco Bell, Tattered Cover Book Store, Hard Rock Cafe, or many other companies featured in this book.

Empowerment allows a company to tap into the creativity, intellect, and emotional energy of nearly everyone in an organization, not just those in the executive suite.[7] Rob Perez, general manager of Hard Rock Cafe Orlando actively encourages servers to bring their individuality to the job. He believes servers will enjoy the work more and perform it better if they remain true to themselves. Perez states: "We want each server to be the best at what he or she can be. Rusty is a showman, for example. Gail is our cleanest, fastest server—and always with a smile. Individuality is what it's all about." Perez calls his management philosophy "the Shtick idea."

Should All Firms Empower?

The subject of empowerment tends to be wrapped in a flag of goodness when it is discussed in the popular press or on the lecture circuit. Accompanying empowerment, however, is the risk of employees making poor decisions, the training and education investment required to prepare employees for empowerment, and the potential for organizational turbulence and turnover during the transition period, among other "costs." An important question, therefore, is whether empowerment is appropriate for all service firms?

David Bowen and Edward Lawler, in a seminal 1992 article, argue that empowerment is not always appropriate.[8] They propose a series of contingencies to help managers determine the degree to which empowerment should be used, if at all. Table 10–1 is a contingency rating scale from Bowen and Lawler's article. The higher the rating of each contingency, and the higher the total score from all five contingencies, the better the fit with an empowerment approach. The authors suggest that both production-line (tight control) and empowerment approaches have particular advantages. They contend that transaction-oriented businesses selling low-priced goods and services in high volumes in stable environments fit the production-line approach better. Examples could include fast-food restaurants and convenience food stores.

Bowen and Lawler's article is valuable because it challenges management to consider empowerment thoughtfully and strate-

Table 10–1

THE CONTINGENCIES OF EMPOWERMENT

Contingency	Production Line Approach						Empowerment
Basic business strategy	Low cost, high volume	1	2	3	4	5	Differentiation, customized, personalized
Tie to customer	Transaction, short time period	1	2	3	4	5	Relationship, long time period
Technology	Routine, simple	1	2	3	4	5	Nonroutine, complex
Business environment	Predictable, few surprises	1	2	3	4	5	Unpredictable, many surprises
Types of people	Theory X managers; employees with low growth needs, low social needs, and weak interpersonal skills	1	2	3	4	5	Theory Y managers; employees with high growth needs, high social needs, and strong interpersonal skills

Source: David E. Bowen and Edward E. Lawler III, "The Empowerment of Service Workers: What, Why, How, and When," *Sloan Management Review*, Spring 1992, p. 37.

gically. This is in keeping with the spirit of this book—the appropriate action depends on the service strategy. Does this mean, therefore, that empowerment is the wrong approach for some companies? Perhaps so, but not for a company that seeks to deliver great service. *Significant empowerment provides a necessary platform for sustained service excellence regardless of the nature of the business.*

Superior service quality is so difficult to achieve in complex organizations, competition in every industry is so fierce, and downward price pressures on undifferentiated offerings are so strong that examples of successful service companies relying on a tight-control model are becoming increasingly rare. Examples can be found, such as McDonalds and United Parcel Service, but these companies may be forced to change their ways. After all, one of McDonalds' toughest competitors is Taco Bell, which used an aggressive empowerment approach to drive growth from 2,900 restaurants and $1.6 billion in sales in 1988 to more than 10,000 points of distribution and nearly $4 billion in sales by the end of 1993. Taco Bell market managers, who were managing five or six restaurants within a region in 1990, were managing, on average, 50 points of distribution (e.g., restaurants, school lunch programs, mobile units) by 1994. By 1994, 90 percent of Taco Bell's company-owned restaurants, averaging nearly $1 million in sales, were team-operated without a full-time manager. Chairman and Chief Executive Officer John Martin writes:

> . . . the key to our success isn't technology. It isn't carts and kiosks and new delivery systems. Those are simply by-products and enablers. Without question, the key to our success has been the empowerment we have given to our people and the results they've achieved.[9]

Companies such as Taco Bell, Starbucks Coffee Company, Tattered Cover Book Store, and Hard Rock Cafe are forging an emerging competitive reality of empowerment in low-cost, high-volume, high-transaction businesses. For these companies, the question is not whether to empower but to what degree. For a service company to fully realize its potential in today's business climate, it must discard the failure cycle of low achievement and high employee turnover. It must develop a culture where employees want to work hard, smart, and fast, a culture characterized by trust and loyalty, a culture where employees feel ownership. Yes, this is a tall order, which is why this book began with the subject of leadership.

Table 10–2 presents a set of continua with the characteristics of unempowered and empowered mind states at each end. The purpose of the exhibit is not to suggest that companies should operate at the extreme right side for all characteristics and for all employees. The extreme right side is actually a moving target. Like so many other topics discussed in this book, empowerment is a journey; there always is further to go. Moreover, senior management must be more empowered than middle managers and they more empowered than front-line servers. Leadership behaviors are important at all levels, but the leadership roles are also different for top managers, middle managers, and front-line servers. Rather, the purpose of Table 10–2 is to demonstrate graphically that companies operating at the far left side of the continua are forfeiting the opportunity for great service. In an earlier era, when customer and employee expectations were different, when competitive pressures were less, when now-popular organizational structures and technologies had not yet emerged, a production-line approach could result in sustained excellence for certain types of services. This no longer is the case today. For a service company to realize its full potential, its employees must realize their potential as well.

Implementing Empowerment

Much of what has been discussed in earlier chapters facilitates an empowerment approach. The conscious effort to nurture service leadership skills and values provides an environment conducive to empowerment. Defining a central service strategy guides empowered behavior. Delivering service through team structures demands empowerment. Technology that supplies information required to perform the service diminishes the need

Table 10–2
EMPOWERMENT CONTINUA

Unempowered State of Mind		Empowered State of Mind
Minimal control over how to perform the job	├──┼──┤	Considerable control over how to perform the job
Limited awareness of company strategy, trends, performance, and service systems	├──┼──┤	Significant awareness of company strategy, trends, performance, and service systems
Little accountability for personal performance	├──┼──┤	Much accountability for personal performance
No responsibility for unit and company performance	├──┼──┤	Shared responsibility for unit and company performance
Compensation unrelated to personal, unit, and company performance	├──┼──┤	Compensation related to personal, unit, and company performance

Source: The characteristics of an empowered state of mind are based on material in David E. Bowen and Edward E. Lawler III, "Employee Empowerment in Service Firms: Answering the Growing Questions," working paper, 1994.

for supervisors to supply the same. Executives gain confidence to push decision-making authority downward into the organization when they compete for talent and invest in skill and knowledge development.

Creating an empowered state of mind in the organization requires a thin rulebook. Thick policies and procedures manuals signify an established way of doing things, a detailed set of prescriptions from the top. Management must determine how much empowerment is needed to implement the service strategy. Companies with a tradition of rulebook management that wish to move to empowerment can appoint project teams to review existing policies and procedures with the mandate to modify or eliminate those that needlessly restrict service freedoms. The thinner rulebooks that survive this process can contain decision zones: *safe zones* within which employees are expected to make independent decisions, *low-risk zones* where employees may choose to consult with a superior, and *high-risk zones* where consultation is required.[10] The high-risk zone typically would concern matters that, if handled improperly, could result in legal problems, harmful publicity, or significant negative financial impact.

The firm's overall strategy and supporting values guide servers in the absence of detailed prescription. A strong, continuous effort to communicate and reinforce vision and values is essential to an empowerment approach. As Harvard Business School professor D. Quinn Mills states:

> Empowerment without a mission is dangerous, and most of us are still not good at missions. Either we don't know what the mission is, or we don't express it in language that helps people understand it and make it effective. And so we fail to empower.[11]

No firm in America more effectively communicates its strategy and values than the Ritz-Carlton Hotel Company, as discussed at length in Chapter 4. Exhibit 4-2 presents Ritz-Carlton's credo card. Employees carry the card and practice its teachings daily. The credo card empowers because it is an honest communication of the expected attitudes and behaviors. The words are genuine; the credo card reflects the organization's reality. Actions speak louder than words in organizations. Ritz-Carlton's credo card—its thin rulebook—works because corporate and hotel executives are true to the words in their own behavior and are personally involved in teaching the words' meanings. Senior executives who personally articulate vision and values—and the empowered state of mind required to enliven them—bring credibility to the cause.

Including empowerment questions in employee surveys underscores commitment and identifies issues that require attention. Both managerial and nonmanagerial employees can be asked in surveys to rate how empowered they feel. The states of mind described in Table 10–2 can form the basis of these measurements.

Including empowerment as part of managers' performance evaluation also sharpens the message. Managers at General Electric are subject to a 360 degree evaluation, involving peer and subordinate ratings in addition to those of superiors. From General Electric's 1993 annual shareholders report comes this rationale:

> This has become a powerful tool for detecting and changing those who "smile up and kick down." To be blunt, the two quickest ways to part company with GE are, one, to commit an integrity violation, or two, to be a controlling, turf-defending, oppressive manager who can't change and who saps and squeezes people rather than excites and draws out their energy and creativity. We can't force that creativity and energy from our teams—they have to give it—but we have to have it to win.[12]

Giving employees a voice in the operations of the company nurtures the ownership feeling of empowerment. John Longstreet, the general manager of The Harvey Hotel in Plano, Texas, convenes "What's Stupid Meetings" with six to eight employees at a time to identify practices to be improved and to symbolize shared leadership of the company. Joyce Meskis, the owner of The Tattered Cover Book Store, holds an open meeting for employees at 8 A.M. on the eighth day of each month. These "8 at 8" meetings give employees an opportunity to make suggestions and raise concerns. Meskis also uses the forum to comment on the state of the company. General Manager Linda Millemann states: "We have to make this an inclusive, participating store where people are heard—or it won't remain a special store."

Directly addressing empowerment in the training and education of both managerial and nonmanagerial personnel increases the capability and confidence to take charge. Managers need to learn the dangers of overmanagement; they need to learn the difference between being a coach and being a boss, between leading and controlling. Incorporating into training and education sessions stories of how empowered employees effectively handled difficult situations can be valuable. A potent learning method is group discussion of the best ways to handle nonroutine service encounters.

As stressed earlier, the trust-empowerment connection is pivotal. Risk-averse managing and serving are unnecessary when trust prevails. Bank One's Judy Frow and Jackie Salazar offer the following advice to managers for creating a climate of trust:

- Hire people you have confidence in, people whom you are willing to empower. Pick people who have a desire to please their customer.
- Create a relaxed, nonthreatening environment. Have an open door for personal and work-related problems. In some environments, you can't feel comfortable—you have to look busy even if you are not. You can't be yourselves.
- Listen to your employees because they know what is going on. Ask us, rather than always hiring a consultant.
- Make all employees feel worthy, no matter what their position level. Solicit their ideas and act on them. Don't exclude the secretaries or the assistants when something is going on. Refer to us by our names.
- Be honest and up-front with employees. If change is coming, tell us. If you don't tell, rumors will take over.
- Give credit where credit is due. It is a wonderful feeling to be recognized for your efforts.

SUMMARY

Creating an empowered state of mind in an organization is a condition of great service. An empowered state of mind includes feelings of control over the job, awareness of the context for the work, accountability for personal performance, shared responsibility for unit and organizational performance, and equity in the distribution of rewards. Management nurtures these feelings by treating employees as part-owners of the business and expecting them to behave like owners.

Innovative companies featured in this book such as Taco Bell, Starbucks Coffee, and Hard Rock Cafe demonstrate empowerment's potential even for low-cost, high-volume, high-transaction businesses. People at work who feel like owners are most likely to work hard, smart, and fast. Empowerment's reach must include managers, not just front-line service providers; companies benefit when managers feel and act like owners, too.

Companies that empower function with thin rulebooks. Strategy and values guide service providers in the absence of detailed prescription. Management must determine the level of empowerment needed to implement the chosen service strategy. Strategy-based decisions for structure, technology, hiring, and training and education should facilitate the needed empowerment approach. The same should be true for teamwork, performance measurement, and reward systems, the subjects of the next chapters.

Managers can broadly assess empowerment in the company with these questions:

1. *Are we a thin rulebook or a thick rulebook company?* What influences employee behavior the most: policies and procedures or strategy and values?
2. *Does top management believe in empowerment?* Is it viewed as a fundamental condition for service excellence, as a management fad, as inappropriate for our business, or in some other way?
3. *Is top management clear on what empowerment means in this organization?* Do senior managers articulate the concept of empowerment and its importance to middle managers and frontline service providers?
4. *Do managerial and front-line employees feel empowered?* Do they feel like part-owners of the business?
5. *Is trust a characteristic of our organization?* Do people in this company have confidence in the competence, judgment, and goodwill of those above and below them in the organizational hierarchy? Does top management recognize the connection between organizational trust and empowerment? Do they recognize that trust enfranchises and mistrust disenfranchises?

CHAPTER 11

WORK AT
TEAMWORK

S till another crucial part of the great service framework is teamwork. Excellent service sometimes is the result of individual heroics. Most of the time, however, it comes from multiple persons performing related service roles in concert. Each step in the service chain must be performed properly for the customer's service experience to be superior. As in a symphony, each instrument has a different part, but when played together beautiful music results.

Although closely related, teamwork is not synonymous with teams. Teams, as discussed in Chapter 6, are structural. Teamwork is values, attitudes, feelings, and skills. Teamwork is central to service excellence regardless of structure. It is critical in a functional structure and no less critical in a team structure. Indeed, a team without teamwork is a team in name only.

Genuine teamwork involves individuals working collaboratively towards a common purpose of high meaning. The collaboration is characterized by regular, open, honest communications; a spirit of helping, trust, and confidence in teammates; and shared responsibility for results. Like empowerment, teamwork involves feelings—feelings of working cooperatively instead of competitively, interdependently instead of independently. The feelings of teamwork include connection to fellow workers, commitment to group effort, and pride in group accomplishment.

Teamwork is not about conformity. Sacrificing individuality is neither necessary nor desirable in teamwork. Rather, teamwork melds individual contributions so that the sum is greater than its parts. Teammates need not look alike, speak alike, think alike, or work alike. Diversity in personality, background, expertise, and outlook brings vitality and energy to collaborative processes.[1] Teammates do need to respect and value one another, understand and believe in their common mission, and consider teamwork as the way to accomplish it.

Dissent does not kill teamwork; selfishness and sabotage kill teamwork. Dissenting opinions can be constructive, laying the groundwork for better outcomes than those untested by debate. Michael Leimbach of Wilson Learning Corporation comments:

> Team members must learn how to air differences, tell hard truths and ask hard questions of one another. When a team is not facing the core issues that prevent it from reaching its goal, its work will not move forward and creative solutions will not unfold.[2]

Teamwork is too important to the delivery of great service not to be the subject of its own chapter. Still, much of what organizations can do to build a teamwork culture has been covered in earlier chapters. Service leadership values and skills create the conditions for collaborative energy. The service strategy provides the direction, the purpose. The principles of reliability, surprise, recovery, and fairness apply equally as well to employees serving each other as to serving external customers. Team structures foster teamwork. Companies can recruit team players and teach team-building skills and values. Empowerment and teamwork are mutually reinforcing; they are bilateral forces operating synergistically. Feelings of ownership, of inclusion, of contributing to the whole are central to each concept. This chapter stresses the importance of teamwork and the need for systematic efforts to encourage it against the background of earlier chapters. Teamwork-enhancing efforts not discussed previously are presented.

THE TEAMWORK IMPERATIVE

Service providers must possess the capability and desire to perform the service customers expect. Teamwork enhances both. Delivering quality service is a group effort. Airline personnel such as ticket agents, gate agents, baggage handlers, refuelers, cleaning staff, flight attendants, and pilots all contribute to an on-time departure. Southwest Airlines demonstrates the power of teamwork in readying a just-arrived plane to depart in 15 to 20 minutes. Southwest personnel swarm onto the tarmac and into the plane to prepare it for departure. A beehive of purposeful activity keeps Southwest jets in the air—the only way an airline can make money.

Southwest Airlines is America's most productive, most consistently profitable airline. It typically is the industry leader in on-time performance and lowest average number of passenger complaints. Southwest Airlines has thousands of employees' photographs hanging in its headquarters building. It publishes an employee newsletter called *Luv Lines*; has made a video of employees, including chairman Herb Kelleher, singing and dancing to rap music; and focuses on having fun as a marketing strategy—Southwest Airlines thrives on teamwork. Teamwork is Southwest Airlines' hidden weapon, its bureaucracy-busting tool, its motivational binding. Other airlines can attempt to duplicate Southwest's short-haul, low-frills, low-fare service strategy; they will be hard-pressed to duplicate Southwest's communal fervor for serving, however. Southwest Airlines' culture is what makes its strategy work.

Numerous studies have investigated the relative impact of cooperative, competitive, and independent behavior within organizations. The results clearly show greater benefits from cooperation. Teamwork encourages employees to communicate directly, to empathize and support one another, to discuss different points of view constructively, to resolve problems effectively, to achieve in their work, and to feel confident and valued as individuals.[3]

Research my colleagues and I have conducted shows convincingly the centrality of teamwork to delivering superior service. Customer-contact personnel in five major service companies who indicate that their organizational units are *not* meeting service standards *disagree* with the following statements:

- I feel that I am part of a team in my unit.
- Everyone in my unit contributes to a team effort in serving customers.

- I feel a sense of responsibility to help my fellow employees do their jobs well.
- My fellow employees and I cooperate more than we compete.
- I feel that I am an important member of this company.[4]

Service work can be physically and psychologically overwhelming. Handling an unrelenting stream of telephone calls in a catalog ordering center; serving drinks, a meal, and picking up trays in one hour on a full flight; or serving a dozen customers standing in a bank teller line during the Friday rush frame the reality of service work. The potential for stress to drain servers' energy and enthusiasm is high. What customers perceive as uncaring or aloof behavior from service providers, in fact, may be coping behavior. Teammates help service providers sustain motivation and energy, maintain professionalism on bad days, and overcome fatigue. Teammates help each other, teach each other, renew each other. Team involvement is another "good tonic."

Teamwork generates control and power. Although power is traditionally defined in terms of dominating others and getting them to behave in a certain way, research has shown the cooperative, constructive face of power. Professor Dean Tjosvold, an accomplished researcher on teamwork, explains:

> Feeling powerful comes from the confidence that one has the abilities and wherewithal to move forward, solve problems, and be successful. In a cooperative team, people feel more powerful because they know that they can use their team members' resources as well as their own. In contrast, when confronted alone with a complex, difficult challenge, people can be demoralized, having to rely only on their own abilities.[5]

Teamwork is an imperative for great service. It nurtures learning as teammates teach each other. It inspires confidence as individual service providers stand with a group, rather than alone. It motivates because it inspires confidence and because service providers know teammates are depending upon them. Teamwork's foundation principles of trusting and respecting others bind individuals together in pursuit of a high purpose.

"Lessons from Geese," Table 11–1, captures the powerfulness of teamwork.

TEAMWORK THROUGH BOUNDARYLESSNESS

So much impedes teamwork within organizations. The causes of poor teamwork are multiple, ranging from the common assumption of managers that internal competition makes people work harder and should be encouraged to the common assumption of individual employees that they must look out for themselves at the expense of others to succeed.

A principal cause of ineffective teamwork is "tightly bounded work." Companies that tightly bind work rely on strict role definitions, lines of authority, and physical separation to organize work. Bosses give orders and subordinates follow them. Dissenting views and discussion of alternatives are discouraged. Organizational units participating in the service chain are separated physically, working on different floors, in different buildings, even in different cities. They communicate by electronic mail, internal memos, reports, telephone, or not at all. Face-to-face meetings rarely or never occur. Strategic, "big picture" information generally is shared only with managers, on the underlying assumption that nonmanagerial personnel would not understand it, would be distracted by it, or would not be interested.

In effect, tightly bounded work denies the natural pathways to teamwork. Teamwork relies on inclusion, frequent up, down, and horizontal communications, big-picture awareness, and an open field for performance. Tightly bounded work processes rely on separatism, top-down communications, small-picture awareness, and narrow spaces for performance. Teamwork's soulmate, empowerment, is restricted. Teamwork is nourished by trusting, respecting, and valuing others. Tightly bounded organizations can function without these traits.

Teamwork cannot prosper in organizations that use the tightly bounded work model. For genuine teamwork to take root and spread in an organization, loose boundaries must prevail. General Electric's Chief Executive Jack Welch has popularized the term *boundarylessness* to denote cooperation across the

Table 11–1
LESSONS FROM GEESE

Fact 1: As each goose flaps its wings, it creates an "uplift" for the birds that follow. By flying in a "V" formation, the whole flock adds 71 percent greater flying range than if each bird flew alone.

Lesson: People who share a common direction and sense of community can get where they are going quicker and easier because they are traveling on the thrust of one another.

Fact 2: When a goose falls out of formation, it suddenly feels the drag and resistance of flying alone. It quickly moves back into formation to take advantage of the lifting power of the bird immediately in front of it.

Lesson: If we have as much sense as a goose, we stay in formation with those headed where we want to go. We are willing to accept their help and give our help to others.

Fact 3: When the lead goose tires, it rotates back into the formation, and another goose flies to the point position.

Lesson: It pays to take turns doing the hard tasks and sharing leadership. As with geese, people are interdependent on each other's skills, capabilities, and unique arrangement of gifts, talents, or resources.

Fact 4: The geese flying in formation honk to encourage those up front to keep up their speed.

Lesson: We need to make sure our honking is encouraging. In groups where there is encouragement, the production is much greater. The power of encouragement (to stand by one's heart or core values and encourage the heart and core of others) is the quality of honking we seek.

Fact 5: When a goose gets sick, wounded, or shot down, two geese drop out of formation and follow it down to help and protect it. They stay with it until it is either able to fly or dies. Then, they launch out with another formation or catch up with the flock.

Lesson: If we have as much sense as geese, we will stand by each other in difficult times as well as when we are strong.

Source: From a presentation by Angeles Arrien at the 1991 Organizational Development Network. Based on the work of Milton Olson.

artificial barriers that can separate people who share a common interest. Welch explains the concept by using the imagery of a house which presents barriers in three dimensions:

- The *horizontal* barriers are the walls—such as functional units and geographic locations—that divide groups of peers into isolated compartments. Why shouldn't marketing speak to design, or Tokyo to Milwaukee?
- The *vertical* barriers are the floors and ceilings that demarcate hierarchy. Organizations do need some layers but when differences in rank block open communication, hierarchy becomes self-defeating.
- The *external* barriers are the outside walls of the company. Beyond these walls are many groups with whom close working relationships are essential, such as customers, suppliers, and venture partners.[6]

George Rieder, a Dallas-based consultant specializing in service businesses, points out how boundarylessness relates to teamwork:

- *mentally and intellectually*—by seeking dissenting views and considering multiple alternatives;
- *physically*—by knocking down walls and locating teammates together in innovative configurations;
- *informationally*—by employing distributed information technology, on-line capability, and user-friendly systems as well as encouraging networking with others both inside and outside the business; and
- *organizationally*—by forming temporary teams, task forces, and strategic issue study groups as well as more permanent team structures.

Unbounded Communications

Free-flowing communication is a keystone of teamwork. Openly sharing relevant information, considering the views of others, shaping decisions with input, meeting people from different units in the service chain—these actions feed the sense of connectedness so essential in teamwork. Tightly bounded internal communications starve connectedness. Free-flowing, give-and-take, up-and-down-and-sideways communication enables people to feel included.

AT&T Universal Card Services, a 1992 winner of the Malcolm Baldrige National Quality Award, practices unbounded communications in multiple ways, including quarterly all-employee business meetings in which senior executives discuss financial results and strategy, quarterly "Lakeside Chats" hosted by senior management and attended by as many as 200 employees at a time, and weekly lunches involving top managers and small groups of employees.[7]

On the last Friday of each month, employees in nearly 500 branches of securities brokerage firm A. G. Edwards listen to a company report on their desk speakerphones. The reports are delivered by chairman, Ben Edwards, who then opens the line for questions. A. G. Edwards has the specific goal of encouraging "full and open two-way communication" where "upward flow of information is just as necessary as the more customary downward flow. . . . It is also important that the information coming from the top be as complete and as candid as possible."[8]

Kemper Service Company in Kansas City practices unbounded communications through an employee exchange program. Front-line service providers and middle managers have the opportunity to visit other units of their choice within the company. During these exchanges, staff from the host department explain their goals, types of customers served, work flows, deadlines, quality indicators, and job skills required. This beneficial program erases departmental barriers and negative stereotypes and clarifies how different units contribute to the service chain. William Fronk, Kemper executive vice president, says the most frequent comment made after an exchange is: "I had no idea they were responsible for so much."[9]

Sharing rallies are another way to stimulate the cross-fertilization of ideas and reinforce the principles of teamwork. Readers may recall from Chapter 2 that Milliken & Company sponsors sharing rallies in which employees from different units formally present the content and results of specific quality improvement efforts before peers and management. Winning presentations are determined by peer voting. Motorola, a Baldrige winner like Milliken and AT&T Universal, sponsors an annual Total Customer Satisfaction Team Competition in which 24 Motorola teams from throughout the world compete in the finals. Each team is limited to 12 minutes to keep them focused on the substance rather than the form of their presentations. Participation in the contest grows each year. In 1992, 24 finalist teams from North America, Europe, and Asia survived a process that began with nearly 4,000 teams involving almost 40,000 employees, up from 20,000 workers two years earlier.[10]

Canadian Airlines International's Pacific Region published its first service quality progress report for employees in 1990. The report contains a two-page section on each operating unit in the Pacific Region: Australia, New Zealand, Fiji, Hawaii, Japan, Hong Kong, Thailand, and the regional headquarters. Presented for each unit are summaries of specific service improvement initiatives, a unit profile, customer satisfaction improvement data, and employee photographs. The report also includes management messages concerning the importance of service quality.

Internal Service Pledges

Bank One Texas Trust Division has broken down interdepartmental boundaries with a process of internal service pledging. The staff of one department meets with the staff of another to discuss each unit's service expectations and to establish standards. For example, the administrative staff meets with the operations staff and begins by declaring its needs, for instance, return our phone calls within one hour, prepare our statements by the 15th of the month. Operations then responds with what it can and cannot deliver. Then operations states its needs and administration responds. The two groups negotiate and agree on service standards (pledges), which are printed and distributed within each department. In addition to the negotiated pledges are universal pledges, which state general expectations of how co-workers are to treat one another. The universal standards are the same for all departments. Each staff member in the two departments signs the agreed-upon and universal standards. The departments meet again in six months to grade each other's performance against the standards and, if necessary, to renegotiate for the next six months. The operations and administrative staffs undergo a similar process with each internal department they serve, as do all other departments. Pledges between the Corporate Trust and Finance departments illustrate the concept (Exhibit 11–1).

Service pledging is a difficult, time-consuming process. It has benefits and drawbacks and will not be right for all organizations. Its purposes are to improve dialogue and teamwork and make departments more accountable for internal service quality. Lynn McCollough, vice president of Corporate Trust, says:

> Most people think it is a good tool to get the service they want. Before we started service pledging, you could ask a department to improve and maybe they would and maybe they wouldn't. Now, expectations and promises are in black and white. How many times does a department sit down with another and say 'this is what we need from you and if you'll do that, we'll do this for you.' Without service pledging, it wouldn't happen.

One drawback is the time investment required for meetings. In addition, although a purpose is to improve teamwork, the opposite may occur in some cases. Some hard feelings are inevitable as departments grade each other with top management receiving comparative (department by department) scores.

Garrett Jamison, executive vice president of the Trust Division, and the architect of service pledging, believes the process is a net plus. He assesses the plusses and minuses in this comment:

> The concept of internal service pledges is simple, but the application is difficult. It permits goal setting and performance measurement at the point of internal service delivery. The service providers and their internal customers jointly define performance standards that are mutually agreeable, deliverable, and measurable. It is both a process of self determination and a demonstration of the power of interdependency. It drives accountability into the heart of the service process and encourages empowerment. It causes communication to take place and improve. And, it addresses a continuing management concern about how to assure reliability of service delivery.

Exhibit 11–1
BANK ONE TEXAS TRUST INTERNAL SERVICE PLEDGES

CORPORATE TRUST pledges to FINANCE

---

1. By the 25th of each month, provide forecast for remainder of current month and for remainder of year.
2. Provide a copy of A/P transmittal and/or T & E Report with explanations of transactions to prepaid expenses or customer reimbursable expenses by the first business day of the following month.

FINANCE pledges to CORPORATE TRUST

---

1. Provide monthly, by the 10th business day, a printout of status on customer prepaid expenses and customer reimbursable expenses.
2. Provide monthly, by the 10th business day, general ledger reports on cost center.
3. Provide procedures or information on what is needed for forecast.

CORPORATE pledges to FINANCE

FINANCE pledges to CORPORATE TRUST

UNIVERSAL MUTUAL PLEDGES

1. Communicate with honesty and understanding; discuss problems with those involved.
2. We will treat each other, regardless of position, with courtesy and respect.
3. All service problems will be treated as "OUR" problem and we will work together on the immediate solution.
4. We will recognize that we are here to serve our ultimate client—the customer—and will focus our efforts on providing unsurpassed quality service.

Corporate Trust:
Department Members

Liz Galindo

Jeannene Gaston

Phillip D. Gatlin

Lynn McCullough

Donna McFarland

Finance Department:
Department Members

Karen Spuria

Fran Toliver

But, be careful. It unleashes powerful human forces, some unexpected. It forces humans to critique each other, face to face, and that's tough duty. Most managers are not very skilled in evaluating the performance of their direct reports, yet the internal service pledge process causes *all* employees to get involved in performance evaluation. It is a self-policing, team building process that can cause tensions and emotions to run high. Frankly, some people just do not want to do it.

Mature, responsible, confident people excel in such an environment, while others may be emotionally distraught by the process. In the end, one would hope that the practice would result in exceptionally powerful teams composed entirely of only the strongest among us. It can result in greatly improved internal performance. Stay tuned! We are still working at it.

Measuring and Rewarding Teamwork

Managers measure and reward what they deem important. Formally measuring teamwork as part of the performance appraisal process—and rewarding team-minded performance—symbolizes the teamwork imperative inside the organization. Managerial and nonmanagerial employees need to know that teamwork is winning behavior and that turfism, selfishness, or noncooperativeness is losing behavior.

The common pattern in performance evaluations is to focus on individual accomplishments. This is not inappropriate. However, if the goal is great service, assessments also should include an individual's contributions to effective teamwork. Although the next chapter discusses performance measurement and rewards in detail, the idea of measuring and rewarding teamwork is stressed here also. Managers who want great service must evaluate teamwork and allocate rewards accordingly.

A former department store manager comments on why measurement and rewards are so important:

> Managers need to be compensated in part on the degree to which the people reporting to them display the positive aspects of teamwork. For instance, when I attempted to improve the teamwork effectiveness in my store it was generally applauded but viewed as 'soft.' In other words, I was judged on my num-

bers. Although teamwork would almost certainly improve my financial results over time, it was an intensive, long-range strategy versus more traditional short-term strategies such as reworking the sales floor. Teamwork as a result received lip service, but not much else.

Staff members of Lakeland Regional Medical Center's Department of Hospital Education are specifically evaluated on teamwork as part of their performance reviews. Employees rate each departmental colleague on a teamwork questionnaire containing 22 questions. All department members participated in the development of the questionnaire. They provided general input on the behaviors important for teamwork, which department director Richard Rees then developed into a series of statements. The staff reviewed the statements and offered feedback and suggestions that Rees used to craft the questionnaire appearing in Exhibit 11–2. Rees states:

> The real value of the team evaluation tool is not just to generate feedback for colleagues, but also to establish the norms by which the team has elected to operate. The items in the instrument provide consistent focus on the behaviors that we value. By incorporating the evaluation in the performance management system, those who behave according to the norms will be rewarded for that behavior.

The department staff adds:

> Our teamwork evaluation is an excellent tool to communicate detailed expectations to the individuals within our team. It allows for consistent and standardized evaluation of teamwork performance. Feedback from each individual provides a framework for directed performance improvement.

In a 1987 speech entitled "Managing for Service Excellence in a Turbulent Environment," marketing researcher Mimi Lieber admonished her audience of managers to "reward cooperative farming rather than the number of pelts."[11] The advice rang true that day. It still rings true. Quality is collaborative.

Teaching Teamwork

Teamwork can be taught. Not everyone will benefit from its teaching in the organization, but many will. Teamwork is values, attitudes, and feelings. It also is a set of skills. Values, attitudes, feelings, and skills can be nurtured.

Great service companies invest in teaching teamwork. These investments range from informal, one-on-one mentoring to formal courses in teamwork. The Bank One Texas Trust Division uses the "Lessons from Geese" (Exhibit 11–1) in new employee orientation sessions. The Trust Division also sponsors half-day scavenger hunts with mixed teams of managerial and nonmanagerial personnel combining talents. Tattered Cover Book Store conducts its two-week "boot camp" for new employees (see Chapter 9) with an emphasis on teamwork. "We teach people that they can get extra points for asking each other for help," states Tattered Cover's Sidney Jackson.

De Mar's plumbing and air conditioning and heating groups meet weekly to discuss technical issues, equipment problems, and solutions. "We are basically looking for everyone's input," states Plumbing Coordinator Don McCann. "Sometimes the guys will call their own meeting. We have an issue and we need to talk about it." De Mar's Randy Newman adds: "We want everyone to work together. We are all out there together. Our people learn that back-stabbing will not be tolerated."

From 1966, A.G. Edwards has taught teamwork to managers in a rigorous six-day course called the Managerial Grid. More than 700 managers and supervisors have attended through 1994. In 1990, the company added a shorter version of the course, called Gridworks, for nonmanagerial employees.

Managerial Grid participants learn to identify the strengths and weaknesses of various styles of managing. They develop understanding of their own management style and its impact on others, learn the benefits of constructive criticism, and improve teamwork skills. With approximately 50 participants per session, most of the seminar is accomplished in teams of seven to nine people. Many of the tasks have time limitations to force effective teamwork or reveal the consequences of its absence. Throughout

Exhibit 11–2
LAKELAND REGIONAL MEDICAL CENTER
DEPARTMENT OF HOSPITAL EDUCATION TEAMWORK EVALUATION

To ascertain the extent _____Debbie Wharton_____ contributes to the overall team spirit and team functioning of our department, please check the space beside each statement which best corresponds to your evaluation of Debbie's teamwork during the last year. PLEASE SEE DEFINITIONS.

	Exceeds	*Meets*	*Does Not Meet*
1. Works toward the understood goals of the organization and the department.	[ ]	[ ]	[ ]
2. Knows individual responsibilities and priorities and how they relate to others.	[ ]	[ ]	[ ]
3. Contributes to an informal, comfortable and tension free workplace.	[ ]	[ ]	[ ]
4. Is enthusiastic about work and exhibits high morale.	[ ]	[ ]	[ ]
5. Displays a high level of productivity.	[ ]	[ ]	[ ]
6. Pays attention to detail.	[ ]	[ ]	[ ]
7. Follows through on commitments.	[ ]	[ ]	[ ]
8. Performs to the best of his/her ability.	[ ]	[ ]	[ ]
9. Takes pride in the team's work record.	[ ]	[ ]	[ ]
10. Shows interest in other team member's achievements.	[ ]	[ ]	[ ]
11. Readily accepts feedback on performance.	[ ]	[ ]	[ ]
12. Shows confidence and trust in other team members.	[ ]	[ ]	[ ]
13. Is cooperative rather than competitive.	[ ]	[ ]	[ ]
14. Encourages others to achieve at high levels.	[ ]	[ ]	[ ]
15. In interactions, does not dominate others.	[ ]	[ ]	[ ]
16. Is able to stay focused on tasks.	[ ]	[ ]	[ ]
17. Exhibits open lines of communications with other staff.	[ ]	[ ]	[ ]

	Exceeds	Meets	Does Not Meet
18. Is sensitive to the feelings of others.	[ ]	[ ]	[ ]
19. Is open to criticism.	[ ]	[ ]	[ ]
20. Is able to resolve conflict effectively.	[ ]	[ ]	[ ]
21. Respects the final decisions of the team.	[ ]	[ ]	[ ]
22. Is eager to try new approaches.	[ ]	[ ]	[ ]

Subjective Criteria:

Exceeds: In the evaluator's judgment and experience, this employee's performance is exceptional and is matched by very few employees. This employee provides a *model* for other staff employees in the unit/area to follow. The employee's demonstrated performance is at a level well beyond that normally expected of the majority of experienced employees in similar positions. Functions as a *resource* for others. Requires little or no oversight or supervision concerning this standard.

Meets: In the evaluator's judgment and experience, this employee's performance meets the Hospital's high expectations for the job and is viewed as performing *very well* on this standard. Requires a normal amount of oversight and supervision regarding this standard. A definite asset to the Hospital.

Does not Meet: In the evaluator's judgment and experience, this employee's performance is *marginally acceptable* and is in need of improvement. This employee is not meeting the expectations of the Hospital in this area. Requires more than the typical amount of oversight and close supervision on this standard.

the seminar, the process a team uses and the results it achieves are critiqued so the team can improve on the next activity. Each individual receives personal feedback from the team twice during the week. With the exception of brief lectures following exercises to clarify learning objectives, the seminar is based on self-learning. A.G. Edwards Vice President Donnis Casey comments on the value of Managerial Grid and Gridworks:

> The Grid programs have had a positive effect on the A.G. Edwards' culture. We embrace the philosophy of open communication, candor, teamwork and critique. The programs have also given us a common base or language. As we continue to grow in size, it aids in holding on to some of the basics that have helped us become the company we are.

Big picture education on what the company believes, how the business operates, and its environment cultivates connectedness and demonstrates the need for teamwork. Stories and anecdotes that feature team accomplishments rather than individual heroes accentuate the organizational value of teamwork. Formal training in problem-solving, interpersonal communication, conflict resolution, leadership, and coaching helps individuals acquire teamwork skills.

SUMMARY

Great service requires great teamwork: individuals working collaboratively toward a common, meaningful purpose. Teamwork values, attitudes, feelings, and skills foster the internal service quality necessary to meet and exceed customers' expectations.

Tightly bounded work processes deny the natural pathways to teamwork. For genuine teamwork to prosper, loose boundaries—what General Electric calls "boundarylessness"—must prevail. Free-flowing communications, internal service pledging, teamwork measurements and rewards, and teamwork teaching are among the investments companies can make to encourage teamwork.

Managers can use the following checklist in discussing teamwork in the organization:

1. *Do we believe in teamwork in this company?* Is teamwork viewed as a key to service quality? Is it viewed as a cultural imperative?
2. *Do we practice boundarylessness?* Do we make special efforts to break down the artificial walls that separate employees and discourage teamwork?
3. *Do we use internal communications to nurture feelings of connectedness?* Is our top management accessible to employees? Does information flow easily in this company? Does it flow upward and sideways, not just downward?
4. *Do internal departments treat each other as customers?* Are internal departments accountable for the quality of service they deliver? Do staff in these departments meet with their internal customers to discuss service expectations and perceptions? Should we consider a formal process such as the one used at Bank One Texas Trust Division?

5. *Do we measure and reward teamwork?* Do managerial and nonmanagerial personnel believe that collaborative behavior is winning behavior?
6. *Do we teach teamwork?* Do we encourage teamwork mentoring? Should we consider a formal course on teamwork? Do we celebrate team achievements in training, education, and internal media?

CHAPTER 12

MEASURE PERFORMANCE, REWARD EXCELLENCE

Great service companies are achieving organizations. Discretionary effort is high. Great service companies measure service providers' performance and reward their excellence. Employees know that they will be measured on how well they do their work, and they know their work is worth doing well. Employees care about doing their best and continually strive to improve. Personal accountability for job execution and recognition for excellent performance contribute to this climate of achievement.

Building an achieving organization requires far more than effective measures and rewards, however. Were this not the case, the earlier chapters on leadership, competing for talent, skill and knowledge development, empowerment, and teamwork would have been unnecessary. Implementing the service strategy through people is a multifaceted journey. Indeed, some companies place too much emphasis on rewards to improve service quality, assuming that employees are single-mindedly driven by them and will respond, robot-fashion, to reward system changes. But organizational life is shaped by the beat of multiple drums, the reward drum making just one kind of sound.

For maximum impact, rewards and the measures on which they are based must be concordant with other inspirations of excellence: service leadership, a mission of high purpose, personal growth, an empowered state of mind, teammates, and teamwork. Excellent service, customer after customer, day after day, requires inspiration that rewards alone cannot provide and discordant rewards stifle.

Performance measures and rewards must be right for the company and its strategy. This is why commission selling works beautifully at Harold's, the Houston apparel store, but was a disaster for Sears Auto Center. Harold's strategy is earning the customers' loyalty through merchandise quality, wide selection, exceptional service, and integrity selling. From their first day, salespeople learn that their roles are to help customers reach good decisions, ensure the clothes fit, and make customers happy. The initial sale to a customer is viewed as the start of a long-term, win-win relationship. Sales commissions, Harold's only form of compensation, multiply when first-time customers become regular customers. Commission selling works just fine at Harold's, whose culture is based on trust.

Unfortunately, Sears Auto Centers had no such cultural foundation for installing a commission selling plan that itself was poorly designed. The result was a pay-for-performance plan that in effect paid for taking advantage of customers. Service advisors drew commissions on every dollar of parts and labor they could sell. Specific high-margin parts were targeted for special emphasis. Whether customers actually needed the parts was of no concern in many outlets. The commission system was strictly a tool to sell more parts and labor; it was not a tool to serve customers well and earn their trust and loyalty.

The combination of a poorly designed incentive system and a weak cultural base for customer service virtually assured that the plan would backfire. Undercover investigations in multiple states resulted in widely publicized allegations in 1992 that Sears was defrauding customers by selling unneeded parts and service. Sears bore huge settlement, marketing, and advertising costs because of the debacle. Most importantly, it suffered a loss of customer trust for its auto service business.

SIGNALING PURPOSE, VALIDATING ACHIEVEMENT

An effective performance measurement system offers timely and useful feedback to service providers, disseminates the information to management, and provides the basis for an equitable, motivating reward system. Rewards extend beyond base salary.

Rewards recognize excellence. Genuine achievement is the barometer for rewards.

Why isn't base salary sufficient? Why are rewards needed, too? Why are performance measurement and rewards down to the individual service provider level necessary? A performance measurement and reward system helps a company communicate its strategic priorities and highest values to employees. And a clear purpose and strong supporting values are integral to great service. Confusion and conflict breed mediocrity; focus with meaning engenders service excellence.

Performance measures and rewards help define internally what a company stands for, what it believes in, its reason for being. They are highly symbolic. Employees know that managers measure and reward what is significant. When management rhetoric about what is important collides with what is measured and rewarded, the rhetoric loses. Employees learn the score by how the score is kept and rewards are distributed.

All Roberts Express employees are eligible for quarterly bonuses contingent upon attaining objectives. The objectives are function-specific and thus vary for different employee groups. Only one objective is common to all employees: customer satisfaction as measured by Roberts Express's monthly customer survey described in Chapter 3. Customer Assistance Team members, operations managers, accounting personnel, secretaries, staff executives such as the human resources manager, the company president—all are accountable for the customers' satisfaction. Roberts Express employees clearly understand the core of significance in their company.

Firms that reward excellent performance rather than just pay for time-in-grade validate achievement. By validating achievement, by celebrating excellence, by raising the performance bar high, companies improve their competitiveness in increasingly competitive markets.

Compensation per se does not motivate most employees to self-actualizing behavior. That too little compensation demotivates employees does not mean that too much leads them to extraordinary effort.[1] For many employees, higher-order needs lie in waiting—to belong, to contribute to the team's success, to feel appreciated by peers and superiors, to celebrate victories, and to be celebrated. For most employees, being recognized differs from and means more than merely being paid. Rewarding excellence helps to sustain excellence. As one bank customer service representative once put it: "When you get recognized for doing good [sic], it makes you go for it."[2]

COMMON PITFALLS

In a controversial *Harvard Business Review* article, Alfie Kohn argues that incentive plans not only do not succeed but cannot succeed.[3] Kohn criticizes incentives for being manipulative ("Do this and you'll get that"), undermining teamwork, ignoring fundamental causes of problems, discouraging creativity and risk taking, and lessening interest in the work. Kohn's article is vulnerable to criticism, and it received an abundance in the subsequent issue of *Harvard Business Review*.[4] The most serious flaw in Kohn's thesis is not that the maladies he discusses don't occur because they do—sometimes. The use of rewards does not produce the maladies, however; misuse causes the problems. Used properly, rewards (and associated measures) can produce effects opposite to those Kohn bemoans. Kohn is condemning the tool instead of the execution.

Many service companies use performance measurement and rewards ineffectively. A common and critical mistake is failing to grasp what employees really want from their work. Reward plans too often are narrowly focused on financial incentives even though employee studies repeatedly show other factors to be more important.

In a study by Dante Personnel Services, employees were asked to choose between an additional $5,000 a year in salary or specific job characteristics. By a margin of 84 percent to 9 percent, respondents selected promotability over the extra money. Eighty-eight percent preferred the opportunity to "learn the business" compared to 7 percent choosing the $5,000.[5]

In a 1991 Gallup Poll, employees were asked to rate the importance of various job characteristics and their satisfaction with them. Health insurance and other benefits, interesting work, job security, and opportunity to learn new skills were rated most important. High income was in the middle of the list,

20 percentage points below interesting work.[6] Considerable disparity exists between importance and satisfaction, suggesting reward plan possibilities more multifaceted and innovative than financial incentives alone. Scores for the full list of job characteristics appear in Table 12–1.

Clearly, the more rewards reflect what is important to employees, the more effectively they will influence performance. Managers make a critical mistake if they consider rewards and financial incentives as synonymous.

Another common mistake is measuring the wrong perfor-

Table 12–1
IMPORTANCE OF JOB CHARACTERISTICS AND SATISFACTION

How important is each of the following characteristics to you?
How satisfied are you with it in your current job?

	Percent of workers who	
	ranked it as very important	said they were satisfied
Good health insurance and other benefits	81%	27%
Interesting work	78	41
Job security	78	35
Opportunity to learn new skills	68	31
Having a week or more of vacation	66	35
Being able to work independently	64	42
Recognition from coworkers	62	24
Regular hours (no weekends, no nights)	58	40
Having a job in which you can help others	58	34
Limiting job stress	58	17
High income	56	13
Working close to home	55	46
Work that is important to society	53	35
Chances for promotion	53	20
Contact with a lot of people	52	45
Flexible hours	49	39

Source: Gallup Poll, Princeton, NJ, 1991. Reprinted in Christopher Gaggiano, "What Do Workers Want?" *Inc.*, November 1992, p. 101.

mances. Performance measurement systems often focus exclusively on *output* measures, such as the number of transactions or telephone calls completed, and ignore *behavioral* measures, such as responsiveness to customers or other employees. Outputs may be more easily measured than behaviors, but this is not the issue. Specific service performances critical to successful implementation of the core strategy are what must be measured and then rewarded. Measuring the wrong performances means rewarding the wrong performances.

US West Communications previously measured customer service representatives and credit consultants strictly on productivity criteria, such as number and length of calls handled. The measurement system hurt quality while frustrating service providers. Winnie Nelson, a US West service-quality manager, comments on the system:

> It drove front-liners to focus more on meeting numbers so they could have good performance appraisals rather than on making sure customers were pleased with the results of their calls. We lost so much in that process.[7]

US West still tracks productivity data but does not use them in performance appraisals. Newer measures incorporate customer feedback.

Chapter 4 discussed the importance of service standards, the explicit types and levels of service required of employees to satisfy customers and to implement the company's strategy. Service standards are the specifics of the overall strategy, the definitions of excellent service that enable employees to understand their roles, judge their own performance, and experience effective evaluation by superiors.

Service standards capture what is important to customers in a way that is meaningful to employees; they form the basis of service performance measurement and rewards. As Craig Eric Schneier and colleagues write: "Companies need a process to help identify and measure 'what counts'—those few activities that lead to success of individuals, teams, units, and the organization."[8] Great service companies focus their measures and rewards on critical success factors.

The absence of an integrated change strategy—a strategy to

implement the strategy—is another common pitfall. Appropriate measures and rewards alone will not, cannot, build a strong service culture and capability. With leadership driving a service mentality, and timely, relevant information guiding decision making, then structure, technology, hiring, training and education, empowerment, and teamwork all must converge with measures and rewards to implement the service strategy. If Sears hopes to materially improve quality in its automobile service business, it not only needs appropriate performance measures and rewards but also an integrated change strategy. The company has taken positive steps. The position of service advisor has been eliminated, and mechanics now diagnose service and repair needs. Customer satisfaction has been incorporated into the pay-for-performance system.

Rewarding performance in the wrong ways, measuring and rewarding the wrong kinds of performance, and overrelying on measurement and rewards to change an organization can contribute to the problems Alfie Kohn associates with incentives. But these are executional issues. Handled properly, performance measurement and rewards are keys to delivering superior service.

GUIDELINES FOR MEASURING PERFORMANCE

Effectively measuring service performance requires a fair process, multiple measures and inputs, simplicity, individual and group evaluation, and an inclusive approach. Measurement guided by these principles provides the basis for an effective reward system.

Emphasize Fairness

Fairness is critical in designing a performance measurement system. Those whose performance is being measured must perceive the system to be fair. An unfair system undermines the credibility of the feedback it produces and the rewards it influences. A measurement system with the following characteristics is most likely to be perceived as fair:

- The measurement criteria relate directly to service standards. The priorities and measures of the service role are consistent.
- Service providers control their own destiny. The measures are sensitive to their actual performance.
- Service providers have been given the opportunity to learn and practice the skills and knowledge critical to successful performance.
- Service providers have contributed input on the appropriateness and fairness of the measures. They have had a voice in the design and implementation of the system.
- The measurement system has been explained effectively and is well understood.
- The measures are administered regularly to minimize the impact of a single measurement encounter. The system is insensitive to atypical encounters.
- Measurement feedback is used positively and constructively to help service providers improve their performance.
- The measures are as uniform as possible among work groups so that people in different jobs play by similar rules.
- Multiple measures and inputs are used to provide a balanced assessment, to compensate for the limitations of any one approach, and to offer different-angled views of performance.[9]

Use Multiple Measures and Inputs

Balanced measurement systems encourage balanced performance. US West's mistake was not that it measured productivity, but that it *only* measured productivity. Thus, productivity concerns dominated service concerns; quality and employee morale suffered as a consequence. Effective performance measurement systems use a combination of measures. The portfolio might measure individual provider's service attitude, accuracy, productivity, teamwork, and skill and knowledge development; group evaluations might include service quality ratings, customer retention, sales, and profits.

Baldrige-winner Xerox uses six mandatory assessments to determine if a manager is promotable: customer satisfaction, leadership through quality, business results, human resources management, teamwork, and corporate values.[10] High performance in each area clears an upward path at Xerox. Xerox managers cannot afford to stress financial results over customer satisfaction or, for that matter, customer satisfaction over financial results. They must balance all factors critical to the company's success.

Customer input is a principal source of performance measurement data. Transactional surveys or mystery shopping reports can be used to assess the service attitude of individual employees or organizational units, for example. Internal company data on service failure rates, response times, customer attrition, and sales and profits also might be used. Input from peers, associates, superiors, and subordinates also can be valuable. Up to one-third of a Levi Strauss employee's merit review depends on peer, client, and subordinate evaluations. Twice a year, six to ten individuals evaluate in writing the employee's performance in the company's core value areas, such as promoting teamwork and trust, embracing diversity, recognizing and rewarding others, behaving ethically, communicating effectively, and furthering empowerment. Each employee may suggest co-workers or clients as reviewers, but managers determine the final list.[11]

Keep It Simple

Convoluted or complicated measurement systems fail to focus employee attention—a principal objective of performance measurement. Simplicity is a key despite the use of multiple measures and inputs. The portfolio of measures should be small. Xerox's six mandatory assessments for managers suggest an upper boundary. Explicitly defined measurement criteria (e.g., percentage of customers who defect for service-related reasons) are simpler than vague criteria (e.g., good service). Data sources—mystery shopper scores, monthly customer surveys, closed-account surveys, teamwork surveys—should be similarly explicit. The relative importance of each measure also must be clear.

A performance measurement index that explicates measures, criteria, weights, and data sources facilitates communication and understanding of the system. Timely feedback also is beneficial. Frequent reports, such as monthly service quality ratings and quarterly mystery shopper reports, enable service providers to keep track of their own progress to a considerable extent. A measurement system is sufficiently simple when service providers need not wait for a formal performance review to know how they are doing.

Measure Individual and Group Performance

Growing emphasis on teamwork and teams does not eliminate the need to measure an individual's service performance. Both individual and group measurements are necessary. Service providers must be accountable for their own performance as well as share responsibility for unit and organizational performance. The absence of individual performance measures hides the poor work of some employees and the excellent work of others. Performance measurement is far more effective when individuals know that their superiors will know how each person is performing his or her job.

Measuring the performance of the work group, such as a service delivery team, department, or field office, also is valuable. Group measurement encourages teamwork, including within-group teaching. It also unleashes peer pressure, a potentially powerful motivator. Consider this scenario: a 300-unit restaurant chain uses several different survey approaches to measure each unit's service quality. Among other rewards, it establishes an annual bonus of $10,000 for units scoring above a predetermined level. The bonus is divided among nonmanagement personnel. In this system, a waiter, greeter, or cook may earn bonuses of $500 or more. Might peer pressure to perform be a factor in this system? Would a hard-working waitress who goes out of her way to please customers have something to say to an associate whose service attitude is poor and discretionary effort is low? The combination of individual and group measurement and rewards can contribute powerfully to a restaurant's culture under these conditions.

Include Everyone

Every employee delivers service. Everyone serves either internal or external customers, and internal service quality affects the quality of external service. Service quality should be part of every employee's performance assessment. No one should be excluded. Not the chief executive officer. Not headquarters staff. Not middle managers. Not internal service personnel. Not front-line service providers. To exclude anyone in the organization from service-related performance measurements diminishes service quality as a cultural anchor. This is why Roberts Express's practice of incorporating customers' service ratings into every employee's bonus plan offers such an important lesson. At Roberts Express, the end customer belongs to everyone in the organization.

GUIDELINES FOR REWARDING PERFORMANCE

An effective performance measurement system facilitates an effective reward system. Reward systems will be ineffectual in moving the company in the intended direction without good information on who does and does not deserve to be rewarded. Supported by solid information, an effective reward system focuses on excellence, uses multiple reinforcers, and recognizes group as well as individual performance.

Reward Excellence

Building an achievement culture involves distinguishing between *competence pay* (compensation for doing one's job) and *performance rewards* (special recognition for outstanding performance). Competence pay is stable, earned by acceptable performance. Performance rewards are variable, earned through exceptional achievement. Rewards reserved for genuine achievement, for excellence, are most likely to stimulate superior performance.

Most service jobs have high discretionary content, as discussed in Chapter 2. The energy and care put into the job are largely up to the service provider's discretion. Service employees are similar to volunteer workers in this respect. Much of this book explains what companies must do to operate at an elevated level of discretionary effort. Going beyond competence pay to recognize excellence is an important step. Great service companies reward employees who "volunteer hard."

Companies increasingly are adopting performance-oriented plans such as gainsharing, commissions, bonuses, profit sharing, and stock options. In a 1993 Coopers and Lybrand study, nearly one-third of the companies in the sample indicated they were considering new pay-for-performance plans. Nearly half of this group reported the plans would be implemented in 1994.[12]

Traditional stepwise salary progression plans do not inspire high discretionary effort. Some employees will exhibit such effort, of course, but not because of the pay plan. Entitlement pay does not foster a desire to improve, to do more, to stretch. Rewarding excellence does foster such a desire. People higher up in the organization are noticing and appreciating superior performance. And being noticed and appreciated fulfills a deep need.

What is the best way to reward excellent performance? Employees provide the answers. Asking employees what they consider to be fair and what motivates excellent performance is a critical early step in designing a reward system. Asking "How can we improve it?" is a critical follow-up step after employees have experienced the new system.[13] In a variable-pay survey by Wyatt Data Services, the effectiveness ratings of pay plans were significantly higher when representatives from the covered groups participated in establishing plan goals.[14] In an American Compensation Association variable-pay survey, plan designs mandated by headquarters resulted in poorer teamwork and higher costs than those developed by employee task forces.[15]

Use Multiple Rewards

The most effective reward systems combine financial rewards, career advancement, and nonfinancial recognition. Each plays a different role; combining them creatively can produce powerful effects.

Financial Rewards. As the studies suggest, pay in and of itself is not inspiring for many employees. High pay is certainly better than low pay, however. And high pay linked to achievement and combined with other rewards can inspire employees to strive for excellence.

Pay often is viewed by employees as a barometer of their value to management. Good pay signifies respect. Poor pay signifies the opposite. Conveying respect to people doing important work and achieving in that work is central to building a serviced-minded culture. This is a principal reason why excellent companies typically pay well. Competence and performance pay potential not only helps companies compete for talent, it helps companies compete for achievement once people are hired. And it helps firms keep their best people.

De Mar service advisors have unlimited income potential based on the revenue they generate, their service reliability (they are not paid for callbacks), and their customers' satisfaction, among other factors. They are among the highest paid in their industry.

Mary Kay Cosmetics has created more female millionaires than any other company in the world. The pay system is simple, generous—and geared to performance. Field saleswomen purchase their products directly from the company, using cash, credit card, or cashier's check. They purchase the merchandise for 40 to 50 percent of the selling price. The discount level is determined by order quantity. A $400 wholesale purchase has retail value of $800. Field sales directors earn additional commissions from the sales of personal recruits and saleswomen in their units. Sales director Mary Beth Slattum comments: "We are paid extremely well. In so many other companies, the money goes to the head people. At Mary Kay, they pay us according to what we contribute."

Star Furniture, a highly successful retailer based in Houston, used to pay its delivery truck drivers hourly wages. Drivers frequently worked overtime and collected extra pay. They had no incentive to improve the quality or productivity of their work. Then Star changed to a commission system that paid the drivers one percent of the retail value of the loads they delivered and customers accepted. Drivers now had an incentive to work efficiently and effectively. The drivers had to pay the company double the value of their commission if they damaged the furniture and were authorized to reject furniture that wasn't perfect before loading it on the truck. The new pay plan worked. President Leonard Gaby states: "Drivers used to try to put as little furniture on the truck as possible and still make it appear full. Now they say: 'Give me 1,100 feet and I can handle it.'"

Career Advancement. Rewarding superior service performance with career-advancing actions is among a company's strongest cultural statements. Employees need to perceive a career stake in delivering excellent service. The best service providers need to progress more rapidly in their careers than others, and the career progress-service quality link must be clear. Paying outstanding servers more *and* advancing their careers is a powerful combination. Add nonfinancial recognition to the mix, and "hard volunteering" becomes exceedingly tempting.

Companies with limited promotion opportunities can consider within-position advancements. Thus, a bank might create three levels of customer service representatives, with each succeeding level involving additional skill and education opportunities, greater income potential, and broader responsibilities.[16]

Superior performers can be rewarded with placement in an accelerated career-path program, appointments to important committees and task forces, invitations to teach in company courses, and selection for advanced training or education courses. Remember what employees would rather have than an extra $5,000 in pay: promotability and the chance to learn the business. As consultant George Rieder states: "The new employee security in today's turbulent business world is skills and competency enhancement."

Nonfinancial Recognition. Extra compensation and faster career progress are potent ways of rewarding excellence. So is a public pat on the back. Genuine recognition conveys respect, gratitude, and admiration; the effects can be profound. Employees receiving the tribute know that they are on the team, that management cares enough to say thank you. Employees observing their colleague's honors want to be honored, too, one day.

Bank One Texas Trust Division gives the Richard M. Hart Service Quality Award annually to one employee whose performance most epitomizes the division's commitment to excellent service. Nominations are reviewed by a selection committee. The division's most prestigious award is presented by Mr. Hart, the founding chairman, to the unknowing winner in front of peers. A $2,500 cash bonus, plaque, and paid day off come with the award. Administrative assistant Jackie Salazar received the award in 1991. In a 1993 interview, she said: "When I talk about it, I still sweat. And it was two years ago. It was the most exciting thing that ever happened to me. I still don't believe it."

Milliken & Company is an ardent practitioner of personal recognition. The Baldrige-winning manufacturer uses four recognition platforms:

- In front of top management, e.g., sharing rallies, hero presentations
- In front of the location, e.g., reserved parking space with the awardee's name visibly displayed
- In front of the department, e.g., colleagues gathered in designated area for presentations
- In front of the individual, e.g., quality performance scoreboards posted near desk

Awards Night at Mary Kay. Mary Kay Cosmetics blends all forms of rewards so brilliantly that this company deserves its own section in this chapter. No company does a better job of celebrating excellence than Mary Kay Cosmetics.

As discussed in Chapter 2, Mary Kay attracts thousands of field saleswomen and sales directors to its annual Dallas "Seminar." The highlight of the event is "Awards Night." Here are my impressions from the Ruby Seminar's Awards Night in July 1993:

> The arena seats 8,000. It isn't big enough this night. Another 3,000 people are in a different room watching on large television monitors. The celebration begins promptly at 7:00 P.M. It will go past midnight.

The Ruby Seminar is one of four held each summer to accommodate all the Mary Kay people who wish to attend—36,000 this year.

The show opens. Singing, dancing, flashing lights. The stage glitters. This is like Las Vegas, only better.

Mary Kay Ash, the company founder, appears on the stage. The audience goes wild. There is love in the air. The emotional bond between Mary Kay Ash and the throng is extraordinary. When the mood finally settles, Mary Kay Ash intones: "I want you to set your goals so that if you are not on stage tonight, you will be next year." The audience erupts again.

Eight thousand fired-up women in one place. This is true motivation. This is the genuine article.

Mary Kay Ash and company president, Larry Harley, present the national sales directors who each receive a rose, a framed certificate, and a kiss from Mary Kay. Each director's achievements are reviewed. The members of the Inner Circle are recognized next. These individuals earned a minimum of $250,000 during the past year. Each recipient may choose $5,000 cash or a $5,000 jewelry "shopping spree."

Shirley Hutton is recognized. She has earned $5 million at Mary Kay, including $800,000 in the past year. Throughout the evening, frequent references are made to "Mary Kay Millionaires."

The first "Queen of the Court" presentation occurs. A throne rises from the floor. The runners-up are presented. Sandy Mann is the first runner-up for "Queen of Personal Sales." She is presented a mink coat on stage. Then Clyneice Ledbetter is announced as the winner. The audience goes wild—again. Everyone is clapping in rhythm. Clyneice is crowned and sits on the throne. Mary Kay says: "This is Clyneice's fourteenth time on the stage, her first time sitting in the throne." Clyneice responds: "Mary Kay has changed my life." Mary Kay Ash makes a personal comment about each member of the Queen's Court. The personal touch is remarkable.

It is time for dancing and music from the sixties. A muscular young man in a bathing suit bounds onto the stage, gyrating to Beach Boys music. The audience erupts—again. At Mary Kay Awards Night, men are sex symbols, not women. The audience claps along to music such as "Born to be Wild" and "Leader of the Pack." Many in the audience are dancing in the aisles. Everyone is having a *really* good time.

Next comes the "Queen of Recruiting" recognitions. Winner Davorah Saleck receives a standing ovation as Mary Kay Ash crowns her. In her acceptance speech, Davorah says: "Thank you so much. You are looking at a 14-year overnight success. Last year I was number five and stood next to the fur coat. I was determined to do better this year." Mary Kay adds: "I am bursting with pride."

Members of the Mary Kay Millionaires Club are recognized in the audience. New members to the Club are brought on stage. The qualification for membership is career earnings of a million dollars. The new millionaires make short speeches. They speak about how they got started, how amazed they are by their success, how they used the money to purchase a new house, care for their parents, or buy something special for children or grandchildren. It is an inspirational highlight in an evening full of inspiration.

Another queen is crowned. She is Judy Caraway, the number one personal sales producer among all sales consultants (nondirectors) in the Ruby category. Judy receives a trophy, diamond ring, wristwatch, and her crown. "I want to thank Mary Kay for this opportunity. There is no way that there is a lady as beautiful as this lady," Judy states. "We all love you, Mary Kay," she adds.

And so the evening proceeds. More entertainment. And many more awards. Before the celebration concludes, more than one thousand women will appear on stage to be recognized in front of their peers. It is a magical, joyous, motivating gala where those who are recognized and those who are not make private commitments to themselves about "next year."

Many companies have awards nights. Why does Mary Kay Cosmetics' Awards Night produce such powerful effects? Its genuineness is the answer. Awards Night is a magnified reflection of how Mary Kay Cosmetics conducts business everyday. This company celebrates opportunity for women and showers them daily with respect, inspiration, and confidence. This is a company founded by a remarkable woman who believes any woman can be remarkable if she sets her mind to it. Mary Kay Ash mails 5,000 personal notes to sales force members each month. Pink Cadillacs are just a small part of a company that relies on hard cash, prizes, praise, respect, spirituality, and love to convince thousands of women to raise their sights. Interviews with sales directors just prior to Awards Night produced these insights:

Mona Holte Butters: "If you are sitting in that audience, it gives you the hope, the dream."

Jessie Logan: "You sit in the audience and you think, I can do it. You see older and younger people, people from small towns and big cities. They all are successful. Mary Kay was such a smart woman when she realized that we would work for the recognition and prizes before the money."

Nancy Moser: "Mary Kay is doing this party for us. She puts us on the stage to say thank you. The last time many women received a round of applause was when they graduated from high school. Mary Kay understood this and built her company around it."

Reward Group Achievement

Reward systems should reflect the collaborative nature of service quality. Mary Kay Cosmetics relies on individual rewards for its field sales force because it is composed of independent contractors operating out of their homes. In its headquarters and factory operations, however, Mary Kay Cosmetics uses team structures and incentives (see Chapter 6 and Exhibit 6-1).

The more important teamwork is to successful service delivery, the more important it is to reward teamwork. Reinforcing team play does not mean eliminating individual rewards. Emphasis on teamwork need not deny individuals the opportunity to shine. Reward systems that combine individual and team rewards usually produce the best results. Individual rewards recognize high discretionary effort and superior performance; team rewards celebrate and reinforce collaborative achievement. The inner satisfaction that can come from personal accomplishment contributing to group achievement suggests the enhanced power of combined individual and group rewards.

Compensation experts Patricia Zingheim and Jay Schuster advocate group variable pay to align compensation strategies with quality-improvement goals. Group variable pay is a cash award for meeting or exceeding goals based on the collaborative performance of an employee group. The awards are made for specific results achieved and are not folded into the base salary. Group variable pay offers the flexibility of focusing on different goals as the business's needs change and the unifying effects of shared rewards. It also moves more compensation cost from fixed to variable status. Zingheim and Schuster write:

> It makes sense to have pay help communicate the goals and measures that are needed to help make TQM important. Group variable pay is the ideal tool because of its flexibility, ability to respond to multiple goals and measures, and encouragement of collaboration and teamwork.[17]

When Salomon Brothers moved its back office support organization from New York to Florida, it instituted Teamshare that allowed employees to keep 10 percent of the savings versus plan. It also recognized outstanding individual performers. Initiated as a one-time event, Teamshare has become an ongoing incentive process.

In the Wyatt Data Services study of the effectiveness of variable pay plans, small group incentives and individual incentives were rated first and second in effectiveness out of the eight pay plans studied. Small group plans also achieved the highest effectiveness ratings for 11 of 15 specific compensation goals, such as "more closely link pay to performance," "increase productivity," "communicate business objectives," "foster teamwork," and "improve customer satisfaction."[18]

Small group incentives may be supplemented by company performance incentives, such as profit sharing, stock purchase programs, and stock options. Reward systems play a key role in instilling an ownership feeling among employees, and corporate-wide risk and reward sharing contributes to this aim directly. Starbucks Coffee Company's stock option plan, Bean Stock, discussed in Chapter 8, illustrates the possibilities of making even part-time workers owners in a literal sense. As Henry Kravis and George Roberts write:

> Ownership focuses attention on the good of the organization like nothing else can. And so, in our view, ownership should

start right at the top, with directors and senior managers, and continue throughout the organization to a broad group of middle managers or the entire work force.[19]

The spirit of the service performance reward guidelines presented in this book is conceptually summarized in Exhibit 12–1: reward excellence, use multiple rewards, reward group achievement. At the base is competence pay. It provides the foundation for performance rewards—financial, career-advancing, and non-financial recognition of superior achievement for individuals, for groups, and for the company ultimately. Company recognition is included with personal and group recognition because of the pride and pleasure members of an organization experience when the organization is celebrated for its excellence. The exhibit is purposely drawn to convey the more pronounced role for performance rewards than competence pay. Entitlement is not the way to excellence; self-actualization and collaborative performance create the way.

Exhibit 12–1
REWARDING SUPERIOR SERVICE
INDIVIDUALLY AND COLLECTIVELY

	Individual Performance	Group Performance	Company Performance
Performance Rewards	• Financial • Career Advancement • Personal Recognition	• Financial • Group Recognition	• Financial • Company Recognition
Competence Pay	Base Compensation		

SUMMARY

Performance measurement and rewards contribute to building a climate of achievement in delivering great service. Service providers know that they will be measured on how well they perform and that it is worthwhile to perform well. Service performance measurement and rewards must be part of an integrated human resources strategy to implement the overall service strategy. Measures and rewards that are right for one company may be wrong for another company.

Measures should capture the behaviors and outcomes critical to delivering excellent service. Rewards should then encourage these behaviors and outcomes. Genuine rewards foster and celebrate excellence; base compensation and performance rewards are different concepts.

Effective measurement systems are fair, based on multiple measures and inputs, simple, and inclusive. Individual and group performance both are measured. Effective reward systems focus on superior performance, use multiple rewards in combination, and recognize group as well as individual achievement.

The following questions are helpful in discussing a company's approach to performance measurement and rewards:

1. *Do our employees feel personally accountable for their service performance?* Do they know how their job performance is measured? Do they know why? Do they believe their performance level makes a difference to the company?
2. *Is superior service achievement part of our company's culture?* Do service providers care about doing their best? Do they strive to improve?
3. *Are we achieving essential synergies in performance measurement and rewards?* Are measures and rewards aligned? Are they in harmony with other human resources practices? Do they fit our strategy?
4. *Are employees involved in the design and implementation of performance measurements and rewards?* Do employees have a voice in a system so central to their well-being and morale? Do they consider the measurement and reward system fair and effective?
5. *Do we use multiple performance measures?* Do we use different lenses to measure performance? Do we encourage balanced performance consistent with our aspirations as a company?

6. *Do we use multiple performance rewards?* Do we use financial, career-advancement, and nonfinancial rewards in combination? Do we recognize the power of personal recognition such as public tributes and awards?

7. *Is our performance measurement and reward system clear?* Is it easy to understand and use, even with multiple measures and rewards? Can our employees determine how well they are doing in the system?

8. *Does our performance measurement and reward system encourage individual and collaborative excellence?* Are we tapping into the fruits of individual effort *and* collaborative energy?

CHAPTER 13

THE ARTISTRY
OF GREAT SERVICE

Companies compete with value in the 1990s. Service quality is integral to delivering value to customers. Value is the benefit customers receive for the burdens they endure. Service quality plays a pivotal role in the value equation by increasing benefits and reducing burdens.

Customers are demanding a good return on their investment of money, time, and energy. The benefits they seek start with— but do not end with—competence. They demand convenience, respect, caring, and integrity as well.

Companies invest heavily, also, to supply these customer demands. They create value by delivering competence, convenience, respect, care, and integrity.

Service quality builds relationships—with customers, with employees, and with other stakeholders in the business. Great companies nurture these mutually beneficial relationships.

Relationship *customers* buy more, are more loyal, and sing the company's praises to others. They develop an attachment to the company. The company becomes an ally.

Relationship *employees* work harder and smarter. They care about the business, its future, its destiny. The business becomes their business.

Relationship *companies* stake their survival on these commitments. The leaders are vested in their customers, in their employees, and in themselves. They love the business and show it. They value people and envision the company as a catalyst for transforming lives. They support, coach, and encourage everyone involved in the process of creating quality service. They celebrate the joy of living out their integrity.

Great service is *serving*. It is defining mutually beneficial goals and trusting during the journey toward attaining them. It is endeavoring to improve the quality of life by creating a meaningful work environment for employees and extending an authentic service product to customers.

Great service is a profit strategy. It is a profit strategy because it differentiates a company from its competitors, stimulates favorable word-of-mouth advertising, and encourages customers to shed mediocre suppliers and consolidate purchasing. It also results in fewer lost customers, lower employee turnover, higher productivity, fewer service mistakes, and, more than likely, higher prices because of higher value. The dozens of companies chronicled in this book for their service excellence are, as a group, highly profitable. It is no coincidence. Excellent service improves financial performance.

Delivering great service is more fun for employees than delivering average service. Excellent service is hard work, but hard work is not what deadens a job. Dull work deadens a job. So does work without a sense of mission, without the opportunity to learn and grow, and without the opportunity to be and feel successful. Great service companies build a culture of achievement. And achieving at work is rewarding.

Great service is not an impossible dream. We have role model companies in every industry, companies whose examples show the way. The research for this book included finding some of these companies and learning their lessons. These lessons are melded with a career-long immersion in the study of service businesses to produce a framework for service improvement, a road map for implementation. Most managers today know that service quality is important to their businesses's performance and future. If they don't know it, they have been living in a cave for the past ten years. The central question today is not whether to improve service but how to improve it. This book is my answer to the second question.

Great service is created. Chapter 1 introduces the framework, and Chapters 2 through 12 develop it. Each part of the framework is crucial; even one missing part limits the potential for true excellence.

Great service is leadership throughout the organization. It is a vision worthy of embrace, exceptionally high standards, and a spiritual energy driven by untouchable values at the core.

Great service is a fundamental belief in the potential of employees to be great. It is a belief in the capacity of people to rise to new heights, to grow and develop, to care about excellence, to become role models and teachers for others in the organization, to serve customers as if their life depends on it.

Great service is attitude. It is extra effort, extra care. It is doing the little things well, using details to be different, striving for perfection. It is serving one customer at a time, listening carefully, interpreting the unspoken as well as the spoken, and finding a way to deliver value, finding a way to please the customer on the spot.

Great service is having a reason for being. It is a clear service strategy that becomes a mission, a calling, a journey of high purpose. It is a direction that moves the human spirit, a direction that becomes a commitment.

Great service is an integrated approach to continuous improvement. It is a puzzle with pieces that fit together. It is investing in the technology that is right for the strategy, right for the mission, not just investing in modern technology to be technologically correct. It is hiring the people who are right for the company, not just hiring good people. It is structuring to implement the strategy, not bowing to the latest organizational fad. Great service is holistic thinking.

Great service is informed decision making. It is knowing what is important to customers, noncustomers, employees, and other stakeholders. It is knowing how well the company is performing service. It is knowing how well competitors are performing. It is knowing what is happening, why, and what needs to be done.

Great service is keeping the service promise. It is an emphasis on accuracy and dependability. It is intelligent design of the service system, searching for and reducing vulnerabilities. It is a passion for performing the service right the first time.

Great service is the element of pleasant surprise. It is doing for the customer what other companies will not do for them. It is demonstrating uncommon commitment to the customers' well-being. It is finding ways to make customers say "wow."

Great service is standing behind the service. It is a sense of urgency when the service system fails. It is making things right for the customer when they go wrong. It is taking total responsibility for what the customer experiences with the company. It is looking beyond the economics of the single transaction and striving to create a customer for life.

Great service is fair play. It is a level playing field. It is helping customers make good consumption decisions. It is treating customers as friends. It is using a standard higher than the law in formulating policy, strategy, and tactics. It is integrity.

Great service is investing in employees' success. It is investing in technology that helps people perform better. It is investing in employees' service skills and knowledge. It is investing in their confidence to serve and their desire to excel. It is investing in their self-actualization.

Great service is creating an ownership feeling within the organization. It is pushing authority and responsibility down into the organization. It is giving employees at every level a voice in how they do their jobs. It is broadening the solution space so that service providers can be "thinking" providers. It is sharing leadership, sharing information, sharing the fruits of accomplishment.

Great service is collaborative. It is employees trusting one another, helping one another, motivating one another, bonding together for a greater good. It is open, honest, frequent communication within the service chain or team. It is old-fashioned teamwork.

Great service is the inspiration to excel. It is dreaming the big dream and pursuing it relentlessly. It is continuous stretching for unconventional solutions, for new paradigms. It is being proud but not complacent.

Great service is artistry. It is people, information, equipment, and facilities, but most of all it is a creative process. It is the artistry that blends these ingredients together and creates a little bit of magic. It is the creativity, commitment, and passion of every person involved in the company.

Delivering great service is difficult. If it were easy, it would be more common. But real companies and real people are providing great service in every industry in America. We can learn from these companies. We can learn from Tattered Cover's Joyce Meskis, who built a bookstore so welcoming and comfortable that customers feel as though they are at home. We can learn from De Mar's Larry Harmon, who hired a helicopter to install an air conditioning unit on a rooftop because it was the only way to keep the service promise on that day. We can learn from Mary Kay Ash, who understands the power of applause. We can learn from Roberts Express's Bruce Simpson, who believes every employee is responsible for customer satisfaction. We can learn from Harold's founder Harold Wiesenthal, who sells customers only what they need and what fits.

The lessons from these leaders and their companies—and from so many other leaders and companies featured in this book—put us on the right path, the path to great service, to a little magic, perhaps even to a poem of appreciation from a customer. We can learn from Oral Bower, who was a patient at Lakeland Regional Medical Center and responded from the heart to great service.

FOR ALL THE ANGELS AT 5 WEST
By Oral Bower

I want you to know you're the very best;
With compassion and skill you are well endowed—
That should make Lakeland Regional very proud.

Ruth, Colleen, and Bonnie, too . . .
Joan and Ted and then there's Lou;
Ollie, Kathy, also Jack,
All of them are on the right track.

Sometimes they're a vampire crew
Doing the things that vampires do.
They apologize for each stick and jab,
Then take more of your blood down to the lab.

They have bags and bottles of every hue
That are constantly dripping into you!

They have needles large and needles small;
They have an endless supply of them all.

I'd like to say my stay was a pleasure,
(But there were many moments to treasure).
I *almost* enjoyed my stay
Because of your "caring" both night and day.

When customers experience service as being delivered by angels, the company has maximized the benefits and nearly eliminated the burdens. The company is great service . . . great service is the company.

NOTES

Chapter 2. Nurture Service Leadership

1. Lee Harkins, "Roadblocks to the Implementation of Quality," Presentation at the American Marketing Association Services Marketing Conference, Orlando, Florida, October 22, 1991.
2. Quoted in Leonard L. Berry, "Middle Managers Can Play a Key Role in Improving Service," *American Banker*, September 23, 1987, p. 4.
3. Daniel Yankelovich and John Immerwahr, *Putting the Work Ethic to Work* (New York: Public Agenda Foundation, 1983), p. 1.
4. See Peter F. Drucker, "The New Society of Organizations," *Harvard Business Review*, September-October 1992, pp. 95–104.
5. Warren Bennis and Burt Nanus, *Leaders: The Strategies for Taking Charge* (New York: Harper & Row, 1985), p. 92.
6. Robert Grudin, *The Grace of Great Things: Creativity and Innovation* (New York: Ticknor & Fields, 1990), pp. 74–75.
7. Grudin, p. 55.
8. William G. Pagonis, "The Work of the Leader," *Harvard Business Review*, November-December 1992, p. 119.
9. Peter F. Drucker, "Leadership: More Doing Than Dash," *The Wall Street Journal*, January 6, 1988.
10. *Boardroom Reports*, May 1, 1991, p. 15.
11. Robert Levering and Milton Moskowitz, *The 100 Best Companies to Work For in America* (New York: Currency Doubleday, 1993), p. 369.
12. *Productivity Views*, July-August 1993, p. 11.
13. Thomas Raffio, "Quality and Delta Dental Plan of Massachusetts," *Sloan Management Review*, Fall 1992, pp. 102–103.
14. "Book Reports Turn Managers On to Change," *Productivity Views*, July-August 1993, pp. 5–6.
15. Ron Zemke, "Mini-Baldrige Can Have Mini-Impact," *The Service Edge*, April 1993, p. 8.
16. Beth Summers, "Total Quality Management: What Went Wrong?" *The Corporate Board*, March-April 1993, p. 23.

17. The material in this paragraph is drawn from comments by Robert Fisher at the meeting "Bridging the Service Quality Gap," held at Milliken & Co., Spartanburg, South Carolina, October 1, 1992.
18. "Executives Go Undercover to Test Service Quality," *The Service Edge*, March 1993, p. 5.
19. "Win the Great Game of Business with Shared Ownership and Financial Knowledge," *On Achieving Excellence*, August 1993, p. 10.
20. Levering and Moskowitz, pp. 38–39.
21. Levering and Moskowitz, p. 38.
22. Remarks by Tom Malone at the meeting "Bridging the Service Quality Gap," held at Milliken & Co., Spartanburg, South Carolina, October 1, 1992.
23. Malone, October 1, 1992.

Chapter 3. Build a Service Quality Information System

1. Julia Nufer, "Using 'Moment-of-Truth' Surveys," *The Marketing Research Report*, Maritz Marketing Research, Vol. 7, No. 3, n.d.
2. "21 Commandments of Customer Service Measurement," *On Achieving Excellence*, November 1991, p. 2.
3. "Focus On: Norrell Temporary Services," *The Service Edge*, April 1993, p. 5.
4. The basic SERVQUAL approach is described in Valarie Zeithaml, A. Parasuraman, and Leonard L. Berry, *Delivering Quality Service: Balancing Customer Perceptions and Expectations* (New York: The Free Press), 1990.
5. Frederick F. Reichheld and W. Earl Sasser, Jr., "Zero Defections: Quality Comes to Services," *Harvard Business Review*, September-October 1990, p. 304.
6. "Report Cards Measure and Improve Inside Services," *Productivity Views*, May-June 1992, pp. 2–3.
7. "Internal Service: How One Company Uses Pay Incentives to Create Enduring Change," *The Service Edge*, June 1993, pp. 1–3.
8. "Travel, Tea, Training for Top Customer Service, Treat Support Staff Like Royalty," *On Achieving Excellence*, October 1993, pp. 2–3.
9. Robert Levering and Milton Moskowitz, *The 100 Best Companies to Work For in America* (New York: Currency Doubleday, 1993), p. 397.
10. John A. Goodman, Scott M. Broetzmann, and Colin Adamson, "Ineffective—That's the Problem with Customer Satisfaction Surveys," *Quality Progress*, May 1992, p. 35.
11. To read more on desired and adequate service expectations, see Valarie A. Zeithaml, Leonard L. Berry, and A. Parasuraman, "The Nature and Determinants of Customer Expectations of Service,"

The Journal of the Academy of Marketing Sciences, Winter 1993, pp. 1–12.

12. Bernard Chudy and Roger Sant, "Customer Driven Competitive Positioning—An Approach Towards Developing an Effective Customer Service Strategy," Taylor Nelson Business Services White Paper, 1993, p. 10.

13. Raymond E. Kordupleski, Roland T. Rust, and Anthony J. Zahorik, "Marketing: The Missing Dimension in Quality Management," *California Management Review*, Spring 1993, p. 87.

14. Brian S. Lunde, "When Being Perfect Is Not Enough," *Marketing Research*, Winter 1993, p. 26.

15. Eli Seggev and Denise Lapnow, "Management Uses of Customer Satisfaction Measurement Systems," a paper presented at the American Marketing Association's Services Marketing Conference, October 23, 1991.

16. As quoted in "Some Ways to Coddle Customers on a Budget," *The Service Edge*, September 1993, p. 4.

17. Interview with Peter F. Drucker, *Harvard Business Review*, May-June 1993, p. 120.

Chapter 4. Create a Service Strategy

1. James C. Collins, "In Pursuit of the Big Hairy Audacious Goal," syndicated newspaper column, May 24, 1993.

2. John E. Martin, "Change. Not If. But How." A presentation to the Center for Retailing Studies Retailing Symposium, Texas A&M University, Dallas, Texas, October 22, 1993.

3. Interview with Chip Bell, *The Service Edge*, January 1990, p. 8.

4. John E. Martin presentation.

5. Leonard L. Berry, Valarie A. Zeithaml, and A. Parasuraman, "Five Imperatives for Improving Service Quality," *Sloan Management Review*, Summer 1990, p. 30.

Chapter 5. Commit to the Principles of Great Service

1. See Valarie A. Zeithaml, A. Parasuraman, and Leonard L. Berry, *Delivering Quality Service: Balancing Customer Perceptions and Expectations* (New York: Free Press, 1990) and Leonard L. Berry and A. Parasuraman, *Marketing Services: Competing Through Quality* (New York: Free Press, 1991).

2. Quoted in Tom Shedd, "UP's Quest for Quality," *Railway Age*, February 1992, p. 22.

3. Shedd, p. 22.

4. Quoted in "Illinois Power Probes the Big-Customer Psyche," *Electrical World*, June 1991, p. 34.
5. Ray Recchi, "It's the Math, Stupid," Knight-Ridder News Service, September 25, 1993.
6. Jane Kingman-Brundage, "Blueprinting for the Bottom Line," in *Service Excellence: Marketing's Impact on Performance* (Chicago: American Marketing Association, 1989), p. 26. This volume contains five papers on service mapping for readers interested in pursuing this subject.
7. G. Lynn Shostack, "Service Design in the Operating Environment," in William R. George and Claudia E. Marshall, eds., *Developing New Services* (Chicago: American Marketing Association, 1984), p. 35.
8. "Pushing the Customer-Service Envelope," *Inc.*, July 1993, p. 24.
9. Mary Jo Bitner, Bernard H. Booms, and Mary Stanfield Tetreault, "The Service Encounter: Diagnosing Favorable and Unfavorable Incidents," *Journal of Marketing*, January 1990, pp. 71–84.
10. Ron Zemke and Chip Bell, "Service Recovery: Doing It Right the Second Time," *Training*, June 1990, pp. 42–48.
11. Quoted in "Improving Service Doesn't Always Require Big Investment," *The Service Edge*, July-August 1990, p. 3.
12. See *Consumer Complaint Handling in America: An Update Study, Part II* (Washington, D.C.: Technical Assistance Research Programs and U.S. Office of Consumer Affairs, April 1986), pp. 34–41.
13. Linda M. Lash, "Complaints as a Marketing Strategy," *The Marketing Strategy Letter*, February 1993, p. 3.
14. "Dell's Customer Advocacy," *The Marketing Strategy Letter*, May 1993, pp. 6–8.
15. Roland T. Rust, Bala Subramanian, and Mark Wells, "Making Complaints a Management Tool," *Marketing Management*, Vol. 1, No. 3, 1992, pp. 41–45.
16. Ron Zemke, "The Perils of Aggressive Service Recovery," *The Service Edge*, June 1992, p. 8.
17. This story is told in the *On Achieving Excellence* newsletter, March 1994, p. 9.
18. "Multiple Measures Give Fed Ex its 'Good' Data," *The Service Edge*, June 1991, p. 6.
19. Sharon B. Schweikhart, Stephen Strasser, and Melissa R. Kennedy, "Service Recovery in Health Services Organizations," *Hospital and Health Services Administration*, Spring 1993, p. 17.
20. "The Other Guy's Goof," *The Service Edge*, August 1992, p. 5.
21. See Linda Cooper and Beth Summer, *Getting Started in Quality* (Chicago: Consumer Affairs/Quality Department, The First National Bank of Chicago, 1990), p. 27.

22. Barbara Caplan, "The Consumer Speaks—Who's Listening?" *Arthur Andersen Retailing Issues Letter*, July 1993, p. 1.

23. Benjamin Schneider, "The Role of Needs in Service Quality," a presentation at the Managing Service Quality Workshop, Institute of Service Management, Manchester Business School, London, England, March 15, 1994.

24. Judith Graham, "Shoppers' Choice: Tattered Cover," *The Denver Post*, March 7, 1992, Business Section.

Chapter 6. Organize for Great Service

1. Leonard L. Berry, "Improving America's Service," *Marketing Management*, Summer 1992, p. 35.

2. "Fedex Involved Employees in Redesigning Courier Appraisals," *Productivity Views*, May-June 1991, p. 8.

3. Claudia H. Deutsch, "Where the Cadre Sets the Pattern," *The New York Times*, June 30, 1991, Section F, p. 23.

4. Richard Y. Chang, "When TQM Goes Nowhere," *Training and Development Journal*, January 1993, p. 26.

5. Geary A. Rummler and Alan P. Brache, "Managing the White Space," *Training*, January 1991, p. 56.

6. Leonard L. Berry, Valarie A. Zeithaml, and A. Parasuraman, "Five Imperatives for Improving Service Quality," *Sloan Management Review*, Summer 1990, p. 34.

7. Jon R. Katzenbach and Douglas K. Smith, "The Discipline of Teams," *Harvard Business Review*, March-April 1993, p. 112.

8. Katzenbach and Smith, p. 112.

9. As quoted in Frank Rose, "A New Age for Business," *Fortune*, October 8, 1990, p. 162.

10. "The Renewal of a Service Organization," a presentation by AAL at the Productivity Forum, Work In America Institute, 1989 Spring Roundtable.

11. Jack Gordon, "Work Teams—How Far Have They Come?" *Training*, October 1992, p. 64.

12. Interview with William C. Byham, "Self-Directed Work Team Magic," *Boardroom Reports*, December 15, 1991, pp. 1 and 8.

13. Thomas A. Stewart, "Do You Push Your People Too Hard?" *Fortune*, October 22, 1990, p. 124.

14. "Integrated Sales Teams Boost Revenue in Recession-Weary U.K.," *On Achieving Excellence*, May 1992, p. 8.

15. Lakeland Regional Medical Center Internal Report, March 3, 1993.

16. Phyllis M. Watson, et al., "Operational Restructuring: A Patient-Focused Approach," *Nursing Administration Quarterly*, Fall 1991, pp. 50–52.

17. Katzenbach and Smith, pp. 114–115.
18. Katzenbach and Smith, p. 115.

Chapter 7. Embrace Technology

1. James L. Heskett, W. Earl Sasser, Jr., and Christopher W. L. Hart, *Service Breakthroughs—Changing the Rules of the Game* (New York: Free Press, 1990), p. 181.
2. Heskett, Sasser, and Hart, p. 183.
3. Gregory P. Hackett, "Investment in Technology—The Service Sector Sinkhole?" *Sloan Management Review*, Winter 1990, p. 97.
4. As quoted in an advertisement.
5. Hackett, p. 100.
6. Thomas Teal, "Service Comes First: An Interview with USAA's Robert F. McDermott," *Harvard Business Review*, September-October 1989, p. 126.
7. Frederick F. Reichheld, "Loyalty-Based Management," *Harvard Business Review*, March-April 1993, p. 66.
8. Faye Rice, "The New Rules of Superlative Service," *Fortune*, Autumn/Winter 1993, p. 52.
9. Rice, p. 53.
10. Christopher Lovelock, *Product Plus—How Product + Service = Competitive Advantage* (New York: McGraw-Hill, 1994), p. 267.
11. Leonard L. Berry and A. Parasuraman, *Marketing Services: Competing Through Quality* (New York: Free Press, 1991), p. 181.
12. Teal, p. 119.
13. Some of the data in this paragraph comes from Faye Brookman, "Innovative Chain Ranks No. 1," *Stores*, April 1993, pp. 21–23.
14. Blake Ives and Richard O. Mason, "Can Information Technology Revitalize Your Customer Service?" *Academy of Management Executive*, Vol. 4, No. 4, 1990, pp. 53–54.
15. Dave Zielinski, "Database Marketing: With Costs Down, More Use It to Pinpoint Promotions, Create Customer Bonds," *The Service Edge*, February 1994, p. 2.
16. Company correspondence, April 11, 1994.
17. As quoted in "Xerox Corp. and Milliken & Co. are this Year's Winners of the Malcolm Baldrige National Quality Award," *The Service Edge*, December 1989, p. 5.
18. "New Kids on the Block," from the report *Creating Value: The New Performance Model in Retailing*, 1993 Spring Management Conference, Management Horizons.
19. Tom Eisenhart, "Interactive Voice Response Used in Bid to Boost Customer Service," *Marketing News*, April 13, 1992, p. 3.

20. "The Appliance of Science Boosts Zanussi," *The Marketing Strategy Letter*, February 1993, pp. 18–20.
21. Simon Applebaum, "The Solution Channel," *Cablevision*, June 29, 1992, p. 26.
22. Lovelock, p. 275.
23. Robert Frank, "Federal Express Grapples with Change in U.S. Market," *The Wall Street Journal*, July 5, 1994, p. B3.
24. Lovelock, p. 271.
25. Myron Magnet, "Who's Winning the Information Revolution?" *Fortune*, November 30, 1992, p. 111.

Chapter 8. Compete for Talent

1. Leonard A. Schlesinger and James L. Heskett, "Breaking the Cycle of Failure in Service," *Sloan Management Review*, Spring 1991, p. 24.
2. Benjamin Schneider and David E. Bowen, "The Service Organization: Human Resources Management Is Crucial," *Organizational Dynamics*, Spring 1993, pp. 39–52.
3. See Valarie A. Zeithaml, A. Parasuraman, and Leonard L. Berry, *Delivering Quality Service: Balancing Customer Perceptions and Expectations* (New York: Free Press, 1990), Chapter 6.
4. Schlesinger and Heskett, pp. 17–18.
5. Leonard L. Berry and A. Parasuraman, *Marketing Services: Competing Through Quality* (New York: Free Press, 1991), p. 133.
6. Frederick F. Reichheld, "Loyalty-Based Management," *Harvard Business Review*, March-April 1993, p. 658.
7. See Andrew E. Serwer, "America's 100 Fastest Growers," *Fortune*, August 9, 1993, pp. 40–56.
8. As quoted in Matt Rothman, "Into The Black," *Inc.*, January 1993, p. 59.
9. Rothman, pp. 62 and 65.
10. Leonard L. Berry and A. Parasuraman, "Services Marketing Starts From Within," *Marketing Management*, Winter 1992, p. 27.
11. Bruce G. Posner, "Taming the Labor Shortage," *Inc.*, November 1989, p. 168.
12. Ron Zemke, "World-Class Customer Service," *Boardroom Reports*, December 15, 1992, p. 1.
13. "Market Leaders are Finding New Ways to Exceed 'Warm Body' Hiring Practices," *The Service Edge*, October 1992, p. 1.
14. Schlesinger and Heskett, p. 26.
15. As quoted in "Companies Striving to Find New Ways to Assess Prospective Managers' Service-Consciousness," *The Service Edge*, April 1994, p. 2.
16. Benjamin Schneider, "Lessons of Service Quality—A Service Cul-

ture Perspective," a presentation at the Managing Service Quality Workshop sponsored by the Institute of Services Management, Manchester Business School, London, England, March 14, 1994.

17. Philip E. Varca, "Power, Policy, and the New Service Worker," *Marketing Management*, Spring 1992, p. 20.

18. Stephan J. Motowidlo, Marvin D. Dunnette, and Gary W. Carter, "An Alternative Selection Procedure: The Low-Fidelity Simulation," *Journal of Applied Psychology*, Vol. 75, No. 6, 1990, pp. 640–647.

Chapter 9. Develop Service Skills and Knowledge

1. As quoted in Tom Cothran and Margaret Kaeter, "Pioneering Quality Training," *Training*, April 1992, p. 16.

2. James L. Heskett, "Lessons in the Service Sector," *Harvard Business Review*, March-April 1987, p. 121.

3. James L. Heskett, W. Earl Sasser, Jr., and Christopher W. L. Hart, *Service Breakthroughs: Changing the Rules of the Game* (New York: Free Press, 1990), pp. 199–201; and "ServiceMaster," *The Service Edge*, February 1992, p. 3.

4. Jeanne C. Meister, "New Employees: How to Help Them Start Strong," *Boardroom Reports*, January 1, 1994, p. 9.

5. "Job Autonomy Keeps Employees Happy, Customers Coming Back," *The Service Edge*, October 1993, p. 7.

6. Michael D. Hartline and O. C. Ferrell, *Service Quality Implementation: The Effects of Organizational Socialization and Managerial Actions on Customer-Contact Employee Behaviors*, Marketing Science Institute, Report Number 93–122, December 1993.

7. Kathleen S. Alexander, "Taking Responsibility for Service," *Arthur Andersen Retailing Issues Letter*, November 1991, p. 2.

8. This paragraph and the prior one are based on material in Leonard L. Berry and A. Parasuraman, *Marketing Services: Competing Through Quality* (New York: Free Press, 1991), pp. 159–160.

9. Leonard L. Berry, David R. Bennett, and Carter W. Brown, *Service Quality: A Profit Strategy for Financial Institutions* (Homewood, Illinois: Dow Jones-Irwin, 1989), p. 160.

10. Source unknown.

11. Harry Bacas, "Make It Right for the Customer," *Nation's Business*, November 1987.

12. "Just-In-Time Training," *Boardroom Reports*, November 1, 1993, p. 11.

Chapter 10. Empower Servers to Serve

1. Based on David E. Bowen and Edward E. Lawler III, "Employee Empowerment in Service Firms: Answering the Growing Questions," 1994 working paper.

2. As quoted by Roger J. Dow, Vice President Sales and Marketing Services, Marriott Hotels, in a presentation at the meeting "Bridging the Service Quality Gap," held at Milliken & Co., Spartanburg, South Carolina, October 1, 1992.
3. See Timothy W. Firnstahl, "My Employees Are My Service Guarantee," *Harvard Business Review*, July-August 1989, pp. 28–34.
4. Timothy W. Firnstahl, "The Center-Cut Solution," *Harvard Business Review*, May-June 1993, p. 64.
5. Linda R. Cooper, "Polishing the Trophy—Enhancing the Service Commitment," *International Service Association Journal*, April 1991, pp. 25–28.
6. See "Hard-driving Boss Challenges Workers to Meet Company Goals and Personal Commitments," *On Achieving Excellence*, December 1993, p. 5.
7. Matthew J. Kiernan, "The New Strategic Architecture: Learning to Compete in the Twenty-First Century," *Academy of Management Executive*, Vol. 7, No. 1, 1993, p. 14.
8. See David E. Bowen and Edward E. Lawler III, "The Empowerment of Service Workers: What, Why, How, and When," *Sloan Management Review*, Spring 1992, pp. 31–39.
9. John E. Martin, "Unleashing the Power in Your People," *Arthur Andersen Retailing Issues Letter*, September 1994, p. 3.
10. Based on remarks by Marshall Roe, Manager of Service Planning and Development, Ford Parts and Service Division, presented in "Effective Empowerment," *Boardroom Reports*, June 15, 1993, p. 9.
11. As quoted in "The Truth About Empowerment According to D. Quinn Mills," *Training and Development*, August 1992, p. 32.
12. Management Letter, *General Electric Annual Shareholders Report*, February 11, 1994, pp. 3–4.

Chapter 11. Work at Teamwork

1. Dean Tjosvold, *Teamwork for Customers* (San Francisco: Jossey-Bass Publishers, 1993), p. 79.
2. As quoted in "How to Overcome Teamwork Blues," *Boardroom Reports*, July 15, 1993, p. 10.
3. Tjosvold, *Teamwork for Customers*, p. 7.
4. See A. Parasuraman, Leonard L. Berry, and Valarie A. Zeithaml, "An Empirical Examination of Relationships in an Extended Service Quality Model," *Marketing Science Institute Research Program Series*, December 1990, Report No. 90–122.
5. Tjosvold, *Teamwork for Customers*, p. 48.
6. Noel M. Tichy and Stratford Sherman, *Control Your Destiny Or Someone Else Will* (New York: Currency Doubleday, 1993), pp. 234–235.

7. "To Wow the Customer, First Wow Employees," *On Achieving Excellence*, May 1994, p. 11.

8. Robert Levering and Milton Moskowitz, *The 100 Best Companies to Work for in America* (New York: Currency Doubleday, 1993), p. 114.

9. As quoted in "Employee Exchanges Improve Teamwork," *The Service Edge*, January 1991, p. 5. The Kemper example is based on material from this source.

10. Barnaby J. Feder, "At Motorola, Quality Is a Team Sport," *The New York Times*, January 21, 1993, Business Section.

11. Mimi Lieber, "Managing for Service Excellence in a Turbulent Environment," speech at an American Marketing Association Conference, Boston, Massachusetts, February 25, 1987.

Chapter 12. Measure Performance, Reward Excellence

1. See Frederick Herzberg, B. Mausner, and B. Snyderman, *The Motivation to Work* (New York: John Wiley & Sons, 1959).

2. As quoted in Leonard L. Berry, Charles M. Futrell, and Michael R. Bowers, *Bankers Who Sell: Improving Selling Effectiveness in Banking* (Homewood, Illinois: Dow Jones-Irwin; Chicago: Bank Marketing Association, 1985), p. 127.

3. Alfie Kohn, "Why Incentive Plans Cannot Work," *Harvard Business Review*, September-October 1993, pp. 54–63.

4. See "Rethinking Rewards," *Harvard Business Review*, November-December 1993, pp. 37–49.

5. "HRM Update," *HR Magazine*, May 1991, p. 19.

6. Christopher Gaggiano, "What Do Workers Want?" *Inc.*, November 1992, p. 101.

7. As quoted in "US West Abolishes Performance Appraisals to Shift Focus to Customers," *The Service Edge*, June 1993, p. 5.

8. Craig Eric Schneier, Douglas G. Shaw, and Richard W. Beatty, "Performance Measurement and Management: A Tool for Strategy Execution," *Human Resource Management*, Fall 1991, p. 280.

9. Based in part on Leonard L. Berry, David R. Bennett, and Carter W. Brown, *Service Quality: A Profit Strategy for Financial Institutions* (Homewood, Illinois: Dow Jones-Irwin, 1989), pp. 175–176.

10. John A. Swaim, "Recognition and Reward: Keystone for World-Class Customer Satisfaction," a presentation to the American Marketing Association Customer Satisfaction Congress, San Francisco, May 10, 1993.

11. "Make the Grade: Live Up to Corporate Values, Not Just Your Job Description," *On Achieving Excellence*, September 1993, pp. 7–8.

12. Coopers & Lybrand Research Study, November 1993.

13. Advice provided by George Rieder as reported in "Farsighted Pay

Plans Return High Yield in Customer Satisfaction and Retention," *The Service Edge*, December 1992, p. 2.

14. Wyatt Data Services 1993/94 Survey of Variable Pay Programs.
15. "Study Offers Useful Benchmarks, Tips for Using Nontraditional Reward Plans," *The Service Edge*, January 1993, p. 4.
16. Berry, Bennett, and Brown, p. 183.
17. Patricia K. Zingheim and Jay R. Schuster, "Linking Quality and Pay," *HR Magazine*, December 1992, p. 59. The material in the preceding paragraph is based on this article.
18. Wyatt Data Services 1993/94 Survey of Variable Pay Programs.
19. Henry R. Kravis and George R. Roberts, "Corporate Rx: Employee Stock Plans," *The New York Times*, May 23, 1993, p. F13.

INDEX